# Occupied by Memory

# Occupied by Memory

## The Intifada Generation and the Palestinian State of Emergency

John Collins

NEW YORK UNIVERSITY PRESS
*New York and London*

NEW YORK UNIVERSITY PRESS
www.nyupress.org

Library of Congress Cataloging-in-Publication Data
Collins, John.
Occupied by memory : the Intifada generation and the
Palestinian state of emergency / John Collins.
p.   cm.
Includes bibliographical references and index.
ISBN 0–8147–1637–7 (cloth : alk. paper)
ISBN 0–8147–1638–5 (pbk. : alk. paper)
1. Intifada, 1987– —Influence. 2. Palestinian Arabs—West Bank—
Social conditions. 3. Palestinian Arabs—Gaza Strip—Social
conditions. 4. Youth—West Bank—Political activity. 5. Youth—
Gaza Strip—Political activity. 6. Memory—Political aspects.
7. Memory—Social aspects.   I. Title. II. Title: Intifada generation
and the Palestinian state of emergency.
DS119.75.C65     2004
956.95'3044—dc22        2004012004

Manufactured in the United States of America
c 10 9 8 7 6 5 4 3 2 1
p 10 9 8 7 6 5 4 3 2 1

*This book is dedicated to my parents, for their boundless love and support, and for their example; and to the residents of Balata Refugee Camp, who continue to bear witness to the Palestinian struggle against the injustices of a world that has not yet learned the lessons of history.*

For an experienced event is finite—at any rate, confined to one sphere of experience; a remembered event is infinite, because it is only a key to everything that happened before it and after it.                                    —Walter Benjamin

We were who we were in our generation, caught between the past and the future, in a society that wants to deny us a present.                                    —John Trudell

# Contents

# Note on Transliteration

In the case of place names (e.g., Balata) or the names and pseudonyms of Palestinians discussed and quoted in the book, I have only transliterated the ayn and the hamza. In the case of authors (e.g., Kanaana), I have simply followed the spelling used in the specific text to which I am referring. There are also a number of Arabic words (most prominently "intifada") that have passed into common English usage, and are therefore not transliterated here. Other Arabic words are italicized and transliterated in accordance with the standard system used in the *International Journal of Middle East Studies.*

# Acknowledgments

That this book exists at all is a testament to the many Palestinians, in Balata camp and elsewhere, who helped me in innumerable ways during the research process despite the trying times in which they were living. Some agreed to be interviewed formally; others offered their time for casual conversations, impromptu Arabic lessons and political debates; many showed me incredible hospitality and friendship in the form of meals and overnight stays; and all left their own mark on me and on the writing that I have subsequently done. Where possible, I have thanked them by name in what follows; in all other cases, their contributions must remain anonymous for reasons of space or personal safety.

I owe a great deal to the many teachers who have challenged me to pursue and make the most of an intellectual vocation. To John Archer, Bud Duvall, Bud Gerber, Ron Harrell, Allen Isaacman, Lisette Josephides, Richard Leppert, Bruce Lincoln, Bruce Masters, David McFadden, Maggie McFadden, John Mowitt, Richard Ohmann, Jim Stone, and Gladys Veidemanis—all of them sources of support and inspiration in their own unique way—I express my deepest personal gratitude. It is a measure of Bruce Lincoln's commitment and patience that he remained solidly behind me as an adviser, a colleague, and a friend from my arrival in Minnesota to the completion of the doctoral dissertation that became this book. To our relationship, Bruce brought the same qualities that distinguish his work as a scholar: an ability to cut to the heart of the matter, to separate the key issues from the marginal ones, to see connections that others miss, and to bring ideas across in a way that is concise, effective, and often revelatory. I remain inspired by his example.

At the University of Minnesota, I found two outstanding intellectual homes: the Program in Comparative Studies in Discourse and Society, and the MacArthur Program on Peace and International Cooperation. Both programs were central sources of funding through several stages of my graduate career. Field research was also assisted by a grant from the

Joint Committee on the Near and Middle East of the Social Science Research Council and the American Council of Learned Societies with funds provided by the U.S. Information Agency, and the Graduate School at the University of Minnesota. I began the writing while I was a Visiting Fellow in the International Studies Program at Denison University, and completed it while teaching in the Global Studies Department at St. Lawrence University.

While in Palestine, I was fortunate to be affiliated with the Institute of Jerusalem Studies; I am grateful to Salim Tamari, May Douani, and Julia Hawkins for the interest they showed in my work and for their assistance whenever I was in Jerusalem. In the early months of my fieldwork, I benefited enormously from my participation in the Palestine and Arabic Studies (PAS) Program at Birzeit University. I carry fond memories of evenings spent with Munir Naser and Sumaya Farhat-Naser, and particularly of Munir's wonderful driving tours of the surrounding countryside. Also at Birzeit, I was privileged to meet and have several helpful discussions with Sharif Kanaana, whose work on Palestinian folklore I have long admired. As I made the transition to working in Nablus, Sa'ed Abu-Hijleh gave generously of his time in showing me the city and introducing me to friends in Balata camp. The staff of the Center for Palestine Research and Studies, particularly Khalil Shikaki and Adnan Odeh, provided crucial assistance in terms of helping me find three talented interpreters (Abdul-Jabbar al-Khalili, Mohammed Odeh, and Muna Shikaki) who helped me bridge the gap between my own Arabic skills and the rigorous demands of qualitative interviews. Each of the three had an important influence on my fieldwork experience and on the present work.

Throughout the long process of preparing for, researching, and writing this book, I've enjoyed the support of friends and colleagues who have blessed me with their generosity and hospitality, challenged me with their critical feedback on my work, and sustained me with their intellectual and political energy. An admittedly partial list includes Rabab Abdulhadi, Mahmoud al-Nayrab, Mehretab Abye Assefa, Amy Bell, Jimmy Bishara, Anita Braun, Bruce Campbell, Arlindo Chilundo, Kenneth Church, Judith DeGroat, Danielle Egan, Christian Fite, Heidi Gengenbach, Ross Glover, Barbara Harlow, Roger Heacock, Frances Hasso, Jim Johnson, Peter Kiernan, Zara Kivi Kinnunen, Mary Layoun, Mark LeVine, Ian Lustick, Erin McCarthy, Joel Morton, Maanda Mulaudzi, Helena Pohlandt-McCormick, Sita Ranchod-Nilsson, Diana Saco, Victoria Sanford,

Claudia Shores Skue, Adam Sitze, Eve Stoddard, Sandra Sufian, Latha Varadarajan, and Jill Zellmer.

Thanking my parents, Don and Edith Collins, feels like a gesture that is at once obvious and terribly inadequate. It is from them that I gained my concern for social justice, my belief in the need for an engaged intellectual life, and the spark for my initial interest in the Middle East; their support, while not always acknowledged, has remained constant throughout the years even when my own resolve has not. Other members of my family were generous in providing me with important logistical assistance during my extended forays abroad, enabling me to carry out my research with a minimum of worries about practical details back home, and in some cases giving me a quiet place to write after I returned.

More than anyone else, Marina Llorente saw me through the completion of this book. With her characteristic verve, intelligence, and humor, she shared with me the ups and downs of the writing (and rewriting, and unwriting) process, the joy of seeing years of work come to fruition, and the beauty of knowing what matters most in life. A true *compañera* and a powerful intellectual, she has enabled the book's existence and buoyed my own emotional health with her love and support in ways that I can only begin to contemplate. Needless to say, like everyone mentioned here, she bears none of the responsibility for the book's shortcomings.

There are five additional people who made a significant mark on this book but who, sadly, did not live to see its publication. Susan Geiger, a truly inspiring teacher and feminist scholar of Tanzanian nationalism, was a steady source of support and encouragement during my years at Minnesota. Shaden Abu-Hijleh welcomed me to Nablus, feeding me an enormous breakfast and introducing me to many of her friends during my initial stay in the city. A well-known peace activist, she was shot to death by Israeli soldiers in October 2002 while sitting on her front porch with her husband and son, both of whom were injured in the unprovoked attack.

Ibrahim Abu-Lughod, one of Palestine's intellectual and political giants, was gracious enough to grant me two fascinating interviews at Birzeit University, where he taught and served as an administrator from his return to Palestine until his death in 2002. Ibrahim's close friend Edward Said, another member of the *jīl al-nakba,* has influenced me more than any other scholar. I met him as an undergraduate, when my interest in Palestine and in intellectual work were both starting to bloom, and he died in September 2003 as I was putting the finishing touches on this manuscript. In the introduction to his 1983 book *The World, the Text and the Critic*, Said articulated the philosophy that I have tried to live up to in my own work: "Criticism must think of itself as life-enhancing and constitutively opposed to every form of tyranny, domination, and abuse; its social goals are noncoercive knowledge produced in the interest of human freedom." I continue to find new challenges, and new sources of inspiration, in the remarkable body of work that he has left us.

Finally, my grandmother, Glenora English McFadden—a true American rebel, a lifelong activist, and a teacher—is, in many ways, the point of origin for the political commitments that led me to work in Palestine. "Peace with justice" is the simple inscription on her tombstone. "That way I can keep teaching after I'm gone," she once told me. I hope that with this book I am helping her in my own small way to fulfill this wish.

# Prologue
## Approaching a Permanent State of Emergency

I've written this story before.
                        —Robert Fisk

This is a book about *the possibilities of memory*. It is rooted in the belief that thinking and talking about the past is a worthwhile enterprise, but one that is inevitably marked by uncertainty. No mere exercise in simple recollection or in repeating received ideas, an active engagement with the past is necessarily about the present and the future as well. It is about open-endedness, not self-assuredness. To approach the past in this way is to embrace what Stuart Hall calls a "politics without guarantees," a politics that assumes that even under the most oppressive conditions, meaning can never be fixed.

This is also a book about *memories of possibility*, memories of a time when the window of opportunity for Palestinian liberation seemed to be more open than ever before. For members of the "intifada generation" (*jīl al-intifāda*), the fact that the window has appeared less open in subsequent years only enhances the power of those memories. As the title of this book suggests, they are "occupied by memory" in the most immediate way: the continuation of the Israeli occupation is a constant reminder of what they experienced, and what they were and were not able to accomplish during their youth. For the rest of us, a close look at their personal narratives, and their relationship to the present realities on the ground, provides its own unique window onto the dynamic, bustling intersection of historical and ideological forces that is the Palestinian struggle.

Like any ethnographer, I come to my research and writing with my own set of memories. When the intifada began in late 1987, I was a second-year undergraduate whose mild interest in the Middle East derived largely from slides my parents had shown me after returning from church-based trips to "the Holy Land." Yet like many observers, including my Lebanese-Palestinian roommate and several Jewish friends who were inclined toward a critical view of the Israeli occupation, I found it impossible to ignore the television images of young Palestinians, rocks in hand, confronting Israeli soldiers in the streets of the West Bank and Gaza. The public face of this remarkable insurrection called to mind the biblical story of David and Goliath, but with a potent symbolic inversion: the Palestinian stonethrowers were both obliterating and appropriating Israel's long-standing self-definition as a tiny, youthful nation surrounded by powerful enemies. Experiencing the intifada via television images—images that were violent, theatrical, sometimes horrific, and ultimately misleading in the sense that they hid much of the popular organizing, social upheaval, and systematic Israeli repression that were going on behind the scenes—led me to develop what I can only describe as a romantic, often envious attachment to the intifada's young activists.[1]

In the relative comfort of my dorm room, I felt like a fraud, and a privileged one at that. Soon I cofounded a group devoted to promoting campus dialogue on Israel/Palestine, an action that generated significant anger at a school where support for Israel had traditionally been strong. I think some people didn't know what to make of me, for I was neither Jewish nor Arab; my interest in the issue derived from my family's commitment to social justice, not from any personal stake in the conflict. For those who were strongly pro-Israel, I may have been more objectionable than any of the three Palestinians on campus, and the more I learned about the history of Zionism and the Israeli occupation, the more confident I felt in playing the role of provocateur. Yet even as I began to find a public voice, and to feel that peculiar mix of adrenaline, empowerment, and self-importance that comes with being an activist during a time of crisis, I was always stopped in my tracks when I saw the latest news from the front lines of the intifada. I was organizing meetings, taking part in debates, and writing articles, but here were people my own age who were speaking to the world in a much more immediate, physical, and dangerous way. They were the "children of the stones" (*atfāl al-hijāra*), and they had my attention.

In many ways, this book is the product of a long process through which I subsequently have come to understand that the notion of heroic, youthful intifada activism I discovered during those years is not just double-edged, but multiedged in ways that reach to the core of Palestinian national identity as it is viewed by Palestinians and non-Palestinians alike. As a result, my own attempts to develop an analytical perspective on "other" people's narratives of the intifada have necessarily involved an increasingly critical engagement with my own reasons for viewing Palestinian resistance in general, and the actions of the "intifada generation" in particular, in the ways that I have up to now. Exposure to critical theories of postmodernism, deconstruction, and discourse analysis led me to question the seductive narratives of national liberation, narratives that so often leave the hierarchical nature of liberation movements unexamined in the interest of prioritizing "the struggle." In addition, by the time I made my third and longest trip to Palestine in 1996 as a Ph.D. candidate, I was fully aware of how the place was saturated with academic and other researchers who help to form what some have called "the Palestine industry." Many Palestinians with whom I spoke had already been interviewed multiple times by journalists, human rights workers, and scholars.

In the process of doing my own interviews and immersing myself in the lives of Palestinian communities—sharing tea on damp winter evenings, enduring days of curfew and violence, talking politics in taxis and coffee shops, enjoying the festive streets of Ramallah during Ramadan—I came to feel a much deeper connection with the young people who had initially grabbed my attention in 1987. Yet as I heard their stories, I kept feeling myself being pulled back into the narrative of nationalism and I wondered, did I really want to produce yet another study that simply oscillated between the twin poles of heroism and victimization? That level of cynicism, and its attendant yearning for something more meaningful than political slogans and stereotypical characterizations, led me to embrace the popular memory approach that insists on a more complex understanding of individual stories and their social significance. During the months after I returned from Palestine, my thoughts moved increasingly, and perhaps inevitably, to a series of more abstract, more "intellectual" issues: the production of social memory, the discursive construction of "youth," the relationship between biography and history.

Current events, however, always have a way of snapping us back to attention. Throughout the completion of this book, Palestinians and

Israelis were locked in a process of what Frantz Fanon, viewing the anti-colonial struggle in Algeria, called the process of "terror, counter-terror, violence, counter-violence." By the end of 2001, of course, the notion of "terror" was occupying a very different place in global political discourse, and long-standing Israeli attempts to tar Palestinians with the brush of "terrorism"—attempts that had been partially undermined during the years of the intifada and the "peace process"—were again receiving a sympathetic hearing from many in the United States.[2] Yet as Israeli Prime Minister Ariel Sharon pursued his own policy of colonial brutality under the cover of George W. Bush's "war on terrorism," the toll of human suffering continued to be grossly asymmetrical, with Palestinians bearing levels of violence and repression unseen even at the height of the intifada. When Sharon launched a massive assault on Palestinian communities in early 2002 (the largest Israeli military operation since the 1982 invasion of Lebanon, a war over which Sharon presided as Defense Minister), refugee camps in the West Bank and Gaza were the primary targets.

That all of this was nothing new was brought home to me one morning in late February of that year, when I turned on the radio and heard that Israeli troops had entered Balata Refugee Camp, where I conducted the bulk of the research for this book. The usual metaphors and euphemisms abounded in news reports that day: the Associated Press quoted an Israeli official as saying that the invasion was part of "an ongoing operation to flush out terrorist cells," while Sharon's spokesman told Agence France Press that Israeli forces were "picking up terrorists with tweezers." Ironically enough, I had spent the previous evening viewing Gillo Pontecorvo's legendary film *The Battle of Algiers* with a group of students. As I listened to the news from Balata, it was as if Sharon had simply stepped into the boots of Mathieu, the colonel who led the French paratroopers into Algiers in an ultimately vain attempt to suppress a movement whose leaders were holed up in the old city. In the film, Mathieu casually labels his mission "Operation Champagne" as he gazes down at a billboard from his perch high above the city; four decades later, his Israeli counterparts were commandeering homes overlooking Balata and dubbing their work "Operation Colorful Journey." Tanks had encircled Balata camp, unable to enter the narrow streets of the defiant, besieged community; were these slow-moving armored vehicles, I wondered, the Israeli equivalent of the French tank that had plodded its way around a street corner at the end of Pontecorvo's film, a lumbering indicator that French power was being eclipsed by the logic of history? Or would Sharon's troops do to Balata what his Lebanese allies had done to the camps of Sabra and Shatila in 1982?

As the news slowly leaked out of Balata, I confirmed what I already knew to be the case: many of those who were fighting the Israelis in the camp were people I had met and interviewed, young members of the "intifada generation" who were now in their late twenties and early thirties. I had to glean information about the dead and wounded from online Palestinian sources, and as I perused the lists I saw family names—Hashash, Odeh, al-Jirmi—that I remembered from my time in Nablus. The invading Israeli soldiers, reports indicated, had done their "house-to-house" search of the camp in a particularly devastating way: fearful of being exposed in the camp's narrow alleyways, they had used a technique they called "walking through walls," methodically using explosives and special saws to cut through the walls separating one home from the next and damaging roughly five hundred dwellings in the process. The "operation" ended after three days, but the people of Balata knew better than to treat it as an endpoint. "The Israelis will not leave the camp like this," predicted one resident. "There will be a massacre here." Less than a month later, Sharon launched his all-out war against Palestinians throughout the West Bank, killing hundreds and systematically destroying the infrastructure of the nascent Palestinian state.

I relate this story not only to give some sense of the place that is home to the Palestinians I interviewed, but also to underscore a larger point about my own relationship to "the question of Palestine." Since 1987 I have gradually come to see the situation in Palestine not—in the manner of the mainstream U.S. media—as a series of "rounds of violence," but rather as violence itself, as something akin to what Walter Benjamin had in mind when he wrote the following passage just months before he took his own life in 1940 while trying to flee from Nazi-occupied France to Spain:

The tradition of the oppressed teaches us that the "state of emergency" in which we live is not the exception but the rule. We must attain to a conception of history that is in keeping with this insight. . . . The current amazement that the things we are experiencing are "still" possible in the twentieth century is *not* philosophical. This amazement is not the beginning of knowledge—unless it is the knowledge that the view of history which gives rise to it is untenable.

The "untenable" notion of history that Benjamin is critiquing here is closely linked with the idea of Progress, and as he suggests, belief in Progress is very difficult to reconcile with the knowledge of what the first four decades of the twentieth century brought to Europe—or, to extend his analysis, with the knowledge of what has subsequently happened in Rwanda, Cambodia, Palestine, Lebanon, Guatemala, Bosnia, and a host of other locations across the globe. The Chilean writer Ariel Dorfman began a thoughtful meditation on the September 11, 2001 tragedy with the words, "I have been through this before." And indeed he had, for it was on the same day in 1973 that a U.S.-backed coup ushered in a horrific period of military dictatorship in his country. How many others can bear similar witness to the horrors that have marked the age of Progress?

In keeping with Benjamin's fundamental insight, I begin from the premise that for Palestinians living under Israeli domination, life is in a permanent state of emergency (Swedenburg 1995b; Taussig 1992). Researchers working in Palestine have traditionally had a difficult time grappling with the nature of this permanence, choosing often to pursue work that is framed, at least implicitly, by the more optimistic, teleological narratives of state building, national liberation, and the "peace process." This is hardly surprising, for as Edward Said has so doggedly and eloquently pointed out, the Palestinian struggle for liberation from Israeli colonial domination is one of the great moral causes of our time. Like many others, I have chosen to take a position on this issue, for I believe that a permanent state of emergency requires a permanent ethical commitment to "speak truth to power." At times this imperative carries with it the need for a careful documentation of Israeli repression with an eye to making the details of this repression public.

At the same time, I believe that one can do this kind of work without putting one's faith blindly in the promises of nationalism; otherwise one runs the risk of mistaking the seizure of state power for the actual practice of liberation. As examples such as Algeria and Mozambique show so clearly, the "emergency" simply takes on different forms after independence. Taking the lessons of this history seriously, then, means recognizing the depth of the crisis we are facing and thus resisting the temptation to provide the sort of "solutions" that "Middle East experts" often toss about so blithely.

## Organization of the Book

The diversity of methodological and analytical frameworks that informs the following chapters reflects the particular challenges and possibilities of a project that cannot be tackled effectively without an approach that is at once historical, sociological, and attentive to the need for critical cultural analysis. In chapter 1 I sketch the intellectual architecture of the book, as well as providing a brief introduction to Balata Refugee Camp and the interviews I conducted there.

In chapter 2 I critically examine the discursive field through which young Palestinians were invested with powerful political, social, and cultural meaning during the intifada. Drawing on the work of David Spurr, I discuss six "rhetorical modes" (heroism, victimization, guilt, potential, testimonial, and empowerment) that run throughout numerous discourses on generation, providing a flexible and varied repertoire for representing the relationship between young people and the nation. Rather than attempting to connect particular modes with particular types of narrators in a mechanistic fashion, I conduct my analysis with an eye to the fact that the same repertoire is, in fact, available to individuals and groups whose political positions may exist in tension, even outright antagonism, with one another. Given the tendency of these various modes to turn up in so many different discursive practices, the materials on which I draw in this chapter are necessarily eclectic, including poems and songs, popular legends, political leaflets and declarations, human rights reports, soldiers' narratives, journalistic and scholarly accounts, legal discourses, even paid advertisements.

The remainder of the book focuses on popular memories of the intifada as articulated primarily by young people in Balata camp. Chapter 3 examines the stories of Isam Abu-Hawila and his mother, Imm Ghassan. Isam remembers the intifada as a time of activism and imprisonment (he was jailed for two years) and a time when social relations were drastically, if temporarily, altered. He also describes it as a time of failed romance, recalling how political events defeated his own attempt to get married during the uprising. Now he speaks of his generation as suffering from a "return to adolescence" as its members struggle to deal with the gulf between their political experience and their emotional immaturity. Imm Ghassan tells a life story organized around a series of tragedies that have taken away her father, her husband, and one of her sons, Nizam, who was an intifada "martyr." Her memories of the intifada, however, are dominated by her own active efforts to defend her sons and all the young men of the camp, and by her determination to maintain her family in the face of economic uncertainty and Israeli repression. Both Isam and Imm Ghassan tell the story of Nizam's death in terms of personal tragedy, but also in a way that emphasizes their commitment to "regenerating" their family by keeping his memory alive. All their stories, I suggest, tell us something important about the complicated relationship between family and nation, and about the subtle ways in which Palestinians come to grips with the receding of the future that their nationalist movement has always promised them.

Memories that suggest processes of political awakening, empowerment, and the disruption of generational hierarchies are the subject of chapters 4 and 5. Here I pay particular attention to the "spatialization" of memory, that is, to the ways in which young people's remembrances of the intifada are closely connected with particular sites where political resistance intersected with struggles over generational authority. In stories rooted in the home environment, for example, the existence of parental authority appears as a limiting factor on the ability of young people to act; hence we find numerous references to passive interactions with soldiers in the home (e.g., in stories of midnight arrests), to parents who forced their children to stay inside, and to children who found ways to sneak out or keep their political activities secret from their parents. By contrast, stories rooted in three other sites—prison, school, and the streets—indicate that through their activities in these spaces, young people succeeded in effecting important redefinitions of generational identity such that biological age came to matter less than one's ability to take on political responsibility. Consequently, these stories are often built on images of generational inversion, with young activists taking the initiative in their interactions with a variety of adults ranging from teachers to prison authorities.

Chapter 6 explores the overdetermination of memory by immediate events and concerns that surrounded the articulation of memory in the interviews. Following the intifada, the beginning of the "peace process," and the establishment of the Palestinian Authority (PA), young people remained bound to one another by the powerful memory of political events witnessed and experienced during their youth; yet their gradual transition into adulthood, occurring in the midst of a national transition from mass mobilization to political negotiation, had left them increasingly fragmented as a generation, with some working for the PA, others returning to school, and still others living uncomfortably as "spectators" who are both unemployed and politically disillusioned. The process of remembering the intifada and assessing its long-term impact, I suggest, generated significant political contradictions both within individuals and between members of the *jīl al-intifāda,* contradictions which these young people were attempting to work through on a narrative level. Most importantly, their general descriptions of the intifada indicate the operation of powerful "moral chronologies," in which later political and social developments are negatively contrasted with the early period of the uprising, which is remembered as a time of optimism, democratic resistance, and pure motives.

As this brief overview indicates, the issue of generation is an evolving and dynamic one in the Palestinian context, subject not only to the workings of memory, but also to an ever-shifting matrix of social forces operating under changing conditions of possibility. With this in mind, I conclude the book with some reflections on key post-intifada developments that have combined to create the present crisis in Palestine. These include deep flaws in the Oslo agreements and the "peace process," contradictions in the relationship between the PA and the "intifada generation," the outbreak of a second intifada in 2000, and the increasingly rightward drift of Israeli and U.S. policy since 2000. These events have demonstrated not only the continuing ability of Palestinians living under occupation to "re-generate" (in both the biological and ideological sense) their struggle for liberation, but also the continuing inability of Palestinians to control the terms through which dominant opinion in Israel and the United States—the two nations whose alliance exerts the most direct control over their lives—discursively constructs that struggle. As I complete this manuscript, Palestinians are facing two simultaneous threats that work hand in hand: a threat to their national existence through unprecedented Israeli state violence; and a threat of symbolic erasure through the post-September 11 reformulation of Palestinian resistance as "terrorism." There is perhaps no greater illustration of the "permanent state of emergency" I have described here than the coincidence of these two threats.

# 1

## Production Notes

My son, oh future! I heard you in the other room asking your
mother: Mama, am I a Palestinian? When she answered "Yes," a
heavy silence fell on the whole house. It was as if something hanging over our heads had fallen, its noise exploding, then—silence.
. . . Do not believe that man grows. No: He is born suddenly—a
word, in a moment, penetrates his heart to a new throb. One scene
can hurl him down from the ceiling of childhood onto the rugged-
ness of the road.     —Ghassan Kanafani, writing to his son Fayez

[T]he nation's biography snatches, against the going mortality rate,
exemplary suicides, poignant martyrdoms, assassinations, execu-
tions, wars, and holocausts. But, to serve the narrative purpose,
these violent deaths must be remembered/forgotten as "our own."
                                            —Benedict Anderson

Each Palestinian is true.
                    —Jean Genet

There is nothing simple about memory. Both seductive and
perilous, memory can be a site of trauma, a place where the past "flashes
up at a moment of danger" (Benjamin 1968c) only to disappear as soon
as we try to grasp it and pin it down. Memory can be a tool in the hands
of emperors, presidents, corporations, and others who seek to extend
their domination by fixing the meaning of the past; yet it can also be a
strategic ally for those who are dominated. It can help create nations, and
it can tear nations apart. It can inspire songs and stories, revenge and revolution. Memory, in other words, is a *process,* one whose outcome is uncertain and always subject to human struggle and creativity. Palestinians,
like all colonized peoples, know this well.

How, then, will the first intifada (hereafter referred to simply as the "intifada") be remembered? Which parts will be preserved in the collective memories of the Palestinian people, the Israeli military, the international media? Which parts will be actively suppressed by one or another of the protagonists? Which parts will remain submerged in fragments of individual memory, only to reemerge during later moments of crisis or reflection? How will the many stories of the intifada be altered, debated, strategically mobilized? These are fundamental questions for scholars of social memory, and they are the kinds of questions that led me to Balata as a place to explore what happens when a period such as the first intifada passes into the realm of memory.

With my focus on the *jīl al-intifāda* (the "intifada generation") came another set of questions rooted in the experience of political activism and political violence. Many of these questions seem profoundly unanswerable. Take the example of Hatem, who was born and raised in Balata and was thirteen when the intifada began. When he went into the streets to face down the soldiers of the occupying Israeli army, what was he feeling? Did he act as a self-conscious representative of his nation? Did he share the political pessimism of many older camp residents? Was he afraid? Did he see himself as one of history's losers? Or as a refugee ready to take revenge for the suffering visited upon his family? Or simply as "one of the guys"? Or, perhaps more radically, was he experiencing something more utopian, something that cannot be contained within the bounds of the national, at the moment of confrontation?

And who, exactly, are the members of the "intifada generation"? They are everywhere and nowhere. On the one hand, they are almost hypervisible, making regular appearances on the evening news and on the front page of newspapers around the world. They are on the cover of many intifada books, stones in hand, giving the "V" for victory sign as they confront Israeli tanks and troops. On the other hand, aside from the occasional quotation, their voices are often strikingly absent from these public venues, replaced by the words of the politicians, pundits, and scholars who are typically called upon to explain what is going on in Palestine. Much like the young activists who led the protests against South Africa's apartheid regime during the turbulent 1970s and 1980s, then, the *atfāl al-hijāra* ("children of the stones") are political caricatures about whom we know surprisingly little. The assumption seems to be that the actions of the "intifada generation" speak for themselves, thus obviating the need for a closer look at the particular kinds of consciousness and social analysis they undoubtedly possess. This book is an attempt to work against the grain of this assumption, and to do so in a way that treats young people as the truly multidimensional human beings they are. This means soliciting their ideas as well as their stories, and it means respecting them enough to engage their testimony critically.

While some researchers have occasionally and effectively used personal narratives as sources for understanding issues of Palestinian history and identity, rarely have such narratives been analyzed *as narratives*— that is, as creative constructions of the past told in particular circumstances for particular reasons that are not always self-evident, even to the teller. Instead, the stories of "ordinary" Palestinians have generally been treated as *evidence,* as documents assumed to bear an unassailable truth-value deriving from a particular relationship to experienced events. This approach is most obviously associated with work that attempts to point out the vast injustices of Israeli settler-colonialism; interestingly, however, it is also available to more hostile analysts who might wish to "prove" that Palestinians are "terrorists." The dominance of this documentary model has often gone unchallenged, closing off other avenues of inquiry.

The approach I use in this book tries to go beyond this dilemma not by ignoring the larger political questions at the root of the conflict in Israel/Palestine, but rather by exploring the politics of memory and narration in their full complexity; not by reifying the fiction-nonfiction divide, but by stressing questions of context and articulation that bear on the production and analysis of *all* narratives; not by eliminating the question of "truth" altogether, but by assuming that "truth" is inseparable from the process of interpretation that is so central to all discourse analysis. I cannot claim to stand entirely outside the documentary model; to do so would be to deny the political commitments I bring to my work. It is perhaps most accurate to say that this book embodies and explores the tensions between the documentary model and the narrative model. It is primarily about the narratives articulated by Palestinians, but it is also about my attempts to develop a perspective on those narratives that is both critical and, in a human sense, sympathetic. And to a lesser extent, it is about my own story as a researcher with my own particular set of experiences in Palestine and elsewhere, experiences that have shaped my whole approach to the research.

The notion of a "permanent state of emergency" described in the Prologue leads to all sorts of interesting possibilities focusing on the space between experienced events and narrated events; between "official" and "popular" versions of history; and between imagined outcomes and observed results. In my own case, I have found the gaps separating the promises of a dominant nationalist narrative and the unsatisfying realities of the present to be extremely fertile ground for research. This book explores the temporal, cognitive, and narrative space between the intifada itself and its later narration and memorialization, in the mid-1990s, by members of the *jīl al-intifāda* and other Palestinians who were attempting to make sense of the past even as they were struggling to "get by" in the present. It is in this space that Palestinians continue to give meaning to their lives in a time of profound, seemingly perpetual uncertainty.

Throughout the book, I explore the "generation" of Palestinian nationalism through a combination of ethnographic practice, discourse and narrative analysis, and ideological critique. I use the term "generation" in two closely related ways. In the strict sociological sense, "generation" refers to age-based social cohorts typically defined in some combination of biological and historical terms. Such definitions are common in Palestine, with the *jīl al-intifāda* preceded by the *jīl al-thawra* (the generation that grew up under the Palestinian revolution of the late 1960s) and the *jīl al-nakba* (the generation formed by the experience of dispossession in 1948), among others (Sayigh 1979, 11, n. 5). Equally important, however, I am drawing on a more discursive notion of "generation" as describing processes through which social identities and political projects are symbolically produced, reproduced, and transformed. Thus I am concerned both with the actions of young Palestinians and with the ways in which the national liberation struggle in Palestine has been, and continues to be, understood and framed through Palestinian, Israeli, and other attempts to fix the meaning of those very actions and the identities (e.g., "hero," "martyr," "suicide bomber," even the category of "the intifada generation" itself) often associated with them.

The intifada embodies the dynamic relationship between these two meanings of "generation." As a social movement and as a historical period increasingly subject to the mechanisms of social memory, it points us to an understanding of recent Palestinian history in which young people are central political actors, *and* to an understanding of Palestinian identity in which the issue of nationhood cannot be "thought" or narrated outside the issue of generation. The intifada represented a point of crisis—and therefore an opening—with respect to the Palestinian national project, leaving the possibilities and tensions of that project exposed and symbolically embodied in the *jīl al-intifāda*. Consequently, it is this group of Palestinians—their actions, their memories, the particular contradictions of their position in Palestine today, as well as representations of them by others—who are located at the center of this book. What emerges is an understanding of the famous "children of the stones" not only as historical actors, but also as a kind of symbolic nexus between the processes of generation, nationalism, and memory.

## Generation-as-Possibility

To be of a particular nation (Lat. *natio*), strictly speaking, is to be *born* (Lat. *nascere*) into a national community. The very idea of nationalism, in fact, implies generation, if only because the successful biological production and ideological incorporation of the young is necessary to the "re-generation" of the national community. The Palestinian use of the term *jīl* nicely illustrates the connection, for while the word technically denotes "age" or "generation," its practical usage (as in *jīl al-intifāda*) clearly suggests that these generations have a *national* significance.

Despite these conceptual and etymological linkages, scholars of nationalism routinely ignore the category of generation altogether, even when discussing issues (e.g., pronatalism) that obviously involve assigning meaning to children and youth.[1] This gap is directly related to the fact that the existing scholarship on generation remains theoretically impoverished when compared with the vast literatures on race, class, gender, and sexuality.[2] Within work on generation, Karl Mannheim's essay on "The Problem of Generations" (Mannheim 1952) remains a foundational text. For Mannheim, shared biological age is not sufficient in itself to establish a collective sense of generational consciousness. A given biological generation becomes "actualized" only when its members can be said to share a "concrete bond" based on their collective experience, as youth, of "a process of dynamic de-stabilization."

Mannheim makes it clear that while the formation of an "actual" generation is a rare occurrence with far-reaching implications in terms of disrupting the prevailing social and political order, *all* emerging generations embody the *possibility* of such a disruption. This possibility derives from the phenomenon of what he calls "fresh contact":

> Fresh contacts play an important part in the life of the individual when
> he is forced by events to leave his own social group and enter a new

one—when, for example, an adolescent leaves home, or a peasant the countryside for the town, or when an emigrant changes his home, or a social climber his social status or class. . . . We can accordingly differentiate between two types of "fresh contact": one based on a shift in social relations, and the other on vital factors (the change from one generation to another). The latter type is *potentially* much more radical, since with the advent of the new participant in the process of culture, the change of attitude takes place in a different individual whose attitude towards the heritage handed down by his predecessors is a novel one. (293–294)

The notion of generation that emerges from such an understanding might be termed *generation-as-possibility,* calling attention to the unique position of young people (Mannheim's "new participants") with respect to processes of social reproduction. This view has important implications for the study of nationalist projects, for it is young people whose "contact" with the idea of the nation is the most "fresh" and, consequently, subject to the widest range of possible responses—from radical reinterpretation to apparently wholesale ideological incorporation. Young people, in other words, are not only the literal products of national reproduction in the biological sense; they are also crucial to the ideological process of "producing the people." However, it is important to note here that while attempts to promote a particular nationalist project necessarily involve efforts to incorporate young people into it, the young people themselves are never entirely constrained in terms of how to conceptualize and articulate the relationship between generational and national identities. Consequently, the study of generation necessarily involves a critical examination of public discourses of generation, for these constitute the universe of meaning within which generational identities are negotiated.

Mannheim also provides a link to the issue of narrative which has been overlooked by many of his commentators, a link that is central to my reading of personal narratives. In one of his most memorable phrases, Mannheim writes that each "actual" generation bears the deep imprint of the particular historical conjuncture that constituted "the drama of their youth." In choosing to describe this lasting impact as a "drama"—rather than simply as a series of discrete "events"—he calls attention to the narrativization of those events, to the ways in which experiences are fashioned, through the mechanisms of memory, into the form of a story that is likely to contain some combination of heroes, victims, and villains;

narrative detachment, ironic juxtaposition, and moral judgment; and themes of romance, humor, and tragedy. This aspect of narrativity confirms, as well, the continuing significance of generation well beyond the moment of its "actualization," for the drama is a *remembered* drama, constantly retold and recreated in changing historical circumstances.

In the Palestinian context it is Ghassan Kanafani who has pioneered the exploration of generation-as-possibility, both in his novels and short stories and in his critical writings on Arab culture and politics.[3] "Our generation used to see in its schoolbooks an unforgettable photograph," writes Kanafani in a 1968 essay (Kanafani 1990):

> This photograph, taken in the second decade of this century, shows a man mounted gloriously on a charger. A shining sword glistens in his hands with which he boldly confronts a Turkish airplane about to destroy him. This was a true picture—not a film, nor mere sensationalism, but a unique and terrifyingly realistic representation of how the Arabs looked on the twentieth century from within the great Arab revolution. (140)

Kanafani, writing in response to the Arab defeat in the 1967 war with Israel, makes it clear that this photograph has a narrative significance for Arabs of a particular generation, representing the turning point from which the great linear, nationalist processes of the twentieth century in the Arab world—the "birth" of nationalism, followed by independence and national "development"—subsequently unfolded. His point in invoking this particular image, however, is not simply to validate the perception of what has changed over the course of decades, but also to suggest that such perceptions themselves are always enabled and limited by the process of generation. "The basic difference separating us from our fathers is unprecedented. . . . The difference between our generations can no longer be measured in years," Kanafani writes, arguing that the "incalculable speed of development" has ushered in a situation where the persistence of patriarchy—which he views in broad terms as a structure encompassing the full range of political and social life—is, in his view, the major obstacle blocking the advancement of Arab society. Despite the apparent rapidity of change, he insists, this society is "really only in its birth phase," a claim that illustrates the continuing appeal and flexibility of generational metaphors for the reconstruction of nationalist narratives during periods of political transition or social upheaval.

Equally important, Kanafani goes on to argue that because of the overwhelming challenges and possibilities facing Arab society, the position of the younger generation is of critical national significance. Here he draws on the link between family and nation, asserting that traditional relations of hierarchical authority within the family constitute "a difficult fetter with dangerous consequences" at a time when the old certainties of national political life are being called into question. The stifling nature of patriarchy, he writes, is preventing the Arab ruling elites—who, it goes without saying, belong to an older generation—from finding ways of tapping into the "dynamism and capacities of the young." Instead, because the younger generation is locked out of the structures of political leadership, the practice of politics in the Arab world remains mired in what Kanafani calls a "blind language," with the major terms comprising the old vocabulary of Arab nationalism (revolution, socialism, justice) having been frozen in a stale, repetitive, meaningless form. What is lacking, he insists, is the "blood circulation system" that is constitutive of true democracy; without the incorporation of the young ("new blood"), this political-biological process becomes stagnant: "Only when our administrative, political and cultural institutions are capable of spontaneously comprehending the youthful strength, its excitement and influence, is there a democratic situation. The opposite has nothing whatsoever to do with democracy." In his own fictional writings, Kanafani suggests that part of the potential of youth lies in the generation of new kinds of narratives, new ways of "imagining" the nation—including the possibility of imagining a binational Palestine/Israel as an alternative to protracted national conflict.

The unspoken, but closely related assumption in Kanafani's 1968 essay is that the combination of political stagnation and the persistently patriarchal nature of social life can also lead to the kind of revolutionary situation that prevailed in Palestine in late 1987. It would be a mistake, however, to assume that the intifada represented the first entrance of young Palestinians into the forefront of their nation's political life. On the contrary, a generational reading of Palestinian nationalism reveals a recurring pattern in which emerging generations, reacting to various threats on the macropolitical level (colonialism, war, diaspora), regularly challenge existing political hierarchies and orthodoxies, push for the exploration of alternative strategies of resistance, and also embody new possibilities in terms of political identity. These periodic insurgencies of youth face in two directions which may seem, on the surface, to be contradictory: on the one hand, insofar as they infuse age difference with a radical political importance, they undoubtedly represent threats to processes of social and cultural reproduction; on the other hand, because they are responses to events and enemies that threaten the entire nation, they also represent attempts to ensure that such reproduction will be possible in the future.

As early as the 1910s, when in many ways the future of Palestine was the most open-ended, it was a group of young activists who sought to advance a radical, pan-Syrian political strategy as an alternative to the narrow Palestinianism of their older, more conservative counterparts.[4] Later, during the British Mandate period in Palestine (1920–1948), young men again played a crucial role as agitators pushing for more radical tactics in the emerging nationalist struggle. Whether in schools, independent cultural associations, Scout troops, armed militias, or informal groups taking part in strikes and demonstrations, the "young bloods" of this period represented a threat not only to the Zionist project, but also to the ideological and material structures of British rule.[5] And in keeping with the open-ended notion of generation-as-possibility, the relationship between these young activists and their elders was a complex one that ran the full spectrum from harmony of interests to open confrontation. Ibrahim Abu-Lughod, the late Palestinian political scientist who grew up in British-ruled Jaffa, recalled some of his own early political activities when I interviewed him in May 1997:

> We engaged in stone throwing, and we were always looking to the side to see if our parents disapproved. Now we were encouraged by our parents to demonstrate, but there was no risk of life. Now in the intifada, there was. We were imprisoned—I mean, the British police and the British Army, they arrested us. The first time I was arrested, I think I was eleven. They beat me up—they just took me to the police station, and the guy had a bamboo stick, and he used to beat us on our asses. And you know, we'd cry—eleven years old, I mean, we thought, it's *fun*. Partly, partly in my case, I know [why] I did it, because my older brother got arrested, and so he was rewarded by my father and mother. So I went out and got *myself* arrested.

There is also evidence, however, to suggest that young people sometimes went well beyond what was "encouraged" by their elders. A major series of demonstrations in Jaffa in 1933, for example, is generally thought to

have been instigated by young activists who saw the older, more established politicians as "always seeking government permission to demonstrate instead of asserting their right to protest," and insisted that
Britain's support of the Zionist project be met with determined mass action (Lesch 1979, 214). The protest in Jaffa turned deadly when young
people began to throw paving stones and police responded with live ammunition, killing fifteen people. News of the violence spread to other
towns in the following days, leading to further demonstrations. The government, writes Ann Lesch (1979), was eventually able to suppress the
protests with the aid of "town elders [who] prevented the unrest from
spreading to Ramlah and Acre" (215).

When a full-fledged Palestinian national liberation movement emerged
after 1967, many of its leaders—including Yasser Arafat, George Habash,
and Salah Khalaf (Abu Iyad)—were men who had begun their political
careers as student activists in the 1950s, building on the wave of Arab nationalism that swept through the Middle East during that decade. Initially
they signed their mobilizational pamphlets with names such as the "Generation of Reform" and the "Young Avengers" before officially forming
the Fateh movement in 1959. They belonged to the *jīl al-nakba,* and even
before they took control of the PLO, they undertook the task of mobiliz-
ing a new generation, the *jīl al-thawra,* setting up training camps for
young guerrilla fighters who became known as *ashbāl* (lion cubs, for the
young men) and *zahrāt* (flowers, for the young women).[6] Much like the
Arab schoolchildren of the 1930s, the members of the *jīl al-thawra* were
in a unique structural position with respect to the ideological field in
which they lived—caught between an idealized past they knew only
through their parents and the very different futures invoked by colonizers, international hegemons, and nationalist leaders. For the guerrilla organizations, the problem was thus one of how to channel the energies of
this emerging generation into activities which furthered the national
struggle. When Arafat was asked in a 1969 interview to comment on
Fateh's efforts in the area of education and other social services, his response—"we know that our struggle is a long-term one and we are
preparing ourselves accordingly"—indicated a recognition that the movement needed to be reproduced, and that education and political socialization were key ingredients in that process (Khadduri 1972, 773).

For those young people who became politicized during the early
phases of the Resistance, the fight against Zionism enabled what had
once been isolated voices questioning patriarchal authority to become

more influential, with the result that, according to Rosemary Sayigh (1979), the leadership of the Resistance was forced to take steps to "prevent mass adolescent revolt" on the part of young people wishing to leave home and take up arms with the *fidā'īyīn* (guerrilla fighters). At the same time, the mass involvement of the population in resistance activities also sparked the articulation of new generational discourses—no less patriarchal, in both the gendered and generational sense, than the old ones—that reestablished other links between the family and nation: the camps, Sayigh notes, were seen by many as "factories of men for the Revolution" (153).

From the perspective of those who have had the power to define the general parameters of Palestine's national history, generation is thus important primarily insofar as it can be mobilized instrumentally in a way that blunts the potentially disruptive force of generational consciousness. When the Palestine National Council drafted the "Proclamation of the Independent Palestinian State" in Algiers in 1988, therefore, it chose to phrase the nation's history in terms suggesting both historical timelessness and generational continuity:

> Palestine, the land of the three monotheistic faiths, is where the Palestinian Arab people was born, on which it grew, developed and excelled. The Palestinian people was never separated from or diminished in its integral bonds with Palestine. Thus the Palestinian Arab people ensured for itself an everlasting union between itself, its land and its history. . . . Nourished by an unfolding series of civilizations and cultures, inspired by a heritage rich in variety and kind, the Palestinian Arab people added to its stature by consolidating a union between itself and its patrimonial land. The call went out from temple, church and mosque to praise the Creator, to celebrate compassion, and peace was indeed the message of Palestine. And in generation after generation, the Palestinian Arab people gave of itself unsparingly in the valiant battle for liberation and homeland. For what has been the unbroken chain of our people's rebellions but the heroic embodiment of our will for national independence?

This rhetoric of generational succession is echoed in autobiographical works, with nationalist leaders often serving as metonyms for the nation as a whole. In *My Home, My Land,* Abu Iyad (*nom de guerre* of Salah Khalaf, one of Arafat's top lieutenants until his assassination in 1990) narrates the Palestinian struggle through his own life story, from his childhood under the British Mandate through his family's dispossession in 1948, to his days as a student activist and a leader in the PLO's armed struggle and, eventually, to the older, more reflective stage from which he writes. The structure of the book, beginning with chapters entitled "Seeds of Hatred" and "Years of Gestation," reinforces the sense of the nation's history as an organic whole, and even the author's warnings about the danger of a rupture in that history are couched in terms which, while ostensibly antiteleological, are no less reliant on the metaphors of generation: "But if a victory in the foreseeable future remains a possibility, so does a catastrophe—the paralysis or even destruction of our movement. It would neither be the first nor the last time that reactionary forces would succeed in *aborting* a revolution."[7] Significantly, this ominous warning is immediately followed by a return to the language of nationalist optimism and regeneration: "Nonetheless, our people will bring forth a new revolution. . . . *It is in the nature of things*" (226, emphasis added). A work of nationalist autobiography such as Khalaf's, I would argue, cannot but make this kind of return, precisely because the mythologizing of generation—the attempt to replace an inherently open-ended process with one whose meaning is fixed—is an integral part of nationalist narration. If the history of the nation is an "unbroken chain," then each generation can only be a link that is effectively identical to all other links; generational discontinuity is not a possibility to be embraced, but a danger to be overcome.

## Narrative and Popular Memory

More than anyone else, Edward Said has written eloquently and persistently about the particular importance of narration for Palestinians. "Facts do not speak for themselves, but require a socially acceptable narrative to absorb, sustain and circulate them," wrote Said (1984) in his classic article, "Permission to Narrate" (34). Zionism possesses precisely this kind of "socially acceptable narrative," drawing as it does on a variety of "metanarratives" including the Judeo-Christian tradition, notions of redemption and return, and structures of Western guilt that are one legacy of the Holocaust. Palestinian narratives, by contrast, have struggled to achieve the same level of legitimacy, especially in the United States, Israel's primary supporter.

The "official" narrative of Palestinian nationalism, associated with the

PLO, is a primarily secular, anticolonial narrative of national liberation. Like all nationalist narratives, it is subject to challenges from within, but its primary challenge has arisen from its unfortunate collision with Zionism.[8] Since the PLO launched its armed struggle in the late 1960s, the Palestinian narrative has been subjected to sustained attacks, including attempts to link Palestinians with Western anti-Semitism and even claims disputing the very existence of a Palestinian people. The repressive policies of the state of Israel during the same period suggest that this narrative "erasure," far from taking place "only" in the discursive realm, is part of a deeply material process of colonization. The playing field, in other words, has never been a level one, and everything Palestinians say and do must be understood in this context.

Popular memory research is an ideal tool for understanding the complexity of the discursive universe within which Palestinians tell their own stories.[9] Unlike the concept of oral history, which often leaves one mired in unhelpful debates about the "accuracy" or "validity" of oral sources, the popular memory approach celebrates the profound explanatory value of personal narratives. "The guiding principle could be that all autobiographical memory is true; it is up to the interpreter to discover in which sense, where, for which purpose," writes Luisa Passerini (1989, 197). In popular memory research, then, what matters is the ways in which people *produce the past* through a dynamic engagement with the present (and even the future). This production involves a range of discourses, official and popular, dominant and oppositional, individual and collective. The analysis of this process, as the Popular Memory Group (1982) notes, is inherently "relational":

> It has to take in the dominant historical representations in the public field as well as attempts to amplify or generalize subordinated or private experiences. Like all struggles it must needs have two sides. Private memories cannot, in concrete studies, be readily unscrambled from the effects of dominant historical discourses. It is often these that supply the very terms by which a private history is thought through. . . . Similarly the public discourses live off the primary recording of events in the course of everyday transactions and take over the practical knowledges of historical agents. (211)

In keeping with this approach, I have attempted to navigate a course between two equally important principles: the need to respect the stories of individuals as creative, purposeful constructions that are always, in some sense, unique; and the need to take seriously the deep structuring of these stories by complex historical forces, including forces that manifest themselves through powerful, hegemonic narratives associated with nationalist projects.

Among historians who work with oral sources, it is most common to solicit testimony either from individuals who have passed well into adulthood or, more commonly, from those who are even older and who are consequently able to reflect back on their youth from the perspective of a full lifetime of accumulated experience. Yet there is nothing inherent in the concept of memory that requires such a limitation; on the contrary, if we begin from the simple but vital premise that "memory speaks from today" (Passerini 1996, 23), no matter who is doing the remembering, then we must recognize that even the relatively young are capable of developing and articulating a historical perspective on the events of their youth. That this is indeed the case was made clear to me even before I began working in Balata, in the following exchange with twenty-six-year-old Hassan, who grew up in Jenin:

J: How did it feel to you personally at that time? Were you excited?

H: Sure, 100 percent. You know, I was a little bit active in the school, in the student unions, trying to convince people, trying to do something to change our life. . . . And this is a good time, a suitable time, because . . . I'm not alone. I feel that there are thousands of people around me. . . . It's really a unique stage in my life. I'll never forget it.

J: Did you feel like you had a responsibility to do something at that time?

H: Responsibility . . . it's a responsibility for everyone. About me personally, yes, we have to do something, we have to change. . . . At that time I was young and full of energy and lots of planning. It's a suitable time.

Hassan's testimony is noteworthy in this context because it eloquently and explicitly identifies the "drama" of his youth: the early days of intifada activism constituted "a unique stage in my life." Equally important, this statement came from someone who, at that point, had made only a partial transition from youth to adulthood: he had completed his university education and had a full-time job, but was unmarried and spent most of his leisure time associating with students. Increasingly on the fringes of the intifada as a historical period but not entirely removed from it, he had nonetheless achieved a certain sense of distance and reflection ("at that time I was young and full of energy"), able to approach his "youth" from the perspective of memory.

This is not to say that these kinds of memories are free from the influence of age; on the contrary, it is precisely the complex relationship between memory and generational identity that distinguishes the self-representations of young Palestinians such as Hassan. Their stories constantly oscillate between the individual and the collective, between, on the one hand, events witnessed personally and often recounted with the conviction that there is no gap between experienced event and remembered event; and, on the other hand, general assessments concerning collective behavior, opinion, and experience. Their stories are also built on an unresolved, but extremely productive, tension between the ideal and the actual, often giving them a quality that is at once didactic and mythic, realistic and performative.

For most of the young people I interviewed, to remember the intifada is to remember a time during which they and their age-mates came to see themselves as the vanguard of the national struggle against Israeli occupation. To put it another way, the uprising was the crucible in which the political "birth" of their generation—and, by extension, the "rebirth" of the nation as a whole—took place. On an individual level, however, intifada stories are also stories of one's own political awakening, of the events through which one came to see that it was necessary to "do something," in Hassan's words. In many ways, then, the key to understanding the *narrativity* of such stories—rather than trying to determine, in a strictly positivist sense, "what really happened" in the intifada—lies in understanding that the relationships between the individual and the collective, and between the ideal and the actual, are fundamentally unstable, negotiated in the act of reconstructing the intifada through memory.

## Balata Refugee Camp

The nineteen Palestinian refugee camps (*mukhayyamāt*, sing. *mukhayyam*) in the West Bank are densely populated communities with a long history of popular organizing against the Israeli occupation. These camps, along with dozens of others in Gaza and the surrounding Arab countries, are administered by the United Nations Relief and Works

Agency for Palestine Refugees in the Near East (UNRWA), established by the United Nations in May 1950. UNRWA is dependent on voluntary international contributions in order to fulfill its ongoing mandate—renewed some sixteen times by the UN General Assembly—of providing a variety of basic educational, health, and other relief services to registered refugees living inside and outside the camps. In the continuing absence of a comprehensive peace settlement which would address the refugee question and other "final status" issues, the camps remain political oxymorons: at least nominally, they are "temporary" locations housing Palestinians who still harbor the dream of returning to their original communities, many of which were erased from the map after 1948; yet the sheer passage of time has forced onto the camps a kind of permanence not envisioned by the international planners who created UNRWA in order to provide a stopgap solution to the Palestinian "refugee problem."

Occupying 252 dunums (approximately one-tenth of a square mile) of land adjacent to Jacob's Well on the southeastern edge of Nablus, Balata is the West Bank's largest refugee camp, with a population of about 22,000.[10] It is also one of the key sites where the intifada got off the ground in the West Bank in late 1987. Most of the camp's original residents fled from the regions of Jaffa, Ramleh, and Lyyda in 1948, settling briefly in Nablus before UNRWA and the Jordanian government created the camp in 1950 on land apparently belonging to the nearby village of Balata. These families initially lived in tents until more permanent structures—first of mud and corrugated iron sheets, later replaced or augmented with cement blocks—were gradually constructed.[11]

An urban camp whose residents have a fierce collective sense of their identity as a community of disadvantaged and politically active refugees, Balata embodies the contradictory social and geographical status of the *mukhayyamāt* in general. On the one hand, Balata is undeniably a part of Nablus, connected to the city by a variety of ties: the municipality, for example, provides electricity, water, and telephone service to the camp, and many students from Balata attend secondary school in Nablus, with UNRWA staffing only elementary and preparatory schools in the camp itself. On the other hand, certain physical features serve to separate the camp from the surrounding community: the primary road coming into Nablus from Jerusalem clearly marks a dividing line between city and camp, and the main street entering the *mukhayyam* features a large, arching welcome sign notifying visitors that they are, in effect, leaving Nablus proper and passing into a significantly different social world. Numerous camp residents with whom I spoke alluded to deep-rooted tensions between the populations of Balata and Nablus, claiming that wealthy Nabulsis have been known to look down on camp dwellers and to demonstrate their class prejudice by using the term "refugee" (*lājeɔ*) as a scornful epithet.

Despite its size, Balata bears a close resemblance to the other camps of the West Bank and Gaza in a number of ways. Entering the camp, one is immediately aware of the severe overcrowding—in terms of both population and the built environment—that places tremendous pressure on the daily lives, financial resources, and emotional stability of camp residents. The sharp increase in the size of the population living under UNRWA's larger mandate in the past half-century is reflected, in microcosm, in Balata, where families struggle to cope with the fact that the camp allows very little room for natural expansion. Aside from the few main streets wide enough to accommodate cars (with some difficulty) and a highly concentrated but vibrant commercial district, the camp is a maze of twisting alleys, many of which barely allow the passage of two pedestrians. Faced with growing numbers of people living in the same space, many families have chosen to extend their houses upward, in some cases ignoring UNRWA restrictions that prohibit building structures more than two stories high; others have built horizontally, encroaching even further on the narrow passageways between blocks of houses. Running down the hill through the center of the camp is a drainage canal that some residents laughingly refer to as "the Mississippi."

While some of the Palestinians who settled in Balata came originally from urban centers such as Jaffa, most were peasants who had previously made their living by farming. With virtually no access to land, camp residents were immediately forced into an entirely new economic situation, dependent on direct UNRWA support, wage work in Nablus or in the camp (where some small-scale industrial enterprises were started), or tenuous work as vendors or informal laborers in the market. Following the advent of the Israeli occupation in 1967, Palestinians from refugee camps and villages all over the West Bank found themselves increasingly ensnared in a dual system of labor migration. First, growing numbers of young Palestinians were already leaving their homeland for work in the Gulf countries and elsewhere, a pattern that was accelerated during the 1970s as the growth of Palestinian universities created a pool of graduates who had few local job prospects commensurate with their level of education. The remittances these workers sent home provided a significant, often decisive source of income for many families. In addition, the first two decades of the occupation witnessed a sharp decline in the number of Palestinians employed in agriculture, owing in large part to a burgeoning Israeli construction sector that relied heavily on Arab labor.

Many Palestinians from Balata, therefore, found themselves in the politically ironic and personally troubling situation of having to spend their working lives across the "Green Line" (the post-1967 border dividing Israel from the West Bank), literally building a new society on the ruins of their own; others ended up laboring on the growing number of Israeli settlements inside the West Bank. Since the start of the intifada, the general trend (with some intermittent exceptions) has been one of declining opportunities for work in Israel, with the Israeli government's periodic closure of the Occupied Territories proving especially devastating to the microeconomies of the refugee camps. More recently, the arrival of the PA, with its growing bureaucracy and network of security forces, has provided some camp residents with a new employment opportunity, but has also generated significant levels of resentment among those who see themselves as not benefiting from the Authority's presence.

While most camp dwellers can be considered poor in the context of Palestinian society as a whole, Balata camp nonetheless has an identifiable (if narrow) class structure. On the bottom are those who are supported largely by UNRWA and by aid from various governmental and nongovernmental welfare sources. On slightly higher rungs of this truncated economic ladder are those who survive by piecing together an ever-shifting montage of income sources, manipulating as best they can the employment opportunities that become available to them. Those with a modest but less precarious situation—for example, shopkeepers and families with access to stable employment in Nablus—constitute the "middle class" of the camp. Finally, as a number of interviewees pointed out to me, Balata has a small but well-known set of comparatively wealthy families, including some who have managed to secure attractive positions in the PA. Overall, in the estimation of Camp Service Officer Taysir Daoud, the unemployment rate in Balata at the time of my interviews was hovering at around 30 percent, though such figures are obviously difficult to evaluate given the complex definitional issues involved and the frequent changes in the employment status of many workers in a place such as Balata. Roughly half of all Balata residents are under the age of fifteen, a figure that correlates closely with existing demographic data on the West Bank and Gaza as a whole.

In my reading, Balata's relative absence from the scholarly literature seems to belie not only its size in terms of population, but also its status as a long-standing center of political activity, especially among young people. Numerous camp residents, for example, insistently told me that the *shabāb* of Balata had "always" been among the most militant leaders of the struggle against Israeli occupation, and that the camp deserved more credit for sparking the intifada. Such claims are undoubtedly made in other camps as well; in this case, the assertion of Balata's primacy may be a function of the attention that the Gaza refugee camps in general, and Jabaliya camp in particular, have received from journalists and scholars who have coalesced around a particular intifada chronology. During one of my interviews with Majid, a Hamas activist in Balata, for example, his friend Ismail broke into the conversation when I began asking questions about who should be considered the leaders of the uprising. "In the West, people think that the beginning of the intifada was December 8, 1987," he offered, "but many in our situation feel that it began before that. In reality, the outbreak was in May 1987, when the Israelis rounded up all the men in the camp between fifteen and sixty years old and put them in the elementary school . . . and there was a kind of revolution in the camp."

As background to understanding this "revolution," Israeli journalists Ze'ev Schiff and Ehud Ya'ari (1989) note that Balata was a particularly troublesome thorn in the side of the Israeli military in the years leading up to 1987. During this period, they argue, the Shabiba youth movement—formed in Balata in 1982 and associated with the mainstream Fateh faction of the PLO—"became the address for almost every matter concerning the youth of Balata," including voluntary work committees, sporting activities, and issues of pressing social and economic concern such as the lowering of the *mahr* (bride price). More generally, the movement established a significant level of control over the daily life of the camp as a whole, taking upon itself the responsibility to "preserve public and national morals" by encouraging unity of political purpose (on strike days, for example) and stamping out drug dealing, prostitution, corruption, and collaboration. In the process, Shabiba went a great distance toward turning Balata into a "liberated zone," a bounded space into which the Israeli Defense Forces (IDF) seldom entered in significant numbers (59–61). Only in late 1987, a month before the intifada began, did the IDF decide to "straighten up Balata" through mass arrests and a major show of force in the camp. According to Schiff and Ya'ari, however, the operation—which prefigures Ariel Sharon's 2002 invasion—"climaxed in

a stunning Israeli defeat" with far-reaching implications for the antioccu-
pation struggle:

> After sealing off the camp, the army sent in motorized patrols to circu-
> late through its alleys and assemble hundreds of men in the school yard
> for identification and interrogation. The members of the Shabiba had
> definitely been caught by surprise. . . . But in the course of sifting out the
> suspects, a buzz of ferment began to spread through the collection of de-
> tainees. One by one, those whose names appeared on the wanted list
> were picked out of the crowd, handcuffed, blindfolded, and ushered
> over to a corner of the yard. At one point the women who were huddled
> around the edges of the area started shrieking wildly and pressing for-
> ward in an angry mass. As if picking up their cue, the detainees immedi-
> ately began to jeer at the soldiers, tearing open their shirts and thrusting
> their bare chests out against the barrels of the Israeli rifles. Soon calls to
> resist actively could be heard from the vicinity of the mosque, and the
> curses shouted at the mosque were punctuated by the thud of stones
> hurled from a distance. (61–62)

When the soldiers eventually backed down on the orders of the head of
Central Command, the residents of Balata had won a highly symbolic
victory in the ongoing battle with the Israeli occupation. In this respect,
Balata proved to be a bellwether of the uprising to come: its defiance
was echoed, in the early months of the intifada, in other camps and villages whose residents declared their communities "liberated" from IDF
control.

Even if we accept the notion that the intifada "began" on 8–9 December in Gaza, Balata also figured prominently in the events that followed
these initial clashes. After the embarrassing failure of its campaign to
crack down on the Shabiba, the IDF had given the notoriously violent
Border Police a free hand to intimidate camp residents, who reported a
sharp increase in random beatings and other confrontations with the
paramilitary units in the days leading up to the Gaza incident. On Friday,
11 December, the twentieth anniversary of the founding of the leftist Popular Front for the Liberation of Palestine (PFLP), a fierce confrontation
took place between the Border Police and Balata men emerging from the
mosque after midday prayers. Given the general atmosphere of appre-
hension and anger in the camp—particularly following the killing of a
seventeen-year-old stonethrower by Israeli troops the day before in the

Old City of Nablus—the clash was somewhat predictable, but also particularly violent, with three Palestinians killed by Israeli gunfire and some fifty wounded.

The camp's first intifada martyr, eleven-year-old Ali Ismail Musaʿed, was killed when soldiers first opened fire on the stonethrowers; Suhaila Kaʿbi, fifty-seven, was fatally shot in the chest when she ran outside and attempted to drag a wounded demonstrator into her house; her fourteen-year-old niece was then shot and seriously injured while trying to pull her aunt to safety. Finally, Sahar al-Jirmi, a seventeen-year-old whose name is still regularly invoked by camp residents as a symbol of young women's heroic activism, was shot to death by one soldier while being beaten by another as she took part in the stonethrowing.[12] Following the fatal confrontation, the IDF sealed off the camp for four days, during which soldiers apparently engaged in a punitive campaign of widespread and indiscriminate retaliation, smashing windows and furniture, sexually harassing women, and storming homes in the middle of the night to take young men away for interrogation. According to one estimate, Balata camp was under curfew for at least 130 days during the intifada's first year, including 26 of the 35 days following the initial demonstrations in December (Al-Haq 1990).

In recent years Balata has continued to be a center of political activity that defies the control of Palestinian and Israeli authorities alike. During the first elections for the Palestinian Legislative Council in 1996, Balata distinguished itself by electing three representatives. One of these, Husam Khader, became a frequent interlocutor for foreign journalists because of his outspoken criticism of Yasser Arafat and his defense of the rights of refugees. By 1999, the power of Balata's activists, nurtured during the intifada and strengthened by the easy availability of small arms, had become a serious issue for the PA. Press reports indicated that the weapons, obtained on the black market from Palestinians and Israeli arms dealers, were for sale in Balata as openly as bread and cigarettes. Caught between its Oslo-enshrined role as protector of Israeli security and its desire to maintain popular legitimacy, the Authority carried out a public but largely symbolic campaign of weapons confiscation in the camp. Given this history, it is hardly surprising that when the intifada flared up again in the fall of 2000, Balata residents were deeply involved in the new groups (including the Al-Aqsa Martyrs Brigades) that emerged in response to continuing Israeli repression and the failures of the "peace process."

*Interviews and Methodology*

By the time I began my interviews in Balata in February 1997, I had already spent nearly six months living and studying colloquial Arabic in the village of Birzeit, a short distance from the West Bank town of Ramallah. I continued to live in Birzeit for the duration of my research, taking advantage of the West Bank's convenient (if somewhat adventurous) system of shared taxis to travel the one hour or so between Birzeit and Nablus on days when I was interviewing in Balata. Between February and June, I conducted approximately fifty interviews, averaging about ninety minutes in length, with a total of twenty-six Balata residents. All interviews were done in some combination of English and Arabic, almost always leaning heavily toward the latter. While my colloquial Arabic skills were suitable for everyday conversation at that point, my desire to avoid missing (or misunderstanding) crucial details necessitated that I solicit the assistance of three interpreters. Abdul-Jabbar, Mohammed, and Muna not only played a central role in the interviews in terms of language, but also took an active interest in the project itself, regularly joining in the conversations to offer their own questions and interpretations.

The majority of those interviewed (fifteen) were young men between the ages of eighteen and twenty-seven; the remainder included six young women aged twenty to twenty-five, one sixty-two-year-old mother, one fifty-six-year-old father, the parents of the young martyr Sahar al-Jirmi, and the Camp Service Officer.[13] In general, I used what has been called the "snowball" method, trying as much as possible to follow existing networks of friendship and social affiliation in order to identify potential interviewees. This method often involved soliciting interviews with individuals whom I met in the course of conducting another interview, or asking interviewees to suggest the names of friends or acquaintances who might be willing to speak with me. Later on, in order to broaden the collective social and political profile of the larger group, I sought out suggestions concerning specific types of people (e.g., someone a bit younger, or someone known to support Hamas).

Of the core group of fifteen young men I interviewed, nine had spent time in prison, with the accumulated time of incarceration for each ranging from a few months to five years. Four of the fifteen identified themselves as devout Muslims, while seven said they were not religious, with the remaining four falling somewhere in between. In terms of their level of education, the group ranged from those who had been prevented from finishing their *tawjīhī* (the Jordanian-administered comprehensive exam given to West Bank students at the conclusion of secondary school), either for economic reasons or because they were arrested, to those who were in their *tawjīhī* year at the time of our interviews, to those who had completed their bachelor's degree and intended to continue with their studies. Of the interviewees who said they were supporters of a particular political faction, the largest number (eight) were pro-Fateh, followed by Hamas (three) and the PFLP (one); three indicated that they had definite political leanings but preferred not to specify them, and one identified himself explicitly as an independent.

Most interviews were technically conducted with a single individual, although in numerous cases there were others (a friend or a brother, for example) present who occasionally joined the conversation. In terms of their level of formality, the interviews varied widely, with the presence of additional individuals in the room often directly affecting everything from the general tone of the discussion to the specific questions I asked. During my initial interview with Issa, for example, we were joined by one of his older brothers, who listened to the entire conversation and broke in at least once when he felt Issa wasn't making himself clear enough. Given that this was my first interview in Balata, I was inclined to read his attendance as designed in some way to "check me out," but also to protect Issa, whose father had died two years earlier. Political affiliation, however, suggested another possible motivation: the older brother is a local official in the PA, and his presence may have had a restraining effect on Issa, who seemed to speak much more freely about his political opinions during a second interview when the brother was not present. In the case of Majid, the twenty-seven-year-old teacher referred to above, the decision to invite a friend and fellow Hamas activist to his house for the first of our three interviews (and the first I did with anyone associated with Hamas) may have been an effort to provide narrative reinforcement (the friend, who spoke several times during the meeting, firmly refused my request for a separate interview, emphasizing that his views were the same as Majid's) or to bolster his own sense of security (the friend took careful notes while I was speaking). In other cases, the involvement of friends or family acted as a catalyst for a more free-ranging discussion, as when several of Sahar al-Jirmi's brothers and sisters popped in and out of my conversation with their parents, often interrupting to dispute details or suggest alternative interpretations.

I went into my initial interviews with a series of subject areas (e.g., intifada experiences, generational dynamics, ideas about nationhood) and, under each of these topics, a lengthy list of possible questions. While these questions continued to be useful throughout the process, it soon became clear to me that in many ways my desire to cover as many questions as possible was not only overambitious, but also counterproductive in the sense that it drastically reduced the possibility of having a discussion driven not by my questions, but by the "answers." As an alternative to this dilemma, I began relying much more heavily on broader questions (e.g., "What do you remember about the early days of the intifada?") as a way to start conversations, with most of the specific issues addressed in my original list of questions held in reserve for use as an interview moved in a particular direction. This movement, the topical flow of our dialogue, varied widely from one interview to another, perhaps most notably along an axis that ran from those individuals who preferred to speak in generalities—deflecting questions seeking information about their personal actions or their family situation, for example—to those who seemed much more confident talking about themselves.

Following the theoretical and methodological insights of scholars of popular memory, I approached these conversations with at least three general goals in mind. First, I wanted to move beyond what might be called the "testimonial" model—a discursive situation in which the researcher, much like the human rights worker or "solidarity" visitor, specifically encourages respondents to narrate experiences of suffering and oppression—to a more open-ended model that leaves room both for multiple kinds of narratives and for critical reflection on the experiences narrated. In particular, I wanted to provide a space for my informants to articulate the kinds of personal, fragmented narratives which, as Passerini points out, are too often deemed "insufficiently political" to be worthy of consideration by researchers. Second, I aimed to treat the interviews as elements of a much wider narrative field in which each narrative always necessarily assumes the existence of others and "makes sense" in part through its relationship to others. Here I found that Ted Swedenburg's work on the 1936–39 rebellion in Palestine provided an excellent model; analyzing the oral testimony of Palestinians who had lived through the rebellion, Swedenburg (1995a) discovered that a single individual's narrative might typically constitute "a complex web of popular-democratic, nationalist, religious, clan, and localist discourses" rather than a simple replication of, or opposition to, "dominant" memory (28). In discussing the intifada with Balata residents, then, I needed to listen for the ways in which personal narratives might contain traces of official discourses while also suggesting important ways of rereading those discourses. Third, I wanted to uncover the generational terms through which Palestinians narrate both the intifada and their personal and collective histories more generally, and to use these stories as a way of specifying the broader relationship between generation, narrative, and nationalism in Palestine.

# 2

# "Gaza Is Ruled by a Child"
## The Intifada and the Rhetoric of Generation

We see lords and patrons, nurses and agents, generals and parents, siblings and lawyers, doctors and pederasts, murderers and uncles —all hovering over the image of the child. Some of these can be trusted, others not. Sometimes you just can't tell. We implicitly count ourselves among the trustworthy. We know what is best— the right distance, the right benevolent power, the right gift for the young. . . . So I write my *essais* . . . to find the right distance between reason and compassion, between memory and forgetting.
—McKenzie Wark

None of us can forget the whispers and occasional proclamations that our children are "the population factor"—to be feared, and hence to be deported—or constitute special targets for death. I heard it said in Lebanon that Palestinian children in particular should be killed because each of them is a potential terrorist. Kill them before they kill you.                         —Edward Said

The emergence of young people as political actors can generate a diverse field of discourses, opening up new possibilities for representing the relationship between the nation and its children. At no time was this more evident in Palestine than at the beginning of the intifada; while sophisticated analysis of the role of young people was lacking at that point, it seems that virtually everyone felt a need to comment on the activists who quickly became known as the "children of the stones" (*atfāl al-hijāra*). For every Israeli government official who argued that Palestinian children were being sent out into the streets as cannon fodder by cowardly parents, there was a young refugee camp resident who expressed a sense of empowerment and insisted on his or her own agency. And for every psychologist or educator cautioning about the long-term ramifications of children's loss of "respect" for adult authority, there was a musician or poet lauding the heroic exploits of the young stonethrowers. All these responses suggest that our understanding of what was "really happening" on the ground in late 1987 and 1988 cannot be separated from the way those events were represented in a variety of discursive contexts. Moreover, the sheer number of interested parties who commented on the early days of the intifada suggests a need to cast the analytical net wide rather than attempting to distill an "authentic" or "pure" Palestinian narrative of events.

In this chapter, then, I provide a topography of intifada discourses on generation. It is through the operation of these discourses—none of which, it should be emphasized, can be contained entirely within the bounds of the uprising itself—that the "intifada generation" came to be constituted as a highly symbolic object of admiration and contestation among a variety of Palestinian, Israeli, and international commentators, as well as an object of intensive counterinsurgency efforts on the part of the Israeli state. Taken together, they constitute a *discursive field* within which the personal narratives examined in the remainder of the book are articulated. There are several reasons for taking this sort of approach. First, scholars of discourse have established convincingly that *what is said* is an important part of *what is* and, further, that all discourse is inherently conditioned—enabled, shaped, limited—by *what has already been said*. Following up on this insight, and given that the Palestinian question occupies a unique position in the world's consciousness, we must acknowledge that the memories that form the core of this book are memories of events that "always already" have meaning—in fact, many meanings. Finally, as I noted in the previous chapter, even a brief survey of the history of the Palestinian liberation struggle indicates that discourses of generation have played a key role in that struggle for decades. In this sense, the discourses that were operative during the intifada stretch backward and forward in time, both drawing on existing notions (e.g., the PLO's "generation of liberation") and providing in turn a kind of narrative palette with which later examples, including popular memories, can be represented on a variety of post-intifada canvases.

## Discourses of Generation as Rhetorical Modes

Much of the existing literature on intifada discourse has tended to identify either social groups (e.g., youth, parents, journalists) or discursive forms (e.g., news reports, leaflets, poems) as the primary unit of analysis. An excellent example is Cohen and Wolfsfeld's *Framing the Intifada* (1993), which uses a communications paradigm and Erving Goffman's general concept of "frames" (Goffman 1974) to explore conflicting interpretations of the intifada. While this constructionist approach is more useful than either a straightforward propaganda or instrumentalist model, the focus on frames also brings with it a number of limitations, most notably the assumption that particular frames are always organically related to particular groups and not others. In Wolfsfeld's words, "Each party who came into contact with the *intifada* created their own set of pictures and frames" (xxvii). From a discourse analytic perspective, this assumption minimizes the possibility that in certain cases groups which are ostensibly on opposite sides of a given political conflict may produce discourses that suggest the operation or internalization of a given frame. In addition, the communications paradigm ignores the extent to which these various "parties" are themselves produced as political and interpretive communities through the workings of the frames they supposedly "create." Finally, as I have already suggested, by implying that "frames" are somehow created *ex nihilo*, Wolfsfeld's model ignores what is perhaps the cardinal rule of discourse analysis: the notion that all communication, from everyday speech to the most complex discursive structures, is necessarily shaped, limited, and rendered possible by a preexisting discursive universe.

As an alternative framework, I have found it useful to focus on the operation of what David Spurr (1993) calls "rhetorical modes."[1] In analyzing colonial discourse in a series of "non-fictional" genres (exploration and travel writing, "literary journalism," narratives of imperial administration), Spurr argues that one should not reify the distinctions between these categories, precisely because *all* are constituted, in part, by their reliance on similar rhetorical modes, including surveillance, aestheticization, negation, and naturalization. Taken together, these modes make up "a kind of repertoire for colonial discourse, a range of tropes, conceptual categories, and logical operations available for purposes of representation" (3). Significantly, the elements of this repertoire are closely related to the devices typically employed in "fictional" genres. Focusing on these modes thus allows Spurr to establish critical linkages *between* genres by revealing certain discursive regularities; it also makes it possible for us to see the wide range of discourses, narrators, and frames associated with the intifada not as natural, distinct entities but rather as intimately linked through their reliance on a similar repertoire of generational metaphors and explanatory paradigms.

In this chapter I discuss six of the most common rhetorical modes (heroism, victimization, guilt-shame, potential, testimonial, and empowerment) through which the actions of the young people who were at the center of the intifada, as well as the young people themselves, have been understood, categorized, researched, and symbolically appropriated. As I noted in my critique of the communications paradigm, no rhetorical mode can be reduced to a singular narrator or subject position; thus the mode of guilt-shame, for instance, is linked not only with some Israeli soldiers who served in the Occupied Territories, but also with some Palestinian parents whose children were involved in dangerous intifada activities. What distinguishes the various modes, then, is not the narrator, but rather the kind of meaning that is attached to young people and their actions. While not unrelated to the others, each mode nonetheless stakes out a distinct position on a constellation of issues related to generation and politics, including the degree of young people's ability to carry out self-motivated political actions; the historical and political contexts within which these actions should be viewed; and the relationship between young people, nationalism, and national identity.

Each mode also contains implicit assumptions about generation itself and about the normative question of where the proper boundaries between generational categories (childhood, youth, adulthood) should be located, both in general and in the more unusual context of a political conflict such as the intifada. These assumptions are embedded in the very terms employed in the various discourses, and they are rarely value-neutral. This nominative variation, however, is not solely a function of competing political agendas. According to folklorist Sharif Kanaana (1993), the involvement of young people in the intifada caused a kind of terminological upheaval in Palestinian society: suddenly no one knew exactly what to call the young activists who were at the forefront of the struggle against the occupation. The meanings of words traditionally used to designate particular age-groups (see Table 1) were either expanded or contracted, highlighting both the arbitrary nature of such categories and the ability of everyday speech to adjust to changing political realities.

TABLE I
*Palestinian Generational Categories*[a]

| Male | Female | English equivalent | Age range |
|---|---|---|---|
| *tifl/atfāl* | *tifl/atfāl* | child | birth–6 yrs. |
| *walad/awlād* | *bint/banāt* | boy/girl | 6–13 yrs. |
| *shab/shabāb* | *sabiyya/sabāya* | young man/woman | 14–25 yrs. |
| *zalame/izlām* | *mara/niswān* | man/woman | 25–60 yrs. |
| *rajul/rijāl* | | | |
| *ikhtyār/ikhtyariyye* | *ikhtyāra/ikhtyarāt* | old man/woman | over 60 yrs. |

[a] The first four columns of Table 1 are taken from a similar chart in Kanaana (1993); however, he only provides information on male generational categories. The age ranges given, therefore, should be read as constructed with these male categories in mind, with puberty and marriage forming the transition points between *walad* and *shab*, and *shab* and *zalame/rajul*, respectively. As I have indicated in expanding the chart to include female categories, there is a rough correspondence between the stages referred to on each side; nonetheless, differences such as the traditionally lower marriage age of women should be kept in mind when comparing the female categories with Kanaana's age ranges.

The main problem, according to Kanaana, is that the "young males" so visibly involved in intifada activities "do not coincide with any traditionally known class or age group with a linguistic designation of its own, either in English or in Arabic," but instead straddle two categories, namely, *awlād* and *shabāb* (42). Yet as we will see below, it is the *youngest* category—and also the only gender-neutral one—that has often been used to label these young activists. Many poets, for example, became fond of referring to *all* young Palestinians, whether five years old or fifteen, as *atfāl,* and researchers writing in English often made a similar move, effectively removing the category of "youth" from the picture and expanding the ranks of those known as "children." On the other hand, as Kanaana notes, many young men found terms such as *atfāl* and *awlād* "insulting" and adamantly preferred to be called *shabāb* (simultaneously "older" and more explicitly masculine), or, in an attempt to place themselves within a longer history of Palestinian youth activism, *ashbāl.*[2] For their part, many adults tended to "snicker" when hearing *shabāb* used in this way, seeing it as "too dignified" a term to be applied to those they saw as mere children; this view led to the creation of a new median term, *shabāb izghār* ("little *shabāb*").

Ironically, the Israeli state, eager to lessen international criticism of its widespread and often indiscriminate repression of young people, at times demonstrated its own interest in breaking down generational distinctions. "The word 'child' is never used in military announcements: they refer to either an infant or a youth, but never a child," observed Anton Shammas (1988) in an early commentary on the uprising. "So a ten-year-old boy shot by the military forces is reported to be a 'young man of ten.'" Clearly, then, the intifada introduced important challenges to existing classificatory systems, signaling a politically driven collapse of the old distinctions between generational categories and, among Palestinians, a growing debate—that sometimes broke down along generational lines—over issues of social and political authority. These linguistic and social dynamics, which are obviously related to assumptions about young people's capacity for political consciousness and agency, provide a crucial context for understanding the operation of the rhetorical modes to which I now turn.

### Heroism: "The Elect Generation of History"

Less than two weeks after the intifada began, the late Syrian poet Nizar Qabbani published his "Children of the Stones," portraying the young Palestinian stonethrowers as heroic, larger-than-life figures single-handedly saving the national movement—and perhaps the entire Arab world—from stagnation. They were heroes not only for resisting Israeli occupation, but also for refusing to countenance the corruption of the Arab leaders who had repeatedly failed to support the Palestinian struggle. "With stones in their hands, they defy the world and come to us like good tidings," wrote Qabbani (quoted in Harlow 1989):

> Ay . . . O generation of betrayals . . .
> O generation of brokers . . .
> O generation of discards . . .
> O generation of debauchery
> You will be swept away—however slow is history—
> By the children of the stones.

For Qabbani, the significance of young people's actions was historical—"sweeping away" an old order and helping to create a new one—as well as political, and their privileged status derived from their determination to take actions that their elders were either unwilling or unable to take.

In an April 1988 lecture in Washington, Palestinian lawyer Jonathan Kuttab picked up on precisely these kinds of arguments, suggesting that children in the West Bank and Gaza "possessed a new spirit" and had "shattered the barrier of fear" between themselves and the Israeli soldiers, with the result that old strategies associated with more "realistic"

Palestinians were rendered obsolete. "Perhaps this is the definition of truly revolutionary action: not that it takes up the gun or is violent, but that it refuses to accept the givens of traditional wisdom, the limits within which everyone feels they must operate," Kuttab argued. "Perhaps only the young are capable of launching that kind of movement." Kuttab's statement exemplifies the somewhat contradictory mode of *heroism*: on the one hand, young people possess historical, even revolutionary agency; on the other, their actions are significant insofar as they contribute to a national cause that has been *defined for them*, even as others have betrayed, abandoned, or failed to live up to it in the past.

Early examples of intifada narratives feature an overwhelming sense of novelty, a conviction that young people were doing something unprecedented. Yet the speed with which the notion of "children of the stones" as heroes crystallized suggests that this particular rhetorical mode was hardly new. Many journalists and other observers, for example, drew on the biblical story of David and Goliath when describing events in Ramallah or Gaza. That such characterizations involved an ironic inversion—with the "young" Israel of the 1950s and 1960s having previously been identified as an underdog David fighting the Arab Goliath—only added to their potency. Just days before the intifada began, young Palestinians could look to the example of the young commando who used a motorized hang glider to carry out a suicide attack on an Israeli military camp near the Lebanese border on 25 November 1987. After landing in a nearby field, he entered the base heavily armed, killed six soldiers, and wounded seven others before being shot dead. According to Kamal Boullata (1990), "the story of the flying boy" had a tremendous impact on Palestinians living under occupation, bringing a "spark of wonder" into their lives and providing a model of youthful resistance:

> That night, as he buckled himself into position, the boy never knew that the heroic accomplishment of his solitary flight was to mark the beginning of an ineradicable moment in the history of his people. The primitive means by which this Palestinian conquered insurmountable odds became the fiber of the uprising. . . . In schools the story of the boy arriving on what looked like a gigantic kite to singlehandedly confront Israeli soldiers within their own military base was overnight becoming a legend. . . . The ground rules of the intifada were set in motion. Schoolchildren were in the vanguard, shaping the events. (26–27)

Boullata's description of the mission as a "solitary" one is significant, because there were actually two commandos involved in the attack, the second of whom landed his glider on the Lebanese side of the border inside
Israel's self-declared "security zone" before Israeli forces captured and
killed him. Both guerrillas were affiliated with the Syrian-backed PFLP-
General Command, and while both went unnamed in news reports, a
photograph in the Palestinian newspaper *al-Fajr* on 29 November seems
to indicate that the second of the two was somewhat older, perhaps making the first more "heroic" by virtue of his young age as well as the military results of his mission.

It was against this backdrop, then, that the rhetoric of heroism
emerged, making a variety of claims on behalf of the stonethrowers while
offering narrative interpretations of the intifada. As Barbara Harlow
(1989) has noted, Qabbani's poem was but the first in a long succession
of odes to the "children of the stones," many of which focused almost ob-
sessively on the image of the stone. In the realm of political discourse, intifada leaflets, known in Arabic as *bayanāt* (sing. *bayān,* "communiqué")
or *mnādā* (sing. *nidāʾ,* "call"), provide an important window onto the
link between rhetorical devices and political mobilization. These popular
texts, produced secretly and distributed throughout the Occupied Territories, functioned both as a mechanism for instructing the population on
particular tactics (general strikes, for example) and as a forum in which
to praise and exhort those who were involved in the uprising.

Discourses of heroism played an important role in the latter process,
with young people regularly singled out for their willingness to fight for
Palestinian independence. Hamas communiqué No. 2 ("The Blessed Uprising"), dated January 1988, is addressed to "patient mothers, righteous
fathers, youth who are fighting a holy war, splendid lion cubs," the latter
phrase reviving the image of the *ashbāl* and establishing both a cross-gen-
erational connection in terms of goals and a generational division between young people who are "fighting" and the elders who are supporting them. The same leaflet argues that Israel "expected the generation
that grew up after 1967 to be wretched and cowed, a generation brought
up on hashish and opium, songs and music, beaches and prostitutes"—
anything but a "generation of liberation," in other words. "Yet what actually happened?" the authors ask rhetorically. "What happened was the
awakening of the people" (Mishal and Aharoni 1994, 205).

Similarly, the United National Leadership of the Uprising (UNLU)
from its inception seized on the image of a heroic, defiant generation of

youth, as in its second *nidāʾ* from January 1988. "O youth of Palestine, O throwers of incendiary stones," the leaflet reads, "the neofascists will undoubtedly be forced to admit the facts forged by your uprising, which is marking the road to national independence" (56). Given that the intifada activists were not formally "trained" to the same extent that the *ashbāl* were, these *bayanāt* read less as attempts to create cadres of young activists than as recognitions and celebrations of the actions that young people were already taking.

Among intellectuals responding to the intifada, descriptions and analysis of the uprising were often inflected with the language of heroism, suggesting that the young stonethrowers were more heroic, and indeed more revolutionary, for being young. In an article written following the Palestine National Council's Declaration of Independence in November 1988, Edward Said (1989, 8) references Qabbani's poem and writes of the intifada activists "with stones and an unbent political will standing fearlessly against the blows of well-armed Israeli soldiers, backed up by one of the world's mightiest defense establishments, bankrolled unflinchingly and unquestioningly by the world's wealthiest nation, supported faithfully and smilingly by a whole apparatus of intellectual lackeys." The heroism of these young stonethrowers, for Said, lies not just in the dangerous act of facing down Israeli troops, but in their perceived ability and determination to take on global structures of political, economic, and military domination at the same time.

Ali Mazrui (1990) takes this argument even further, linking the intifada's activists with their counterparts in China as playing "a fundamental vanguard role" in a world-historical sense, as "the elect generation of history." There is ample evidence to suggest that intellectuals such as Mazrui were not the only observers who viewed the intifada through such a global prism: indeed, for many community activists and liberation movements from Los Angeles to South Africa, the intifada provided, in much the same way that the Algerian resistance had done three decades earlier, a useful model either to invoke or to emulate.[3]

## Victimization: "It Is a Confiscated Childhood"

Unlike the rhetorical mode of heroism, which was used primarily by Palestinians and others sympathetic to the Palestinian struggle, the mode of *victimization* is available to a wider variety of narrators, including hawkish Israelis. Similarly, whereas the first mode relies on what we might call local or regional images (e.g., David and Goliath) to highlight the national significance of young people's actions, the second mode relies heavily on appeals to international standards of human rights. Discourses of victimization thus constitute an arena of struggle linking occupier, occupied, and a host of experts (lawyers, psychologists, case workers) in a highly charged contest over who is the true defender of the rights of children and who merely "uses" children for political ends, a contest whose audience is global.[4]

Discourses of victimization emerged during the intifada partly as a response to the aforementioned collapsing of distinctions between generational categories. For those concerned with the plight of young people during times of political violence, this situation presented a serious dilemma. On the one hand, children and youth of all ages were clearly suffering the full range of Israel's counterinsurgency strategy: they were shot, beaten, teargassed, arrested, tortured, denied their right to education, and subjected to curfews and other forms of collective punishment. On the other hand, when asked, many of these young people exhibited a profound sense of empowerment and insisted that because of their actions in support of the national cause, they should not be referred to as "children" (*atfāl*) but should instead be treated with the respect normally given to adults.

The mode of victimization, in other words, is built on a paradox that becomes clear when we look at the many studies aiming to document the "effects" of the intifada on children and youth. Given that young people played a crucial role in creating the intifada in the first place, can we really isolate these "effects," even for analytical purposes, from the agency of those who are supposedly "affected"? The general privileging of structural explanations as a response to this paradox is reflected in the impressive amount of human rights research on children and the intifada, in which the empowerment of young people is regularly acknowledged, but almost always subordinated to what is clearly seen as the larger moral imperative: the need to document, in as much detail as possible, the victimization and suffering of Palestinian "children." One of the most widely cited sources, the massive 1990 study undertaken by Swedish Save the Children (Nixon 1990), devotes three volumes to child death and injury and collective punishment, including month-by-month reviews of Israeli actions and hundreds of case studies. According to the report's introduction, the issues of "empowerment through the intifada, and resulting challenges to traditional authority" were to be explored only in a single section of the fourth and final volume which, to the best of my knowledge, was never completed. Similarly, James Graff's *Palestinian Children and Israeli State Violence* (1991), which synthesizes material from the Save the Children report and a number of other sources, discusses the "positive" aspects of the intifada for young people only in the last of its thirteen chapters.

The reasons for this emphasis on passive victimization are clearly related to the audience for whom these texts are generally intended, namely, international readers who are assumed to be in a position to influence events in Israel/Palestine, either by pressuring their own governments to oppose Israeli policies or by contributing to organizations working on behalf of young people.[5] Given this goal, it is not surprising that many human rights reports refer almost exclusively to "children" even when discussing Palestinians as old as nineteen. Such work does not always contain an explanation of how a particular definition of "child" was arrived at, nor does it acknowledge the fact that the labeling of teenagers as "children" might be inconsistent with the self-identification of the people involved. The Palestine Human Rights Information Center (PHRIC), for example, reported that "children" accounted for 40 percent of intifada-related deaths in the period up to May 1989, but included in this figure Palestinians aged seventeen to nineteen, who represented just over half of the total (Rouhana 1989, 111). This decision to expand the category of "child" upward in age—as opposed to extending the category of "youth" downward—effectively uses the youngest members of the group to stand for the whole. In the process, some of the most active participants in the intifada—young people in their mid- to late teens—are reduced to the status of passive, innocent "children" instead of the self-motivated activists many saw themselves to be.

Moreover, the framework suggests that from a moral standpoint, there is something more offensive about killing, beating, or arresting a sixteen-year-old than a twenty-year-old (or, indeed, anyone older than twenty). While this view is undeniably persuasive, it can also have unintended consequences: when the victimization of a certain age group is highlighted, the focus is taken away from the Israeli occupation as a *total system of domination*—subject, in its entirety, to moral standards enshrined in relevant international laws, UN resolutions, and so forth—and transferred to a select group of cases where, presumably, the occupying power has exceeded the bounds of what is morally permissible.[6] Graff, who defines children as those under the age of seventeen, summarizes the ethical argument typically offered in support of human rights work on children:

> [T]here are compelling reasons to focus on Palestinian children. First, people and governments have special obligations to protect, educate and nurture children. As adults, we have special responsibility to do what we can to help make it possible for children to live in dignity and freedom as adults. . . . When a government pursues a course of repression in which children become major targets, as in this case, people of conscience . . . are morally bound to take political action.

In support of such a position, most human rights reports provide extensive testimony by young people themselves. But this testimony almost always takes the form of responses to highly circumscribed sets of questions concerning the interviewees' status as victims of Israeli state violence. Other texts arising out of the intifada, such as news reports and sociological studies, including my own, suggest that when given a chance to talk about political issues of their own choosing many young Palestinians often focus not on their own victimization and that of their age-mates, but rather on the larger political grievances at the root of the intifada.

We find similar dynamics in the large psychological literature covering the "effects" of the intifada on young people.[7] Despite the high levels of violence experienced by Palestinians of all ages, many of these researchers found it difficult to document what was assumed to be the inevitable negative impact of this environment on the behavior and emotional well-being of children and youth, particularly when the young people themselves were interviewed. The problem, once again, is that if one assumes that "the intifada" is essentially a separate entity acting upon young people, it is impossible to see the ways in which the "behavior" of young people is itself constitutive of what we know to be "the intifada." Varying responses to this chicken-and-egg problem are reflected in the diverse definitional and methodological approaches employed in a number of these studies. Nariman Awwad's (1992) study of Dheisheh Refugee Camp, for example, partially brackets the problem in two ways, first by looking only at children aged thirteen and under, and second by relying on questionnaires administered not to the child, but to a close relative who was asked to speak for the child. The design of the questionnaire itself—focusing on "degree of exposure to violence" and on the incidence of various psychological and somatic aftereffects of this exposure (sleeplessness,

aggression, headaches)—ensures an emphasis on the passive victimization of young people; possible elements of empowerment are alluded to
only in a concluding section of the report.

In other work, such as Ahmad Baker's (1990) study based on an eval-
uation of nearly eight hundred West Bank and Gaza children (aged between six and fifteen) in 1989, we see a more explicit ambivalence about
the gap between research expectations and results. "[O]ne would hy-
pothesize that the prevalence of psychological problems among Palestinian children would be high," observes Baker. "Palestinian psychologists
have noted, however, increased self-esteem displayed by Palestinian youth
during the Intifada; some psychiatrists even reported a reduction in
pathological symptoms among some youths following the onset of the Intifada" (497). After administering two standardized tests and asking
mothers to describe the occurrence of various symptomatic behavior patterns, Baker found a variety of problems, including disobedience, sleep
disturbance, and fear of leaving the house. He concludes, however, that
"no serious pathological conditions were detected on a scale beyond that
expected in the general population" (502). Concerning the impact of the
intifada in particular, he was unable to correlate negative behavior patterns with the uprising itself; certain positive trends, however, appeared
to be directly related to the political action of young people:

> The onset of the Intifada . . . seems to have provided Palestinian youth
> with a mechanism that strengthens self-esteem. . . . Palestinian children
> who are actively engaged in the events of the Intifada tend to perceive
> themselves in a powerful role because they confront the Israeli Army. So-
> cial support and high esteem are transmitted to the children by adults
> and peers for their "bravery." Furthermore, subjective data collected on
> these children tend to suggest the absence of defeatist attitudes among
> them. (504)

Baker notes, appropriately, that a preliminary study conducted in the
midst of the intifada is hardly the last word on psychological effects,
which often take years to manifest themselves. Nonetheless, studies such
as his are significant not only for their specific findings, but also for what
might be seen as the collective refusal of young people to cooperate with
a rhetorical mode whose raison d'être is their status as victims.

Outside the realm of published research, popular discourse from
the early period of the intifada indicates that even as images of young

Palestinians boldly confronting Israeli troops were being beamed around the world, many older Palestinians were already wondering how the younger generation would be negatively marked by the intifada experience. Just as Qabbani's "Children of the Stones" and similar poems focused attention on the historically significant actions of young people, Hussein Barghouti's "A Song for Childhood" (1989), recorded in 1988 by the Palestinian group Sabreen, highlighted the price that the "intifada generation" was paying, as a generation, for its activism:

> The moon rose
> over childhood
> And childhood was hills
> gathering sparrows and flowers
> in baskets under the moon
> I'll pursue it, weeping and
> falling on jagged stones.
>
> It is a confiscated childhood.
> From books and oil lamps, sometimes,
> to prison and release, sometimes,
> sometimes my life is counterfeit
> Inside a city besieged by guards.

The suggestion that childhood can be "confiscated" indicates Barghouti's concern over whether the *jīl al-intifāda* will end up being a proverbial "lost generation." As is the case in South Africa, site of recent debates over the fate of the young people who were at the forefront of antiapartheid activities in the years after the 1976 Soweto uprising, the "lost generation" discourse in Palestine is marked by an emphasis on the ways in which children were forced to be (or act like) adults before they were ready to do so. "From the shoot-to-kill policy and the breaking bones policy to the night raids and beatings, the children are forced to face the new challenges of a new time," writes Eyad Sarraj (1993). "They simply cannot afford the luxury of childhood and have to assume the worries of adulthood."

One of the Israeli military's initial responses to the storm of international criticism that accompanied its repression of the uprising was to echo its critics, albeit for very different (and, one might suspect, more cynical) reasons, by claiming that the young people being killed and wounded in intifada confrontations were, in fact, victims. In this case, of course, the accused "victimizer" was not the Israeli occupation, but rather a whole range of Palestinian authority figures, including parents, teachers, and political leaders. An early Israeli Justice Ministry report, for example, argued that the uprising "has exploited children by placing them in harm's way" and charged "the PLO and extremist Islamic elements" of deliberately recruiting young people to put their bodies on the line in street clashes (quoted in Nixon 1990, vol. 1, xiv). This general argument resurfaces in the Ministry of Defense's 1993 defense of Israeli military and legal policy during the intifada (Yahav 1993). Perhaps recognizing that earlier Israeli claims had been discredited, notably the claim that the PLO was itself responsible for starting the uprising, the book presents a modified argument focusing on the status of young people as political pawns:

> One of the most significant developments in the "Intifada" was the large number of juveniles, including small children, who took to the streets during the rioting. Initially, this seems to have been a spontaneous response. Over time, however, leaflets of the "Intifada" leadership issued explicit and highly detailed instructions on the use of children in the disturbances. This was a highly cynical attempt to use small children as a screen behind which to attack the IDF; on some occasions it has resulted in the tragic loss of life by—or injury to—youngsters. (95)

The bulk of the book's treatment of issues related to young people, however, concerns official Israeli attempts to deal with "juvenile offenders" within a military justice system which the authors describe as "marked by a judicial awareness and a degree of sensitivity to law and due process unprecedented in the modern history of belligerent military occupation" (15). In this legal context, the book presents young people as victims not of their political leaders, but of parental neglect. An excellent example is the 1988 "Order concerning the Conduct of Minors" (Military Order 1235 for the West Bank/951 for the Gaza Strip), which empowered the military to hold parents "criminally liable" for the actions of their children by imposing a fine or jail sentence on the parents, with the assumption that the money paid will be returned only if the parents succeed in preventing a recurrence of the child's action.[8]

The inspiration for this policy was clearly practical, namely, to deter political resistance activities (and, as an ancillary effect, to raise money through the widespread levying of fines) while avoiding the international criticism that would likely result from putting young people on trial. In explaining the policy, however, the book's authors attempt to provide a *moral* justification: "The Israeli government position on this question," they note, "is that parental liability is based not merely on the actions of the minor but on the parent's own conduct in failing to provide parental supervision sufficient to keep the child out of trouble. . . . [T]he liability stems from the parent's omission in regard to the child's upbringing" (97). They conclude with the curious assertion that these policies, which plainly had the potential to exacerbate intrafamily tensions, were in fact designed to help reverse the "loss of parental authority" in the West Bank and Gaza.

In this case we see how the mode of victimization gave Israeli authorities a language with which to carry out a project of linking state and parental authority, both perceived as embattled. Ironically, in positing such a common interest with Palestinian parents, the state also demonstrated how tenuous this rhetorical mode can be, since accusations of parents mistreating their children quickly slip into a different discourse which implies that the children were actively refusing to obey. Narrators more sympathetic to the Palestinian cause run into a similar problem when using this mode, for claims of passive victimization are constantly confronted with evidence indicating that not all young people who suffer violence are equally "passive" in terms of their own relationship to political events. Some are caught in the wrong place at the wrong time, others join in peaceful demonstrations with the knowledge that the military response may be deadly, and still others actively seek out violent confrontations with soldiers. I do not wish to argue, for example, that certain killings carried out by Israeli troops are more "justified" than others; rather, I am suggesting that as a rhetorical mode often employed in the most all-encompassing terms, victimization may provoke others to make precisely the same kind of argument.

*Guilt and Shame: "Vulgar, Unnecessary Situations Which Humiliate Them and Degrade Us"*

One of the most interesting moments during my time in Balata camp occurred when I went with Abdul Jabbar to interview eighteen-year-old Ayman. Just as we were beginning our conversation, Ayman's father, Abu

Nimr, came into the sitting room to greet us. After he introduced himself, I asked if he might be willing to let us interview him in the near future. He agreed, but seemed disappointed when I told him the topic of my research; he suspected that he would have little to contribute, he said shyly, because it was young people like Ayman who had "made" the intifada.

When we returned to interview him, he spent the first half of our conversation detailing his family's flight from its home in Kfar Saba in 1948, the difficult conditions that prevailed in Balata in the years following the *nakba,* and the economic imperatives that forced him to leave school in the sixth grade and begin a series of low-paying jobs culminating in his current work as a laborer in the Nablus vegetable market. More than any other Palestinian I interviewed, Abu Nimr seemed to harbor a quiet bitterness that surfaced most clearly in his attempts to draw out my own feelings of guilt as an "outside" visitor who was asking for his time and his stories, but was able to offer very little in return. He told me the story of a journalist who came to Balata shortly after 1948 wanting, in Abu Nimr's words, to "take pictures of the barefooted little children," but who balked when challenged to explain how his pictures would really help anyone, saying, "I'm only a journalist." Given that Abu Nimr knew not only of my identity as an academic researcher, but also of my specific interest in young people, his observation was especially pointed and revealed some of the connections between the mode of victimization and the mode of *guilt-shame.* On the one hand, he was attempting to provoke feelings of guilt on the part of an outside visitor who was able to offer little in return for his stories; on the other hand, his story "worked" precisely to the extent that I was inclined to see Palestinians as victims.

As I learned later in the interview, there was also a close correlation between the appearance of guilt and shame in Abu Nimr's personal narrative and the victimization of children, including his own. When I asked him to speak about some of the events and experiences he remembered most from the intifada, he immediately invoked the name of one of the camp's young intifada martyrs, then suddenly broke into tears and left the room, unable to hold his emotions back. This memory seemed to constitute, for him, the tragic underside of his contention that young people had been at the forefront of the intifada. His own life story was one of hard work and suffering rather than one of activism; nowhere in our conversations did he mention taking part, at any point in his life, in the kinds of resistance activities in which his sons were involved on a daily basis during the intifada, or, indeed, in any other kind of self-generated political action.

In talking with Abu Nimr, I found myself face to face with what Eyad Sarraj calls the "helpless" Palestinian father, "sitting in the corner" while his wife and children are out confronting the Israeli occupation. "Now at the beginning of the intifada, women went out into the streets to protect their children, basically, and in the process they were in confrontations with Israeli soldiers, and that encouraged young girls also to go out," Sarraj told me in a May 1997 interview. "But soon after that, when men were feeling so insecure that they have lost the control over the family—because boys were out, and now women are out, and young girls are out—the man, the father, was sitting in the corner so helpless." Just a few months before our interview, Abu Nimr had seen Ayman shot in the leg during the September clashes near Joseph's Tomb in Nablus; years earlier, during the height of the intifada, another young son was seriously wounded in the head by a rubber bullet while he and other elementary school students were stoning soldiers at an observation post set up near their school. For this father, then, discussing the intifada and its effect on other young people may have been an uncomfortable reminder of his own inability to prevent such tragedies from befalling his own children.

Like all the modes discussed in this chapter, the mode of guilt-shame is obviously not limited to discourses about young people. Yet as the example of Abu Nimr suggests, the combination of children and violence can inspire the most intense feelings of guilt and shame among adults. This is even more evident in the narratives of Israelis, particularly certain Israeli soldiers who are directly involved in the violence, than it is in existing Palestinian narratives. Once again it is the young people—whether viewed as passive victims or active agents—who are the link between narratives that might otherwise appear to be purely antagonistic. The mode of guilt-shame appears primarily in discourses that are oriented toward internal conversations rather than international audiences, constituting a kind of inner monologue for several groups of narrators who are both observers of, and participants in, political conflict. The key to understanding the examples presented here lies in the recognition that while the feelings of guilt and shame described in them belong to adults, it is young people who are regularly credited with inspiring these feelings. As such, narratives that use this mode contribute a unique element to the composite picture of the "intifada generation" that is constructed through the entire group of rhetorical modes.

Surveying the variety of texts produced during the early days of the intifada with an eye to issues of guilt and shame, it is difficult to find extensive examples of Palestinian adults talking about the actions of young people in ways that explicitly reveal the operation of this particular mode. Given Israeli attempts to foster feelings of guilt in Palestinian adults—whether by shifting the blame for "security offenses" onto parents accused of failing to "supervise" their children, or by deliberately humiliating fathers in front of their children—this absence is quite understandable. The sort of collective nationalist euphoria that accompanied the start of the uprising also meant that while many adults were undoubtedly feeling a complex mixture of pride, fear, and guilt over their children's activities, the overwhelming popular mood mitigated against the expression of the more "negative" emotions. Moreover, the initial stage of the intifada, when resistance was less directed and more open to the spontaneous intervention of "ordinary" Palestinians, provided ample opportunities for parents, particularly mothers, to work side by side with their children in the streets rather than "sitting in the corner."

Nonetheless, it is possible to see, in some of the other modes discussed here, traces of the extremely painful feelings of guilt and shame that would surface later in the memories of fathers such as Abu Nimr. In Qabbani's "Children of the Stones," for example, the simple use of the second-person ("O generation of debauchery/*You* will be swept away . . .") effectively indicts the poet's entire generation, even as it blunts this sense of collective guilt by shifting the reader's attention onto the heroism of the young stonethrowers. Similarly, human rights narratives focusing on the victimization of Palestinian children are built on a solid foundation of adult shame, but enable that shame to be submerged under, or channeled into, the more active process of exposing Israeli responsibility for Palestinian suffering. For those sympathetic to the Palestinian struggle, then, the mode of guilt-shame initially operated through a kind of displacement, allowing uncomfortable feelings to be recast in more positive light.

For many Israeli Jews and for many of Israel's international supporters inclined to be critical of the occupation, the intifada led to a different sort of displacement, providing another occasion for what some Israelis refer to sarcastically as "shooting and crying."[9] In this discourse, which appears in reaction to policies aiming at the violent suppression of Palestinian resistance, shame is transformed into a kind of moral soul-searching focusing on a national loss of innocence (suffered, perhaps, as Israel "comes of age" as a nation): soldiers "shoot" Palestinians, then "cry" over the implications of their actions for Israel's collective conscience. Singer-songwriter Si Hyman captured this move in a song written in response to the uprising:

> The world that I had is no longer, and the great light is gone.
> Boys play with lead, girls with steel dolls;
> Life looks different in the shadow of filth.
> Shooting and crying, burning and laughing,
> When did we ever learn to bury people alive?
> Shooting and crying, burning and laughing,
> When did we ever forget that our children too have been killed?[10]

In the United States, liberal observers with a long tradition of supporting Israel were quick to pick up on this discourse, issuing a flood of columns lamenting not the fate of the Palestinians bearing the brunt of Israel's military response, but rather the policy's corrosive effect *on Israel*. In suppressing the intifada, the *New York Times* opined in January 1988, Israel was "betraying its own values" and revealing that "the state that once promised deliverance to the oppressed has truly lost its way."[11]

For many Israeli soldiers called on to carry out the government's counterinsurgency policy in the West Bank and Gaza, the issue of guilt was considerably more pressing, and more personal. "I—we do . . . bad things, lady, bad things," said an eighteen-year-old soldier to Robin Morgan during the American feminist activist's visit to Dheisheh Refugee Camp early in the intifada (1989, 270). "What did you do in the Occupied-Territories riots, Daddy?" asks a young boy of a soldier-father who sits slumped in a chair, hand clamped over his eyes in shame, in a cartoon published in the *Miami Herald*.[12] As oral historian Alessandro Portelli notes, the question of what one's father or grandfather did "in the war" is one of those archetypal questions that often cuts to the core of personal and collective identity, especially for children socialized into a highly militarized view of history.[13] In this case, the father's shame at having to answer his own son effectively mirrors the source of his guilt, for it is the issue of facing *children* in the streets that lies, spoken and unspoken, at the core of many soldiers' narratives of their intifada experiences.

One remarkable example is the diary of Jonathan Kestenbaum, who served in an IDF reserve battalion charged with enforcing a brutal twenty-four-hour curfew on the village of Qabatya in the northern West Bank in August 1988. Qabatya had become famous in February of that year for the lynching of Mohammed Ayyad, a resident of the village who had been collaborating with the Israeli military; when confronted by a crowd demanding that he repent, Ayyad had opened fire from inside his house, killing a four-year-old boy before being dragged from his home and executed by the crowd. The mission of the IDF battalion, Kestenbaum records his commander as telling the reservists, was to keep Qabatya under curfew until its people were "broken." Kestenbaum's diary of his unit's three-week stint in the village (1988), excerpted in the *Jerusalem Post* the following month, is worth quoting at length:

August 8: We had arrived at our training base, laughing and nervous. . . . One sign of things to come—amidst the jokes and nervous laughter there were signs of genuine excitement by some soldiers at the prospect of "teaching them not to raise their heads."

August 12: Hour after hour of numbing patrols. An obscene situation as I chase down a side road after a nine-year-old who had spotted a piece of bread in the gutter.

August 13: The biggest disillusion for me are the officers. I think they actually enjoy it: the power, the control, and, above all, the humiliation. . . . One young officer pulled up with a glint in his eye, bringing in two nine-year-old boys strapped to his jeep, in the back seat and on the hood.

August 17: We are being placed in all sorts of situations which I find quite unbearable. . . . Under the steely eye of armed soldiers, elderly women and five-year-old children clear rotting garbage out of the gutter. Not one of the IDF's most auspicious moments. . . . Two soldiers: One man is almost ashamed of where he's serving and what he's doing. "The whole curfew is absurd and terribly painful," he says. "When a child of three looks at me with hatred, I feel ashamed at what I'm doing." Another man feels the patrols shame him. The pain, poverty, and disgrace of the residents causes him great distress.

August 18: Another scenario from the other side of hell. Patrolling in the fields we spot a young boy coming out of the orchard. Two soldiers run after him, at which point he throws his hands up and says, "Don't shoot me." His identity card shows him to be nine years old. Same story: "I'm hungry and came to collect apples." . . . Another day hounding old women and children. Vulgar, unnecessary situations which humiliate them and degrade us. They look at us with a mixture of hatred, contempt, and disdain.

August 21: With the curfew lifted, there's a semblance of village life, but the smouldering of hatred in the eyes of the kids is plain.

August 26: For four days we have been at a roadblock, partly to breathe a little, and partly to avoid having contact with the "locals." Meanwhile, in Tubas, five miles away, a fifteen-year-old boy was shot and killed by a member of our unit. . . . Why are we using live bullets on teenagers throwing stones?

In these excerpts, we find that Kestenbaum's feelings of guilt are prompted time and again by his interactions with women, old men, and particularly children; if there were men his own age in the village (he was twenty-nine at the time), he apparently took little notice of them, or at least failed to see their presence as generating the same troubling ethical questions he faced when confronting young people.

In the intifada narratives of Israeli soldiers, and in the numerous studies analyzing the strategies of soldiers in dealing with the "moral dilemma" of serving in the Territories, one regularly finds the army's task of quelling the uprising juxtaposed with the more traditional kind of military campaigns that loom so large in the collective memory of Israeli Jews. Eyal Ben-Ari (1989), an anthropologist who wrote about his reserve duty in Hebron, notes that when his unit was given its instructions prior to leaving for the West Bank, they soon realized that in contrast to soldiers carrying out more conventional missions, they were being "ordered to become policemen," issued with "nonstandard gear" designed for the suppression of large demonstrations. Yet as his article makes clear, the reservists were also able to deflect any sense of moral ambiguity they may have felt initially by relying on a variety of psychological mechanisms, including a shift in terminology that helped close the gap between the role for which they were trained and the role they were being asked to perform. "What happened . . . was that in the space of a few short days everyone—officers and soldiers—reverted to the typical mode of *military* thinking and perception," he observes (381). Using military terms—for example, referring to the practice of clearing streets of debris left by demonstrators as a "clean-up" or "mop-up" (*nikui shetach* in Hebrew) operation—served to "clean" the conscience of men like the reservist who told Kestenbaum, "When a child of three looks at me with hatred, I feel ashamed at what I'm doing."

Even in the early days of the intifada, Israeli discussions of the uprising demonstrated the existence of significant divisions over how soldiers should respond to their own feelings of guilt.[14] "Shame, said Marx, is a revolutionary feeling," wrote one leftist in a biting commentary on the "shoot and cry" syndrome. "Take your tears, soldiers, the tears of shame and disgust, and turn them into a weapon."[15] Yet as Ben-Ari notes, a hegemonic institution such as the Israeli military can easily blunt and circumscribe such radical possibilities: "If anything . . . what I witnessed at that time (a few months after the uprising's beginning) was the basic resiliency of the situation" (384–385). For their part, Israel's military policy makers, faced with soldiers who were speaking openly about their feelings of moral ambiguity, took concrete steps to reverse what they saw as a dangerous erosion in morale. Defense Minister Yitzhak Rabin's infamous January 1988 policy of using "force, might, and beatings" to quell the uprising had the potential to turn "shoot and cry" into "beat and cry," but it also served as an officially sanctioned opportunity for soldiers to channel their previous feelings of powerlessness into a violent campaign of indiscriminate bone breaking. Perhaps it is most accurate, then, to say that in terms of the political responses they generate, guilt and shame are inherently ambiguous, simultaneously embodying not only the possibility of turning into "revolutionary feelings," but also the possibility of serving as incentives to further violence. Viewed as elements of this particular discursive field, however, guilt and shame are very much about constructing young people in particular ways, for within this mode it is young people—through their actions, their suffering, even (in Kestenbaum's narrative) their mere presence—who serve as the catalysts for these feelings.

## Potential: Demographic Dreams and Nightmares

Nationalist discourse, in Palestine as in much of the world, typically genders national territory as female and figures women as both the metaphorical "mothers of the nation" and the literal vessels through which the nation is reproduced. Nationalist discourse is also pronatalist, and thus

operates on a generational level, investing children—those who are produced, as it were, when the nation is reproduced—with powerful symbolic meaning. Consider, for example, Mahmoud Darwish's "Identity
Card" (1973), a poem whose writing roughly coincided with the rise of
the PLO in the mid-1960s. With its combination of humility ("My father
/ is from the family of the plough / not from a noble line") and defiance
("Beware beware of my hunger / and of my anger"), the poem was in
many ways a perfect inaugural statement for a movement attempting to
speak and act in the name of a newly diasporic community of refugees,
dispossessed peasants, and angry students. The opening stanza,

> Write down
> I am an Arab
> and my I.D. card number is 50,000
> and my children are eight in number
> and the ninth
>     arrives next summer.
> Does this bother you?

is widely known among and quoted by Palestinians for its powerful sense
of self-assertion. It is also an excellent example of how pronatalism can
function as a means of rhetorical struggle: the narrator's eight children—
and, even more provocatively, the suggestion that another "arrives next
summer"—constitute weapons capable of instilling fear in the enemy, in
this case the state of Israel, not only demographically but also in terms of
the political possibilities they call to mind.

The rhetorical mode of *potential* reminds us of the etymological connection between nation and generation discussed in chapter 1. Procreation, in this light, is the quintessential nationalist act, and children the
most basic and irrefutable constituents of the nation. In Israel/Palestine—
with its century-long history of Zionist, Arab, and international attempts
to engineer particular demographic outcomes through military means,
the manipulation of borders, and the promotion or prevention of immigration—to be a child is to be, through the simple fact of one's birth and
existence, a small but important addition to a statistical category with national importance. As the intifada made clear, however, children are more
than signifiers of national strength; they also embody the potential for active, even revolutionary participation in the life of the nation and the cre-

ation of different futures. The mode of potential, then, is similar to the mode of guilt-shame in that the dualistic question of young people's agency or passivity is less important than their symbolic value. A child, in this mode, may be viewed as a protoactivist or protoadult inherently capable of playing a political role in the future, but his or her significance in the here and now is primarily *ontological,* serving as a reminder of the power of reproduction.

Discourses employing this mode are generally directed either internally—that is, at the nation itself—or at the "other side," or (as is the case with Darwish's poem) at both. As we shall see, both Israelis and Palestinians employ the rhetoric of potential in ways that are rooted in the colonial situation itself. More than any of the other modes considered here, the mode of potential effects a powerful symbolic reversal in the relations between the two national communities. Potential plays on the fears of the colonizers, suggesting that the power they currently enjoy is always tenuous and may, in fact, be fleeting; similarly, potential allows the colonized to feel comforted in the knowledge that "time is on our side." These differences help explain why discussions of birth rates in Israel often take on a defensive tone bordering on national panic while, conversely, Palestinians employ the rhetoric of potential with a kind of nationalist defiance that ranges from the grim to the celebratory.

"One time when the town [Gaza] was under curfew, a pregnant woman started to have labour pains," begins one humorous story recorded during the uprising:

> The soldiers took her to a military hospital to give birth there. It turned out that she was pregnant with twin boys. The head of one of the babies came out, he looked around and saw all these [Israeli] military uniforms, turned back to his brother and shouted, "Ahmed! Ahmed! We are surrounded, get some rocks!"[16]

In this case, the image of newborn babies preparing to join the *atfāl al-hijāra* playfully capitalizes on the notion that Israeli soldiers are afraid of mere children. During the intifada, however, Palestinians also had ample opportunity to employ the rhetoric of potential in a much more serious vein: well-publicized cases of infants dying from tear gas exposure, for example, generated especially strong public outrage, and statistics of gas-related miscarriages were often cited alongside those related to deaths from gunshots, beatings, and other forms of violence, implying that Israel was even reaching into the womb to prevent the production of more Palestinian nationals.

Not surprisingly, the link between nationalism and procreation also has a long history in Zionist and Israeli discourse, and in Israeli policies toward the Palestinians. David Ben-Gurion, Israel's first prime minister, set the tone by emphasizing the absolute need for a Jewish majority in Palestine, and since then the continuing goal of demographic superiority has been an issue of national consensus in Israel, even if the question of how to maintain such a favorable situation has regularly generated heated debates over political philosophy and public policy. According to Nira Yuval-Davis (1989), the notion that Israeli Jews are in a "demographic race" with Palestinians (or with Arabs in general) has led various Israeli governments to try boosting the Jewish birth rate through symbolic monetary rewards for "heroine mothers" (those bearing ten or more children) in the early 1950s; cheaper housing for large families under the "Fund of Encouraging Birth," begun in 1968; and additional subsidies allowed under the 1983 "Law on Families Blessed with Children."

The discourse of demography in Israel has also focused attention on Palestinian children as symbolic reminders of Israel's perceived inferiority in the realm of procreation. "Sovereignty over the land of Israel will not be settled by guns and hand-grenades, but rather in two domains: the bedroom and the universities—and it will not be long before the Palestinians surpass us in both," opined one Israeli academic (Arnon Saffir) in 1986 as the Knesset was debating a proposal to declare 1987 a sort of national "year of child-bearing" (Elmessiri 1996, 12). Alarmist pronouncements concerning comparative birth rates have become a staple item in the rhetoric of right-wing politicians who advocate the "transfer" (a racist euphemism for forced expulsion) of Palestinians from their homeland.[17] Indeed, as Kanaaneh (2002) argues, Israeli "nationalist biopolitics"—including the world's largest per capita system of fertility clinics, a conservative approach to family planning for Jews, and aggressive provision of contraceptives and abortion services for Palestinians who live in Israel—are simply another type of "transfer" consistent with Israeli practice in the political and military arena.

The notion of Palestinians outnumbering Jews in Israel proper, of course, is only a possibility if one insists (as right-wing Israelis often do) that the West Bank and Gaza are part of the state of Israel. Within the internationally recognized boundaries of the state established after the

1948 war, Palestinians currently number approximately 20 percent of the total population. It is the question of what to "do" with the West Bank and Gaza, in other words, which holds the key to racist Israeli fears about the Palestinian "demographic time-bomb," and roughly half the population of these territories is under the age of sixteen.

In this context, it becomes easier to see why the intifada—in which large numbers of Israeli soldiers regularly found themselves confronted by crowds of young Palestinians—not only gave added urgency to debates in Israel about the future of the territories, but also caused an intensification in the use of pronatalist discourse. Just days after the Palestine National Council declared an independent Palestinian state in November 1988, for example, the *New York Times* ran a full-page advertisement placed by El Al, Israel's national airline, using the image of a very pregnant Jewish woman to promote airfare discounts for large families. The text next to the woman reads, "With our new family fares to Israel, your first kid flies for 25% off. Your second flies for 50% off. Your third kid flies for 50% off. Your fourth kid flies for 50% off. Your fifth kid flies for 50% off. Your sixth kid flies for 50% off. Some kids, of course, fly free" (Faris 1989).

The intifada also sparked the formation of a new right-wing political party in Israel, Moledet, explicitly dedicated to the "transfer" of Palestinians from their homeland. In a speech to party supporters, Moledet leader Rahavam Ze'evi used slightly veiled references to the higher Palestinian birth rate to lay out his assessment of Israel's dire predicament:

> Look around here, as we've done. Every [Arab] settlement is becoming a village, every village a small town, every small town a city. In a dozen years, according to the statisticians, the numbers will be equal. In a democratic state where everyone has the right to vote, they'll be the majority. In 13 years, the prime minister, minister of defense and chief-of-staff here will be Arabs. (Quoted in Brown 1989, 22)

Many "moderate" Israelis have also contributed to pronatalism as a hegemonic discourse through the use of the more palatable rhetoric of demographic "problems," and again it seems that the intifada provoked more discussions along these lines. Yehoshofat Harkabi, a former hawk and chief of military intelligence in Israel, argued in an influential 1988 book that the ruling Likud Party and its traditional allies—the parties advocating neither expulsion nor withdrawal, but rather a kind of creeping annexation through increased Jewish settlement in the Territories—were guilty of "the height of irresponsibility" for ignoring the "problem" posed by the higher Palestinian birth rate. "Were the Arabs of the West Bank to somehow disappear, Israel could annex the West Bank with equanimity," he notes. "But the Arab population will not only not disappear, it will continue to grow. . . . [And] by the year 2000 there will be 20 percent more Arab than Jewish children in this age group [under age four] west of the River Jordan" (46–47).

A book such as Harkabi's, which was enthusiastically reviewed in the United States, essentially trades the mode of guilt-shame for the mode of potential: the intifada, in his view, calls for political and territorial concessions not because it forced Israelis to confront the colonial nature of their own national project, but because it made Israelis aware of just how many Palestinian children are living in the West Bank and Gaza. The uprising, to put it another way, represented the arrival of former Prime Minister Golda Meir's famous nightmare concerning Palestinian reproduction: according to Yuval-Davis (1989), Meir once spoke of her fear that she would "have to wake up every morning wondering how many Arab babies have been born during the night" (92). The continuing significance of Meir's statement becomes clear when it is placed in the context of the more openly racist discourse that has succeeded it. For Palestinians, such pronouncements are not easily forgotten; on the contrary, to the extent that Palestinian nationalists also see themselves as fighting a "demographic war" with Israeli Jews—and many do—pronatalist statements from mainstream leaders such as Meir are as likely to be preserved in popular memory as are right-wing calls for "transfer."

It is worth pointing out that in my interviews in Balata, I found no unified position on the issue of pronatalism. One woman, twenty-five-year-old Leila, explained a rise in early marriages by insisting that "in time of war" it is necessary for "any nation" to replace the men (*rijāl*) who are killed while fighting. At the same time, she said firmly that she would not let such national imperatives, whether defined in political or cultural terms, dictate her own decisions concerning marriage and family. Leila's obviously complicated relationship to the nationalist discourse on demography points to the fragile, contradictory nature of potential as a rhetorical mode. While this mode may typically operate on the most basic level of nationalist hopes and fears—stressing the biological continuity of the nation—it can also be used in ways that are more subversive with respect to the construction of militant nationalisms, for the idea of children

*Figure 1.* In this Naji al-ʿAli cartoon, Hanzalla watches as an old man damages, but fails to clear, an American flag. (Naji al-ʿAli)

growing up to continue the national struggle represents only one kind of "potential" among many. During the intifada, for example, peace groups regularly attempted to bring together young people from both sides of the Israeli-Palestinian divide for "peace camps," working from the assumption that the "potential" of children is in fact open-ended rather than inevitably locked into the national roles of occupier and occupied. Accounts of these cross-national efforts joined Israeli discourses of the "demographic war" and Palestinian legends of stonethrowing babies in a crowded narrative universe, each employing the generational rhetoric of potential.

## Testimonial: "Faithful Witnesses"

The famous political cartoons created by the late Palestinian artist Naji al-ʿAli each feature the figure of Hanzalla, a young boy, standing with his back to the viewer and silently observing a world dominated by Arab corruption, Israeli repression, and American imperialism (see Figure 1).[18]

While it is clear that the artist, himself a refugee, used Hanzalla as a vehicle for depicting the desperate situation of the poorest Palestinian refugees, it is equally significant that he chose to create a child to fill this role. In effect, Hanzalla is a dynamic combination of innocence and wisdom, young in age and small in stature but old in terms of what he has seen and experienced.

In the *testimonial* mode, young Palestinians are represented as witnesses in two related ways. First, they are witnesses to injustice because, like Hanzalla, they have seen it with their own eyes.[19] Second, they are witnesses capable of providing evidence before the court of world opinion, evidence that is presumably more valuable because of the "innocence" of the witness. Were Hanzalla ever to speak, for example, he could only speak the truth, and could "convict" all those who have been responsible for the disasters of Palestinian history. There is a parallel here to the mode of victimization: just as the child is typically the victim most capable of arousing the sympathy of adult viewers, he or she is also the most authentic witness. With adults, as McKenzie Wark (1994) wryly notes, "There is always the suspicion that they may be adulterated by impurities—such as politics."[20] The irony of this mode is that once young people do begin to speak, they run the risk of undermining the sense of innocence so often attributed to them.

Although Naji al-ᶜAli died just before the intifada began, his famous creation survived and played a role in shaping the visual landscape of the uprising. In general, we might say that the confrontations between Israeli soldiers and young activists were not only structurally asymmetrical, but also semiotically overdetermined, saturated with powerful symbolic meanings belonging to a wider universe of discourse. When soldiers entered Palestinian communities during the intifada, for example, they found young people who not only were openly defying the authority of the occupation, but who also represented the negation of the Zionist dreams of winning the "demographic race." In refugee camps such as Balata, soldiers may also have found themselves face to face with the equally symbolic figure of Hanzalla. As I learned during my field research, the figure of Hanzalla is omnipresent in many camps—idly drawn by students in their notebooks, spray-painted on cement walls such as the one outside the UNRWA school in Balata (see Figure 2), worn as necklaces and carried as keychains—suggesting a level of subcultural popularity that can be read in a number of ways.

*Figure 2.* A spray-painted rendition of Naji al-ᶜAli's Hanzalla figure joins other graffiti on the outside wall of the UNRWA school in Balata camp. To the right of Hanzalla is the stylized design which serves as both acronym and logo for the Popular Front. (John Collins)

On the one hand, the fact that Hanzalla is so often on public display may indicate a kind of generational solidarity in resistance, the collective refusal of the young to submit to received wisdom and historical "realities." At the same time, Hanzalla is a strangely passive counterpart to a group of young people who are best known for their political action; observing but never speaking, he is the silent mascot of the *jīl al-intifāda.* His silence, of course, may be the most unnerving attribute of all for Israeli soldiers who are not used to being surveilled, even by cartoon characters. One can easily imagine Hanzalla drawing the attention of soldiers who were charged with stamping out intifada graffiti by forcing Palestinians to paint over it.

Kamal Boullata's *Faithful Witnesses* (1990), a collection of artwork by a select group of West Bank and Gaza Palestinians (none older than fourteen), is another excellent example of the testimonial mode. The book presents a picture of Palestinian children as simultaneously embroiled in and innocent of the political conflict which provides the backdrop—and, in many cases, the subject matter—of their paintings. John Berger's preface to the book, for example, relies heavily on a notion of youthful innocence, and of children as rendering unfailingly accurate representations of the world around them. "The first marks on paper are ahistorical. . . . It speaks of the painter's own experience, uninfluenced by any other," writes Berger of the art produced by the youngest children:

> The first language of painting tells everything it tells as if for the first time. The "voice" with which it speaks of tear gas or submachine guns is the same as it uses to speak of a cloud or a house. Consequently its evidence is incontrovertible, as would be the evidence of a stream or a tree if suddenly they acquired the gift of making signs. (9)

At the same time, he makes the somewhat paradoxical observation that children who live a daily reality of military occupation "grow up fast" and that, consequently, some of the paintings in the collection "are already fully adult." Berger's interpretation of the artwork, in other words, exemplifies one of the tensions inherent in the testimonial mode: the claim that children are the best witnesses *because they are children* sits uneasily with the assertion that because of their political surroundings, *they have ceased to be children at all.*

Like the PLO, which declared a "generation of liberation" in the 1970s, Boullata presents the young artists in *Faithful Witnesses* as narrators eminently capable of telling *national* stories. In one painting, a horse carrying two Palestinian flags is chased by an army jeep, suggesting, in Boullata's words, the "dauntless heroism which prevails in Palestinian popular fables" and "the Palestinians' trust in ultimately winning freedom, no matter how long their struggle lasts." In another, a winged horse also draped with a Palestinian flag flies over Jerusalem in a child's rewriting of the Prophet Muhammad's famous journey from Mecca to Jerusalem. Boullata, citing the young artist's careful rendition of churches and mosques in a panoply of bright colors, argues that the painting supports the "Palestinian national vision" by depicting "a Jerusalem for everyone." In this light, the adjective in the book's title takes on a double meaning, suggesting that the child artists are not only "faithful" in the sense of giving accurate depictions of what they have seen, but also "faithful" to the national project and the narratives that typically sustain it. With this combination of veracity and authenticity, the child takes on the role of a primary "national signifier," much like the heroic peasant often celebrated by middle-class Palestinian nationalists (Swedenburg 1990).

Internationally, Palestinians have too often been rhetorically reduced to two figures: the bomb-wielding, airplane-hijacking "terrorist" and the pitiful refugee. Where such stereotypes have served to mark Palestinians in terms of their difference—as stateless persons acting outside the norms of international politics—the image of the child in *Faithful Witnesses* enables a process of rehumanization and normalization: Palestinians are children who paint like children all over the world, and they are a national community just like any other. For Palestinians, however, assertions of national identity rarely go unchallenged, and the children's art project did face its share of difficulties. The UN Exhibitions Committee, according to Boullata, decided "to censor 11 of the children's paintings for 'offending a member state,' [and] to omit the titles of all the works that were exhibited" (20–21).[21] Nonetheless, the project appears to have been quite successful, with the artwork appearing not only at the United Nations, but also in *Life* magazine and on the ABC News *Nightline* program. It is difficult to imagine these mainstays of the American mass media giving similar space to other forms of cultural production associated with less "innocent" Palestinians.

As I argue in the following chapter, the practice of Palestinians acting as witnesses to their own oppression and testifying for the benefit of "outside" audiences—for example, by narrating stories of martyrdom (the word "martyr," significantly, is derived from the Greek *martyros*, meaning "witness" in the sense of one who bears testimony) or displaying wounds suffered at the hands of Israeli troops—is a crucial mechanism through which the very idea of "Palestinianness" is performed and reified. This "stockpiling" of evidence, I suggest, feeds directly into the state-building project of the nationalist elite and mitigates against popular empowerment and the development of a democratic political culture. While the presentation of the children's paintings depicting scenes of violence in *Faithful Witnesses* may be seen in this light, it is striking that throughout my interviews, young people consistently tried to deflect attention *away* from the specific injuries and injustices they had suffered personally. Rather than step into the role of passive witness—a role associated with young children and grieving parents—they regularly stressed their own empowerment during the intifada, thereby distinguishing themselves as a generation of action. In the following section, I explore some of the ways in which a variety of observers attempted to come to grips with the power of this new generation.

## *Empowerment:* Balad hākimha walad

As we saw earlier in this chapter, heroic characterizations of the "children of the stones" are generally associated with observers whose relationship to the intifada and its activists is, for the most part, an external one based on observation and admiration from afar. Among some journalists and others who were immersed to a greater degree in the daily events in the West Bank and Gaza, a rather different mode emerged soon after the uprising began. Here the focus was also on the power of young people, but power was understood in a much more localized way, as residing in relationships between and among Palestinians rather than simply in the dynamics of the larger conflict with Israel. Consequently, an act such as throwing a stone or enforcing a commercial strike could be read not only as expressing nationalist defiance, but also as embodying a rejection of certain hierarchical structures active within Palestinian society, chiefly those relating to the exercise of generational or, more broadly, patriarchal authority.

The mode of *empowerment,* then, represents young people as gaining power and influence within their own society at the expense of the older generation, making the intifada a sort of zero-sum game with respect to the issue of authority. Much of the early commentary on the uprising picked up on this notion of generational upheaval, often drawing sweeping conclusions concerning the far-reaching implications of this shift for Palestinian society. Some, like journalist Said Aburish (1991), hailed the empowerment of young people as a long-overdue and revolutionary development capable of overturning not only the authority of a specific generation, but indeed the very idea of generational authority. While Aburish often crosses into what I have called the heroic mode when stepping back and assessing the larger significance of this social revolution ("The *intifada . . .* is a revolt against the old, obsolete ways of the Arabs in general"), the interviews he conducted in the West Bank suggest that Palestinians were conceptualizing generational issues in terms of the specific relationships they were living every day. "[T]hey don't trust us," said one mother when asked about the younger generation. "They don't share anything with us; in fact they don't share anything with anyone who is older than twenty." One young activist essentially confirmed this observation: "We learn from the Israelis, from TV, and from each other, and we don't follow the uneducated ways of the older generation," he said. "They don't have anything to teach us" (172).

The first-hand literature on the intifada, while admittedly contributing to an overall slighting of young people's perspectives, nonetheless contains a steady stream of similar comments illustrating the apparent inability of adults to exercise control over the young. Not all observers, however, shared Aburish's optimistic characterization of the uprising as bringing about a kind of progressive social liberation. To many, the new-found freedom and authority of the *jīl al-intifāda* constituted a double-edged sword that could potentially shred the Palestinian social fabric far into the future, and damage the lives of countless young people who were growing up without the benefit of a stable, traditional socialization process. "The family pecking order has been turned on its head," wrote freelance journalist Kate Rouhana (1989) in an early article on children and the intifada. "Parents are struggling to handle aggressive children and to renegotiate the family relationships, as children increasingly respond to a locus of authority outside the home, and the parents' authority is reduced" (117).

Like Aburish, Rouhana sees the generational upheaval as profound and far-reaching, but where the former highlights the democratic idealism and self-reliance of youth, the latter quotes the much more apocalyptic view of Francis Azraq, a Palestinian psychiatrist who sees the breakdown of generational authority as signaling, ultimately, "the destruction of society." According to Rouhana, even the intifada's early period demonstrated these darker possibilities:

> [Y]ounger children are starting to show signs of disturbance in unruly and aggressive behavior. In Nablus and Jenin, for example, there were reports that the shabab were organizing the younger children into marching formations with "uniforms"—black garbage bags over their heads and white socks pulled up over their shoes—because they were out of control, "stoning anything that moves." (119)

The empowerment of young people, in this view, is desirable only insofar as it can be harnessed in the service of more "acceptable" activities.

Given the extent to which these kinds of analytical discourses were circulating in the West Bank and Gaza during the early stages of the intifada, it is easy to understand why, for many Palestinian adults, the notion of children as the ultimate arbiters of social and political power might have had a certain ironic, even humorous appeal. In Gaza, for example, psychiatrist Sarraj told me that the uprising led to the development and popularization of a telling proverb, *balad hākimha walad* (the ruler of the country is a child). Popular legends and other stories from the intifada period also draw on this theme, often portraying Israeli soldiers and Palestinian adults as equally beholden to the dictates of the *jīl al-intifāda*. One such story relies on the understanding, on the part of the listener, that it is young people—referred to, in this case, as the "Palestinian military governor"—who are in charge of enforcing commercial strikes (see chapter 5):

> [A] man from Hebron . . . has closed his store and stands in front of it defying the orders of the military to reopen it. The Israeli military governor comes and asks him who gave him permission to close his store, and the man from Hebron insists it was the military government. They argue back and forth, until finally the military governor says, "I am the military governor and I did not permit you to close your store!" And the man replies, "I do not mean you, I mean our Palestinian military governor."

On one level, such stories illustrate the ideological failures of the Israeli colonial project, with the intifada having overturned whatever modus vivendi may have once existed, however tenuously, between occupier and occupied. On another level, however, stories about child rulers are also documents of a perceived shift in the internal relations of power among Palestinians: to stay with the example just quoted, the Hebron shopkeeper defends himself not by appealing to his own authority as an adult male, or simply as a Palestinian, but instead by referencing the "permission" given by the local *shabāb*. Finally, the influence of young people on everyday matters in these stories is also striking as an alternative model of political authority more broadly, for the long-standing national leadership—the PLO—is nowhere to be found. Here it is useful to note that many younger Palestinians refer dismissively to the older generation of leaders as "the Abus" (the fathers), referring to revolutionary *noms de guerre* such as Abu Ammar (Yasser Arafat), Abu Jihad (Khalil al-Wazir), and Abu Iyad (Salah Khalaf).

The very suggestion of generational tension in the early stages of the intifada, of course, implied a lack of national unity at a time when such unity was obviously crucial to the success of the struggle against Israeli occupation. This would be no small irony, for in many ways the intifada helped reduce, at least temporarily, many of the larger political divisions that had plagued the Palestinian national movement for decades. Observers who characterized the intifada, even partially, in terms of social upheaval thus put themselves directly at odds with a prevailing nationalist discourse which was fueled by the initial accomplishments of the uprising, a discourse in which the delicate issue of generational tension was largely ignored and other developments in the realm of social relations were treated only insofar as they were seen as positive. Edward Said (1989), for example, in a somewhat uncharacteristic moment of nationalist euphoria, hailed the "profound social and moral achievements" of the intifada, listing a number of progressive social changes (the absence of "noisy rhetoric," a sense of "organic nationhood" leading to an increased emphasis on "the public good and the collective will," the participation of women as "equal partners in the struggle") and leaving out the issue of generation altogether.

Similarly, the aforementioned intifada leaflets (*bayanāt*)—composed, by all accounts, through a process of collaboration between the PLO leadership outside and the clandestine local leadership—understandably stress both the necessity and the existence of social and political unity among Palestinian residents of the West Bank and Gaza, generally singling out only "collaborators" (ʿ*umala*) as examples of those who might be working against such unity. In such nationalist texts, the mode of empowerment is effectively present by virtue of its absence: silence on the issue of generational authority speaks all the more loudly when placed alongside reports of children "stoning anything that moves," stories of shopkeepers obeying the orders of teenage "military governors," and popular notions that the country is "ruled by a child."

Palestinian parents and journalists, however, were not the only observers who commented on evidence of generational upheaval during the intifada. Many Israeli analysts were quick to pick up on the generational angle and, more broadly, to emphasize the extent to which the mass mobilization of the Palestinian population was either a result of, or a cause of, profound changes in social relations. In one of the earliest books on the intifada to reach a wide audience, veteran Israeli journalists Ze'ev Schiff and Ehud Ya'ari (1989) refer to the initial protests of December 1987 as "an awesome outburst by the forsaken and forgotten at the bottom of the social heap" (79), and later highlight the fragility of the bonds normally linking the old and the young. "Boys of twelve and thirteen or even younger publicly defied their parents," they argue. "Teenagers turned viciously on their fathers even in the more conservative villages, and in one incident a group of girls stoned their own parents for trying to stop them from demonstrating" (126).

The keen interest Israeli commentators showed in the issue of generational dynamics may help explain why nationalist-minded Palestinians might have chosen to minimize their acknowledgment of young people's empowerment vis-à-vis their elders. Of perhaps greater significance, however, is the way in which a certain notion of generational empowerment played directly into Israeli military and judicial treatment of young Palestinians detained and/or charged with "security offenses" during the uprising. These policies, in and of themselves, represent a kind of discourse on generation, one which plays an important role in the Israeli Ministry of Defense's 1993 book on Israel's legal response to the intifada. Relying heavily on the Israeli sources just cited, the report's authors offer five underlying causes of the uprising's outbreak and its staying power, four of which turn, significantly, on the issue of young people's social and political empowerment. First, they reference the "profound dissatisfaction with the PLO" felt in the West Bank and Gaza, and argue that young people in particular "concluded that it was incumbent upon them to take matters into their own hands." Second, in a well-worn and highly debatable colonial construction, they claim that the "new generation" of Palestinians—those born after 1967—had "grown up under the leadership of Israeli democracy" and were therefore inspired to engage in political activity without fear of military reprisal. Third, they argue that Israel's policy of "maintaining a benevolent leadership" in the Occupied Territories "produced a feeling of absence of rule among the young Palestinians," leading them to the "misguided belief" that Israel would not fight to retain control over the Territories. Finally, the authors note that the young intifada activists succeeded in taking over the public relations role normally occupied by older political leaders: "The Palestinian youths that had guided the uprising since its inception had become well-versed in manipulating the press. They were able to exploit the media, particularly the foreign press, by projecting the image of a 'violent' IDF attacking an 'innocent' civilian population" (Yahav 1993, 28–29).

Reading this list, one is struck by the extent to which the IDF authors were willing to grant a significant level of agency and political consciousness to the young activists of the intifada. Yet later in the book, as we have already seen, the same authors attempt to refocus attention on the *victimization* of young people at the hands of cynical politicians and neglectful parents, implying that Israel's military policies were carried out in order to shore up a system of social "authority" that was beneficial to Palestinians as well as to the maintenance of the occupation. In the end, what appears to be a contradiction between two rhetorical modes (victimization and empowerment) is in fact an attempt to operate on both sides of one central assumption, namely, that the intifada did indeed witness a fundamental collapse in the patriarchal structure of Palestinian society. While it may make sense, then, to read the denial of generational empowerment in Palestinian nationalist discourse as a response to the general readings offered by Israeli analysts such as Shalev (1991), or as an attempt to mobilize the population through the constant invocation of national unity, it is also important to recognize the ways in which this particular denial might also represent a reaction to an Israeli counterinsurgency effort whose architects openly cited the breakdown of generational authority and other forms of social "lawlessness" as justifications for their repressive policies.

In this chapter we have seen that in the process of reporting, assessing, characterizing, and memorializing the intifada, a wide range of narrators—journalists, politicians, psychologists, soldiers, and young people themselves—consistently returned to the use of powerful generational metaphors, categories, and lines of analysis; all, to return to McKenzie Wark's provocative essay quoted at the start of this chapter, found themselves "hovering over the image of the child." But which child? The heroic stonethrower immortalized in poems and underground leaflets? The helpless victim forced to endure the brutality of Israeli soldiers? The innocent witness providing unimpeachable testimony to a global audience? The confident teenage activist, defiantly usurping the authority of his parents? The answer, of course, is that all these figures are at play in the complex discursive field I have explored here, and that the very idea of *jīl al-intifāda,* the "intifada generation," is best viewed as a collection of ideal types, produced through the workings of multiple rhetorical modes, all masquerading as a neat sociological category. It is significant to note, in this context, that of all the Palestinians I interviewed during my field research, no two were in precise agreement as to the definition of *jīl al-intifāda* or the criteria by which one might judge who belonged to this famous group. Most attempted to give an age range (e.g., those who were between fifteen and twenty-two at the start of the uprising), while others offered qualitative descriptions that were often more expansive (e.g., "anyone who suffered" or "participated" in the intifada). This diversity of opinion illustrates the futility of attempting to specify the "intifada generation" as a purely objective category located outside its narrative construction.

In the remainder of this book, I give analytical prominence to the stories and interpretations of young Palestinians who have begun the process of re-creating the intifada, and their role in it, now that the uprising has passed firmly into the realm of memory. While there is no question but that the voices of the younger generation have been given too little space in much existing scholarship on the intifada, my intention here is not to simply add another set of narratives to the equation. Rather, I strongly believe that approaching the intifada through the lens of personal narratives has the potential to effect a radical transformation in our understanding of what, in the broadest sense, the intifada "means" to Palestinians of all ages. In the context of the foregoing discussion, for example, the self-representations of Balata's young people provide important challenges to a number of the rhetorical modes I have examined, revealing in many cases the profound political contradictions embedded in these modes. These young narrators give us ample reason, for example, to question liberal notions of the inherent passivity of children living in situations of violent political conflict. To put it another way, without these personal narratives, it would be much more difficult to see the ways in which the entire idea of the "intifada generation" is built on an unresolved tension between structure and agency, between victimization and empowerment, between the imprint of childhood and the impact of "growing up"—in short, between history-repeating and history-making.

# 3

# Between Romance and Tragedy
## *A Balata Family Confronts the Present*

"Marhaba," I begin. "Are you Ali Imawi's mother?" She pauses.
Her squint becomes a fast twitch. "Yes," she sighs. "I am Ali's
mother." She invites me in. In the dim light a man rises in greeting.
Ali's father. With a gesture of his hand he asks me to sit on the
mattress across from him. "She has come here to talk about 'Ali,"
the woman says matter-of-factly, as if I am not here. "She must be
a journalist like the ones who came here after Ali's martyrdom."
I look down, embarrassed to be brooding on the pain of others to
get a story.
— Lamis Andoni

Treating everyday cultural phenomena as important does not
mean isolating them from politics; on the contrary, [it reveals] the
temporary and shifting nature of the boundaries between politics
and everyday life, pointing to the considerable areas previously
segregated and marginalised that became open to politicisation.
— Luisa Passerini

Everything ends to prepare for this wedding,
An entire era . . . an age comes to an end.
This is the Palestinian wedding,
Never shall lover meet lover
Except as martyr or fugitive.
— Mahmoud Darwish, "Blessed Be That Which Has Not Come!"

My initial entry into *mukhayyam Balata* was accomplished in
part through the assistance of Ashraf, a twenty-four-year-old resident of
the camp whom I met while he was working in Ramallah. Having just
graduated from An-Najah University in Nablus, Ashraf took an immediate interest in my desire to interview members of his generation. Perhaps

because he was a sociology major, he quickly began peppering me with the sorts of questions I had always imagined anonymous committee members asking when reviewing grant proposals that suggested some intellectual or practical uncertainty: What did I hope to find out? How would I decide whom to interview? Why had I chosen this particular age range? His questions had the effect of getting the ball rolling, of helping me begin a necessary conversation, with myself and with others, about how I would actually conduct the interview portion of my project within the rather limited time period I had available to me. In later conversations, including three formal interviews, Ashraf consistently refused to let my questions go unquestioned, and seemed to take the need to disturb some of my most naive political assumptions as his personal challenge.

Given the impulse, common to most anticolonial nationalisms, to paper over the "cracks" in the edifice of national unity—a centripetal tendency which the physical expanse of the Palestinian diaspora has perhaps intensified—I was surprised to find Ashraf, from the beginning of our relationship, insisting on Balata's political *diversity*. Several times in our initial conversations he expressed the conviction that in my cohort of interviewees, I needed to include individuals whose social biographies—in terms of political faction, religious beliefs, level of education, economic status, time spent in prison, and other life experiences—were "different," and who were therefore likely to have "different" perspectives on the intifada. Yet one of his first suggestions was that I speak with his friend Isam, a twenty-five-year-old who, from what I could gather at that point, seemed a lot like Ashraf himself—serious, well-educated, and secular.

In the course of my interviews, however, I soon discovered that where Isam was concerned, I shouldn't read too much into these connections, and I began to pay attention to several important differences between the two friends. First, whereas Ashraf is the oldest son in his family and is therefore under some pressure to contribute to the family's income (particularly in the absence of his late father), Isam is the youngest of nine children. Second, unlike Ashraf, who steadfastly refused to link himself with any political faction and was never arrested for involvement in the intifada, Isam proudly identified himself as a supporter of the leftist Popular Front for the Liberation of Palestine (PFLP), and spoke of his two-year imprisonment during the uprising as a life-changing experience. Finally, as Ashraf pointedly mentioned to me when he first suggested his friend as a possible interviewee, Isam was the brother of an intifada

*Figure 3.* Poster commemorating residents of the Balata
Refugee Camp who were killed during the intifada. (Tara
LaFredo)

*shahīd* (martyr, pl. *shuhadāʾ*) and thus had a special status in the camp
(see Figure 3).[1]

I soon learned that Isam, like Ashraf, had been raised by his widowed
mother, his father having died when he was young. This was a fairly common situation in the camp, one rooted in a basic demographic fact—
women in Palestine tend to marry older men and to outlive them—that

*Figure 4.* Isam and Imm Ghassan Abu-Hawila at their home in Balata camp, May 1997. (Heidi Gengenbach)

pushed me to broaden my interview base and examine, in a limited way, the perspectives of Balata parents. In this case, the two mothers reacted quite differently to my presence and my interest in interviewing them: Imm Ashraf[2] politely but firmly declined my request, but Isam's mother, Imm Ghassan, was eager to talk about herself and her family.

In my conversations with the Abu-Hawilas (see Figure 4), I found narratives which operate in complex, shifting relationship—at once complementary, tangential, and critical—to the narratives of "official" Palestinian nationalism.

Isam and Imm Ghassan's intifada stories certainly embody the internalization of particular nationalist categories, but they also speak to the existence of profound ideological fissures. To be sure, they harbor bitter memories of tragedies and indignities suffered throughout their lives, most prominently the death of their son and brother, Nizam. Indeed, as will become clear in the following pages, the memory of Nizam's martyrdom is one of the most important mechanisms through which they articulate their relationship to each other and to the various social worlds—

the camp, the troubled terrain of Israel/Palestine, the international arena — of which they are a part. Tragic memories such as this, however, exist side by side with a range of other stories and remembrances which evoke images of sacrifice and regeneration, resistance and romance. What ultimately emerges from their stories is a sense of generation and memory as similarly open-ended processes that provide, in a present moment seemingly dominated by outside forces, a way to preserve the possibilities of the future.

## Narrating Tragedy, Performing Identity

I made the first of several visits to *dār Abu-Hawila* (the Abu-Hawila house) in late February 1997 when Ashraf led me across one of the two main streets that trisect the camp, up the hill and into a narrow alleyway until we stood in front of the door to Isam's house, staring at a small poster identifying this as the home of Nizam, the martyr. I had intended this initial meeting to be a purely social visit, a chance to get to know Isam before possibly returning for a formal interview. Shortly after my arrival, as we were drinking tea in his family's sitting room, Isam disappeared for a moment and returned with a series of photographs of Nizam, taken in the hospital just before his death near the end of the intifada's first year. As I looked at the pictures (probably twenty-five in all), it seemed to me that the photographer had carefully walked around the hospital bed, taking pictures of the wounded body from every possible angle, in some cases also capturing another young man at the bedside giving the "V" for victory sign made famous by young activists during the intifada. In what was perhaps the most striking photo, a poster of a Naji al-ʿAli cartoon was draped across Nizam's chest. The image of the young Hanzalla, fashioned by an artist who had himself been a victim of political assassination only two years earlier, called attention not only to Nizam's youth — he died at age twenty-four — but also to his political experience: according to his mother, he became an activist by the age of ten or twelve, and was routinely detained and tortured as a teenager before joining the ranks of the *shuhadāʾ*.[3] The poster was hanging prominently in the Abu-Hawila home along with various pictures of and other tributes to Nizam.

In the course of the subsequent interviews I conducted with Isam and Imm Ghassan, both spoke at length about Nizam and the events that led up to his death. For her part, Imm Ghassan talked of the tragedy almost as if it were expected given her family's troubled history in general, and its relationship with the state of Israel and its security apparatus in particular. "What can I say? I have lots of stories, and there have always been problems in my life, from when I was little," she said when I interviewed her for the first time in mid-April. She spoke for nearly an hour in response to my initial open-ended question ("Tell me a little bit about yourself and your family"), summarizing her life as a series of violent tragedies which had befallen her and various members of her family. Her father died in battle in 1948, when she was six years old, and the surviving members of her family were forced to flee their home in Jaffa, eventually ending up in the newly created Balata camp. Of the fourteen children in her family, she was the only one to stay in the *mukhayyam*, marrying and starting a family while her brothers and sisters all went to Jordan following Israel's capture of the West Bank in the 1967 war. Then in 1973, just three months after Isam was born, her husband was killed when a runaway truck crashed into a shop where he was drinking coffee just outside the entrance to the camp. Throughout the first two decades of the Israeli occupation, her older sons were in and out of political detention and interrogation; one was arrested for five years at the age of fourteen. These experiences, she says, taught them "hatred" for their occupiers: "If there is someone who tortures you, would you love him?"

When I asked Isam to tell me about Nizam, he began by insisting that his brother was a "normal" young man who always treated others well and who, like many of his friends, left school of his own volition before completing his *tawjīhī* (secondary school certificate). "Nizam wasn't well-educated," he says. "He used to work for a day, or a week, and then when he got some money in his pocket, he would stop working." In terms of political activity, he points out that Nizam was arrested a total of twenty-two times, all prior to the start of the uprising. One memorable arrest occurred in 1986, when soldiers came to the house to search for weapons, but found only books and kitchen knives; for possession of these items, Nizam was jailed for a month and a half, and the family was fined 70 Jordanian dinars.

After December 1987, as the level of Palestinian resistance and Israeli repression steadily increased, Nizam lived for months as one of the *mutaradīn* ("wanted"), young activists who spent their time on the run from the Shin Bet, the secretive Israeli internal security force known to Palestinians as the *mukhābarāt*. Isam and his mother both remember that during the time when Nizam was "wanted," he never slept at home. "He would go and sleep in the mountains, or at friends' houses and so forth," says Imm Ghassan. "This happened every day during the intifada . . . [young men] going, coming by the house, going, coming, going, coming." Meanwhile, Israeli security officers also made regular visits to the house to look for Nizam, led by the officer responsible for Balata, a man known to camp residents as "Captain Abu Shawqi." During one of these visits, Abu Shawqi confronted Isam's sister Hala, who was studying for her *tawjīhī* exam, and accused her of membership in an illegal organization when he found political slogans written in some of her books. "That time he said to my mother, 'I swear, if Nizam doesn't come [to turn himself in] . . . I'm going to want her instead,'" recalls Isam. "[He said] 'I don't want Isam or Marwan or Bassam—I want Hala.'"

Clearly Nizam's flight from the *mukhābarāt* was placing a tremendous strain on his family—Imm Ghassan says that she and her children were routinely threatened by Abu Shawqi while Nizam was in hiding—and in this the Abu-Hawilas were not alone. A number of Nizam's close friends were also on the run, and Isam tells the story of one incident which perhaps symbolizes how Israel's counterinsurgency policy encouraged—and also relied upon—a kind of tug-of-war between parents and children:

> I remember there was one *shab* whose father used to beat him a lot. . . . The father was a taxi driver, and he convinced his son to turn himself in. So they drove to the edge of the camp, and [the young man] asked his father to stop so that he could buy cigarettes. But he didn't buy the cigarettes—he ran away.

Even this young man, however, eventually surrendered at the urging of his family; in fact, according to Isam, one by one, all of Nizam's comrades came out of hiding and made themselves available to the Shin Bet for questioning or arrest. With the pressure growing on Nizam to do the same, he finally gave in—but only after his family appealed to what might seem an unexpected source: a young woman with whom Nizam was apparently in love, and who convinced him to come out of hiding. According to Imm Ghassan, Nizam placed one condition on his willingness to surrender: there was a major feast approaching, and he told his mother, "I don't want to be in prison and have all of you celebrating the feast alone. . . . Let me see you for the feast—we'll have fun and eat meat, and then I'll go to the prison. Don't worry—everything will be fine." After two days of the feast, he went to the intelligence headquarters, but he was not detained as expected; instead, as Imm Ghassan carefully described in our interview, he was threatened by Abu Shawqi:

> When he went to turn himself in, Abu Shawqi said to him, "Abu-Hawila, why did you come here? Do you think this is a hotel where you can just come when you want to and not come when you don't want to?" He said, "Listen"—he slapped him twice and said, "I don't want you in good shape, I don't want you alive—I want you dead."

Isam, who was understandably surprised to see Nizam in the street only two hours after he had gone to turn himself in, tells essentially the same story, adding that Abu Shawqi punctuated his words by touching his moustache—a kind of oath—thereby demonstrating his intention to carry out the threat. Indeed, as I learned from speaking informally to others in Balata about Nizam, the image of the hated Abu Shawqi foreshadowing Nizam's martyrdom is a constitutive element of the story. One of Isam's friends, a long-time Fateh activist named Khaled, insists that Nizam's death was the result of a "personal" matter between Nizam and Abu Shawqi, and that this was a common occurrence during the intifada. Many people were targeted for punishment or assassination, he said, simply because they had made one or another of these officers angry.

Regardless of the motivation behind it, the actual incident in which Nizam was killed bears all the markings of the kind of premeditated assassination described in a 1993 Human Rights Watch report, which details the Israeli government's use of undercover hit squads as a tool for targeting Palestinian activists. The report effectively debunks the official Israeli claim that these forces were operating under law enforcement-type rules of engagement, demonstrating instead that the undercover squads functioned more as military units that regularly followed what amounted to a shoot-to-kill policy, deliberately using lethal force against a variety of Palestinians they had no interest in capturing alive. Moreover, the report also indicates that many of these killings were preceded by death threats against the "wanted" persons and by the harassment and violent intimidation of their families, as occurred with the Abu-Hawilas.[4]

The Israeli newspaper *Hadashot,* citing Palestinian sources, reported on 6 October that Nizam "was shot by Shin Bet members when they took him from his house [on 26 September]."[5] If true, this would make Nizam's death one of the intifada's earliest cases of undercover assassination, given that, according to Human Rights Watch, the killing of *mu-*

*taradīn* did not become a systematic element of Israeli government policy until early 1992.[6] While I was only able to obtain second-hand testimony about Nizam's death, which happened at night under murky circumstances, there did seem to be a consensus among camp residents that he was singled out for murder by a special unit, rather than being randomly killed in a clash with a regular army patrol in the camp.

Following his confrontation with Abu Shawqi, Nizam resumed his pattern of staying out of sight and sleeping outside the house. According to Isam, his brother must have known that some sort of operation against him was afoot, because on the day of the shooting he came home for the first time since his trip to the intelligence headquarters the week before and warned Isam not to sleep in the house that night (though he refused to say why). Imm Ghassan remembers that the atmosphere in the camp was tense that day because there was some sort of Hamas activity going on. Nizam appeared unexpectedly:

> He came to the kitchen window . . . and said, "Mother, what are you doing?" I told him that I was making dinner—I was frying potatoes. He said, "Well, I'll come in and eat with you." So we made dinner—even to us, God is merciful—and we ate. Then he said, "By God, they're going to come and imprison us right now," and I said, "Well, only God can help you." He went outside, because he knew [the soldiers] were coming, they were coming to the house. A group came from over there, another group from up there, and so forth.

At that point her three sons who were in the house—Isam, Bassam, and Nizam—ran "zigging and zagging" in all directions; Isam remembers scraping himself on walls as he tore through the darkness, unaware of what was happening to his brothers, until he finally ended up at the home of a neighbor who took him in. Meanwhile, says Imm Ghassan, she wrestled with one of the soldiers, trying to hold his gun to prevent him from firing at her children; in the end, however, she could not stop them from chasing after Nizam and shooting him. At this point in the interview, Muna, my interpreter, interrupted Imm Ghassan to ask, "They shot him with what?" This may seem an odd question, but it is not an uncommon one in Palestine, where Israeli forces have used a variety of types of ammunition ranging from plastic and rubber bullets to so-called "live" ammunition. Imm Ghassan's answer, directed to Muna, suggested impatience at the question, but also a determination to provide, as much as possible, exact details of the shooting: "*Bullets*! 'Dum-dum'![7] Two 'dum-dums' in his head. A bullet in his shoulder. A bullet in his waist. A bullet in his stomach. A bullet in each leg. He saw it, John did—he saw the pictures!" Isam's list of Nizam's wounds was slightly different, though equally precise: six bullets in his legs, one in his waist, one in his shoulder, and one fatal "dum-dum" bullet to the head. Additional details I gathered from other camp residents suggest that the assassination of Nizam may have been even more brutal and calculated than his brother and mother had indicated. According to Isam's friend Khaled, for example, the soldiers intentionally shot Nizam once in each leg to prevent him from fleeing, confirmed his identity, then shot him seven more times before tying him to the back of a jeep and dragging him for several hundred meters down a street just outside the camp.

Imm Ghassan didn't see the shooting, but heard her son call out "Mother! Mother!" after being wounded. She wanted to run and find Nizam, but was prevented from doing so by soldiers who shoved her back into the house while, unknown to her, the assailants removed her son's body from the camp. Her attempts to locate Nizam were futile, and later she learned that he had been taken to the intelligence headquarters:

> They called an ambulance driver and told him, "Come to the gate of the building and pick up this dog here." And he said, "That one is not a dog"—the ambulance driver said this—"he is better than all of you. He is more honorable than you are." Later Bassam came to me and said, "Mother, do you know that ambulance driver, the one who carried my brother's life?" I said, "Yes." He told me, "He was martyred—they killed him." Do you see how they treat us?

As Isam tells the story, the medical personnel who responded to the call to pick up a "dog" arrived to find Nizam being treated by a soldier who was crying. They eventually took him to a hospital in Nablus, but because of the serious nature of his injuries, doctors there decided to send him to al-Maqassed Hospital in Jerusalem, where he underwent several surgeries before his death nine days later. It was during Nizam's days as a "living martyr,"[8] according to Imm Ghassan, that a friend managed to talk his way through an Israeli checkpoint with his camera in order to photograph Nizam so that evidence of the shooting could be printed in the newspapers; these are the photos I was shown when I first visited the Abu-Hawila house. After Nizam's death, Bassam succeeded in bringing the body back to Balata by way of Jericho, and a process of negotiation between the family and the Israeli military authorities began over the issue of burial. The Israelis, said Isam, wanted to take the body in order to prevent the holding of a nationalist funeral, but the family and other camp residents refused to give up the body. In the end a compromise was reached: the military allowed a small funeral to take place at night, attended only by Imm Ghassan, Bassam, one of Nizam's friends, and the *shaykh* of the camp's mosque.[9]

As jarring as it was for me to be shown the photographs of Nizam's body, and as incongruous as it may seem to show them, or to tell such stories, to a first-time visitor, these practices make perfect sense if we view them in the context of existing Palestinian conventions of political narration and memorializing, particularly in dialogue with visitors seen as representatives of the "outside" world. As a crossroads of traders and conquerors and a beacon for religious pilgrims and other tourists, the Holy Land has long been a highly "visited" place; most recently, as the site of an extremely visible and volatile political conflict, Palestine has also become one of the most researched and reported areas of the world. Palestinian residents of the West Bank and Gaza, therefore, have a great deal of experience in being visited, observed, and interviewed by a steady stream of journalists, human rights workers, academic researchers, and solidarity delegations. All these groups became an increasingly common sight in the West Bank and Gaza during the intifada. The body of written material they have generated (books, dissertations, op-ed pieces and news features, articles in organizational newsletters, and informally circulated personal travelogues) continues to grow, with individual accounts frequently featuring descriptions of visits to the homes of Palestinians wounded or killed during the uprising.

As someone who has engaged in "political tourism" (Stein 1995) in Palestine myself, I have lived the sharply contradictory reactions that such public narrations of suffering can elicit from "outside" visitors. On one level, the experience can be an almost perversely empowering one: when I first went to Palestine in 1990 as part of a solidarity delegation, I did so with the rather selfish notion that *I* would be the one to document the injustices occurring in the West Bank and Gaza, and that *I* would somehow use this information to influence public opinion and government policy back home. Like most such delegations, we spent time in hospitals and refugee camps literally viewing—and, in the case of one member of our group, videotaping—the suffering of young Palestinians who obliged us by ritualistically displaying their wounds and recounting how they had been wounded. When I returned six years later to conduct the research for this book, I continued to meet many Palestinians who expressed the hope that I would pass their stories on to others when I returned home so that "America" would understand why the intifada occurred. Young people in particular were fond of insisting, half-jokingly, that I "go and tell Bill Clinton" what I had seen and heard.

When I stepped back from these encounters, however, I also saw that they can be read as cultural practices through which both parties, by playing a particular role, participate in the constitution of Palestinian national identity. In the presence of "outside" visitors, Palestinians are expected to perform examples of what the visitors view as the essence of "Palestinianness"—namely, stories of suffering and victimization.[10] The visitor, in turn, is expected to observe and record (in writing, on tape or film, in his or her memory) the "evidence" of suffering. The parallel between these encounters and the paradigmatic intifada event—the confrontation between stonethrowing youths and Israeli soldiers—is both striking and ironic, given that many of the wounds displayed to visitors were originally inflicted in these skirmishes. In making such a comparison, I certainly don't mean to minimize the fact that street demonstrations inevitably carried with them the potential of injury or death for those involved. My point here, however, is that these clashes were also constituted by their status as a kind of routinized political theater, a performance which could not take place without the willingness of each side to play its part.

Similarly, the kind of interaction I had with Balata residents such as Isam and Imm Ghassan is its own type of ritual characterized by a kind of symbolic violence—inflicted when the experience of suffering is narratively reenacted—and by an uneasy cooperation between visitor and visited. This is not to say that both parties have no choice in the matter; on the contrary, as I will argue in greater detail below, there is a kind of calculation at work in which the motivation for taking part in the ritual lies not in the present moment itself but in an imagined future when the suffering will be redressed. Such calculations, in other words, are necessarily and fundamentally shaped by the situation itself.[11] How else to explain the fact that once I entered their house and was shown the photographs of Nizam, I felt that I *had* to ask them to tell the story? And how else to explain the fact that despite their having told and retold this painful story—the close resemblance between each of their narratives suggests a kind of formal repetition—both Isam and Imm Ghassan were willing to tell it yet again when they spoke with me?

### Activism: Confronting Soldiers, Speaking to the World, and Growing Up

More than most people I spoke with in Balata, Imm Ghassan moved almost effortlessly between narrative modes, creating an engaging mix of the serious and the comic, the testimonial and the epigrammatic. At a particularly somber juncture in our first interview, for example, she launched into an attack on "the British" and "the Americans" as those responsible, through their support of Israel's creation, for her long history of suffering:

> Who brought the Jews [to Palestine]? America and Britain. The British Mandate was very important. In the British time there were weapons, there were planes, there were military stations, there were police dogs— *all* for the Haganah [the underground Zionist military forces]! All the weapons went to the Haganah . . . and the Haganah used these weapons to kill us. To the Arabs, [the British] gave nothing! Who brought Israel? Britain, America.

She made this point immediately following her description of Nizam's death, effectively providing her own assessment of the larger international context in which the major events of her life should be viewed. She would repeat this gesture in a later conversation when discussing Isam's unsuccessful attempt to get married during the intifada: after reasserting her desire to help Isam find a wife, she looked directly at me and said forcefully, "John! My father and my son are martyrs [at the hands of] Israel, but it is not from Israel. It is from *America*!" Then, however, perhaps sensing my rather grim reaction to this accusation and to some of her more sobering personal experiences, she gave me a mischievous look and said wryly, "So I want to make an intifada against America!"

Imm Ghassan told several stories involving her interactions with Israeli soldiers, who, she claims proudly, are almost universally afraid of her. These stories bear a close resemblance to many intifada legends and jokes, brief narratives that tend to present a conflict between two opposing forces nearly always represented by Israeli soldiers and Palestinian civilians. The Palestinians inevitably defeat their occupiers through trickery, moral superiority, or simply by refusing to submit to the soldiers' demands, even if death is the result. In one of the most famous such stories (which I was told more than once during my stay in the West Bank) soldiers capture a young boy of seven or eight and accuse him of throwing stones. When he admits to the charge but says his brother made him do it, the soldiers demand to be taken to talk with the brother. The boy obliges, takes them to him home and presents to them his brother, the ringleader—a smiling four-year-old.

In her own stories, Imm Ghassan portrays herself as almost always getting the better of the soldiers, often by openly haranguing them without showing any fear of possible reprisal. During the intifada, she recalls, soldiers were constantly coming to her house to search for weapons and harass her family, sometimes fining her for possession of kitchen knives and other "illegal" items. One day she got up early to pray and found soldiers surrounding the house; she woke her sons to alert them, and then the soldiers forced her and her daughters to stay in the living room while they tore the house apart, claiming there were weapons hidden in the walls. "It was the iron [bars] the house is made of," she told me triumphantly:

> But because they used the sensor to see what was inside, they thought it was weapons, not the iron. And I told [one of the soldiers], "You brother of a whore! This is the iron in the house!" And so they went into the kitchen and they took all the tiles out until they came to the pipes, and that's when they knew that there was nothing there. . . . [T]his is what they did, and they didn't find any weapons. What would've happened if they *had* found weapons?

At one point in this argument she demanded that the soldiers tell her the whereabouts of her son Marwan, who had been arrested recently. They replied that they were going to "hang" him, so she turned to one of the soldiers, a Druze—she was deliberate in pointing this out, indicating that his participation in the raid was particularly offensive to her—and said, "They should hang *you!*"

All of Imm Ghassan's sons were in and out of prison throughout the uprising, and many of her stories involve verbal skirmishes in what amounted to an ongoing war of position between her and the Israeli security officers in Nablus. Intimidating parents as a way of encouraging them to stop their children from engaging in intifada activities was an important, though largely unexamined, element of Israel's counterinsurgency strategy during the uprising. In Imm Ghassan's case, this intimidation often took the form of summoning her to the military intelligence headquarters, where she would use a variety of verbal tactics to indicate her refusal to cooperate. When one of her sons was arrested upon returning from a trip to Jordan, she confronted a security officer who had been a neighbor of her family in Jaffa before 1948, saying, "You know us, you're like my uncle, so why aren't you helping us?" Later she was ordered to appear once again before the intelligence officers, who told her that there was something wrong with her sons' minds—to which she shot back, "It's because of your torture!" and threatened to kill one of them. This incident led to another situation which illustrates the cat-and-mouse quality of her relationship with the military occupation: the officers put her in a cell with one of her sons, apparently hoping that he would say something incriminating to his mother. She correctly suspected, however, that there was a prison guard hiding in a cabinet in the cell, so she and her son said nothing, foiling the officers' plans. Afterward, when she learned that the guard was using the Arabic name "Zaki," meaning "clever," she mocked his choice of name in front of his superiors, saying triumphantly that his "cleverness" wasn't working with her.

Imm Ghassan's confrontations with soldiers were not limited to circumstances involving her own sons; on the contrary, time and again during our two interviews she insisted that she felt a responsibility to defend *all* young people, because all of them were her children. One day when she was shopping in Nablus, for example, she saw a group of soldiers harassing a young boy; afraid that he would be arrested, she intervened, claiming that he was her son. Everything was going well, she recalled with a smile, until the boy's real mother arrived on the scene and almost ruined the rescue attempt! As Giacaman and Johnson (1989) note, and as numerous young people told me in interviews when I asked them about women's activism, rescuing a child by claiming to be his or her mother was one of the signature roles women played in the intifada. Much of the literature on women and the intifada has picked up on precisely this notion of activist motherhood, in which large numbers of Palestinian women were able to engage in public confrontations with soldiers by reformulating and expanding their identities as mothers.

What I want to point out here is that the kind of identity created through such political activism is not only gendered, but also generational. In this respect, Imm Ghassan's twofold explication of the reasons for women's activism, and of her own motivations for taking an active role in the intifada, is instructive. First, she painted such a vivid picture of the political activities of Balata women—confronting and intimidating soldiers, helping the camp survive prolonged periods of curfew, working together to free other women who were harassed or arrested by the army—that I finally asked, half-jokingly, "Where were the men?" The answer, she said, was that many of the men were either dead or in prison, or had gone outside the camp to find work in Nablus and beyond, leaving a vacuum that widows and other women like herself were able to fill. This reading suggests that in her mind, the actions themselves were not necessarily gendered male or female, but were definitely the responsibility of adults.

Second, she also located women's activism explicitly in relation to the actions of young people who were themselves at the forefront of the uprising. When I asked her how it felt to see young children taking part in demonstrations and placing themselves in danger, she replied, "I should be the one fighting . . . because I am tortured when I see them." In these kinds of statements, Imm Ghassan linked the defense of young people with the defense of the wider community and nation. The willingness to put oneself at risk in order to defend other people's children was for her a supreme mark of patriotism (*wataniya*), a badge of political authenticity worn by all women except, she said, those few who were "afraid" or who didn't "feel" for their nation.[12]

Isam's memories of activism are closely linked with his involvement in the Popular Front, a faction claiming only a small number of supporters in a camp traditionally dominated by the mainstream Fateh movement. He was initially attracted to the PFLP because he felt that its Marxist ideology appealed to the poorest members of society and might constitute the best means to achieve liberation. Now, however, he says that while he is still with the PFLP "intellectually," he cannot support it "practically" because it has failed to adjust to the new realities of the post-intifada situation, most notably the ongoing "peace process." The resignation with which he speaks about these "realities" stands in sharp contrast to his memories of the intifada, memories which are particularly vivid for its early period, when optimism was high and resistance activities were more spontaneous. This was, to return to Karl Mannheim's image, the "drama of his youth."

Like many of the young people I spoke with, Isam insists that in many ways the intifada began well before December 1987 in Balata, where the

IDF had been testing out a version of the bone-breaking policy made official in early 1988 by then-Defense Minister Yitzhak Rabin.[13] Nonetheless, he says, there was something different about the demonstrations that followed the December 9 events in Gaza: as the barrier of fear was broken, resistance to the occupation quickly became a mass movement, and Israel was put on the defensive. In our initial interview, Isam recalled the first major intifada demonstration in Balata:

> The first day of the intifada was a Friday, December 11, the anniversary of the Popular Front. . . . The army was there in the camp. I remember well that some of the young *shabāb* of the camp were throwing stones [at the soldiers]. Then a young *shab*, a child, was martyred—he was ten or eleven years old. Then a lot more young people came . . . and after that, two more were killed, Sahar al-Jirmi and Suhaila Ka'bi . . . and after that there were more demonstrations and many people were injured.[14]

During the four-day curfew that followed, the IDF reinforced its presence in the camp, staking out positions on rooftops and drawing volleys of stones from young Palestinians in what Isam described as a daily game of minor skirmishes that occasionally escalated into more deadly confrontations. As we discussed his recollections of those first days and weeks, he returned several times to the idea that he often felt "victorious" vis-à-vis the soldiers he encountered in the streets and alleyways of the camp:

> J: How did it feel at that time, when it started?
> I: It's hard to say exactly, but . . . when I picked up a stone and threw it at the army, there was a real feeling of comradeship—I alone, or my group of *shabāb*, was standing up against armed soldiers who had all kinds of weapons, fully-armed soldiers. . . . And the Israeli army defeated the whole Arab world in 1967, and before that in 1948—Egypt, Syria, Jordan—and we alone, as people or as a group, we achieved something important. Regardless of what it was, we achieved something for ourselves and for our society.
> J: You felt like you were defeating the Israelis?
> I: Sure. Why? Because we were just kids, and even when the soldiers were young, they were older [than we were] and they were armed. And sometimes we wouldn't run away from them—they ran away

> from us. . . . He [i.e., the Israeli soldier] was afraid of me because he
> was coming into a land that wasn't his.

In the context of these memories, age matters for Isam, who was sixteen at the end of 1987: a significant part of his pride in having taken part in the intifada from its inception derives from the knowledge that he and his friends were young at the time. When I hypothesized aloud that many of the soldiers serving in the West Bank must also have been young, he quickly responded in a way that demonstrated his awareness of exactly how age matters. "That's true, but it's well-known that in the [Israeli] army, a young man enters after he turns eighteen, so there is a difference of two years between him and me," he pointed out. "Plus they had weapons and training, which makes a big difference."

All of his emphasis on what should have been the superiority of the IDF—surely one of the strongest armies in the world should be able to brush aside a few angry teenagers!—serves as an effective way to set up the following stories, in which he illustrates how he and the *shabāb* were able to humiliate the IDF in two different ways:

> One time they came to the school so that we could clear the air between us. They put down their weapons, one [soldier] stayed to guard the weapons, and we played football. So we started to ask them things like, "Why do you kill our people?"—you know, childish questions—and they didn't know how to answer. They said, "Well, you're always throwing stones at us." They themselves didn't even know why they were there! I remember another time, we were playing football at the school, and they [i.e., the soldiers] were playing with us. So we all withdrew one by one from the field [i.e., leaving the soldiers alone] and started stoning them!

On one level, the image of Palestinians and Israelis suspending their battles and playing football together calls to mind accounts of similar games that took place in the "no-man's land" between lines of trenches during World War I. For Isam, however, telling stories of intifada games has little to do with the possibility of coexistence or the futility of the fighting. Instead, the stories derive their meaning from the spectacle that is made of the older, better-armed Israeli soldiers who, despite their numerous advantages, prove unable to answer the most "childish" questions and fall prey to an impromptu ambush concocted by the very young people they were sent to pacify. They are clearly stories with a particular moral attached to them, and they would not "work" (at least not to the same extent) without the element of generational contrast, a contrast Isam skillfully incorporated when he set the stage for the stories by informing me of the age difference (however small) between the *shabāb* and the soldiers.

During the uprising, Isam worked with what he calls his "group" (*majmūᶜa*, in his case a small team of PFLP supporters) in a variety of activities, from organizing demonstrations and throwing stones to solving local disputes and confronting camp residents suspected of collaborating with Israel. Unlike his mother, however, he was less inclined in our conversations to discuss particular encounters he had with soldiers, unless doing so (as in the football stories) for humorous effect; similarly, he was somewhat reluctant to relate the specificities of his personal involvement in resistance activities. Instead, he spent a good deal of time speaking in general terms about the internal dynamics of the uprising and its impact on everyday life in the camp. In response to my questions about changes in intergenerational relations—questions that contained within them the implication that traditional generational hierarchies had broken down during the intifada—Isam insisted that the mass character of the movement, as well as the nature of Israel's repression of it, actually strengthened social relations by encouraging and necessitating greater cooperation among all social groups. He notes, for example, that the restrictions on freedom of movement and economic activity which accompanied the intifada (in the form of curfews, strikes, and extended periods of closure) meant that fathers were able, or were forced, to spend more time at home with their children, a trend which he says improved relations between husbands and wives.[15] He also argues that pressing issues of personal security and political strategy led to more mixing of the sexes among young people, as when a young man and woman who did not know each other held hands (pretending to be married) in order to get the man past a military patrol or checkpoint.

In Isam's view, however, whatever social and political successes the intifada may have achieved were clearly confined to its early period. Assessing the uprising's development over time, Isam traces a steady decline in what were its greatest strengths—mass involvement and unity of purpose—and a gradual increase in internal tensions. There were fights over money sent into the West Bank and Gaza by the PLO in Tunis, fights which he says led to the formation of armed, semiautonomous "strike forces" identified with particular factions. These groups, such as the Red Eagles (associated with the PFLP), engaged not only in violent actions against Israeli targets (and each other) but also in the intimidation of the Palestinian population at large. By the time Isam was arrested during the 1991 Gulf War, the intifada had essentially been stalled by a combination of factors: the withdrawal of Arab support for the PLO in retaliation for the latter's support of Iraq; the loss of remittances sent by Palestinians working in Kuwait and the other Gulf states to their families back home; the devastation of the Palestinian economy as a result of Israel's military closure of the West Bank and Gaza; and the increasingly violent factionalism to which Isam referred. Given that he had been "inactive" for some time because of disagreements with his "group," his arrest came as a surprise; he was charged with being a PFLP organizer, throwing stones, writing graffiti, and investigating collaborators, and was sentenced to two years in prison.

"I was a prisoner—what can I say?" was Isam's initial response when I asked him what it was like to be in prison during the intifada. He went on, however, to argue that the prison experience for many young Palestinian men served as a rite of passage, a period of fundamental personal transformation (see chapter 4). Spending two years in the newly created "Ansar III" prison in the Negev Desert brought him into close, daily contact with political detainees from all factions across the ideological spectrum.[16] It also introduced him to a new kind of confrontation with Israeli soldiers, one in which his options were starkly limited: "The clashes were much more dangerous," he says, recalling one particular day when soldiers fired on the prisoners with tear gas and live ammunition. During clashes in the camp, he explains, one could always "go back home, close the door, and escape the tear gas. But in the prison, there aren't any rooms, there is nothing to close behind you. So either you die, or you do something."

The most important "education" Isam received while in detention, however, was social rather than political. "Socially [I learned] how to deal with people in a correct way . . . and more than this, I learned how to control myself," he says, by way of illustrating how he was a "different person" (*insān tāni*) when he came out of prison. When I asked him whether his family and friends also saw him differently as a result of his imprisonment, he explained how he was gradually able to gain the "respect" of his older brothers. Before his arrest, he says, "there were a lot of problems in my family between my brothers. I tried a little bit to help solve them, but I wasn't able to do so at first." After his release, however, he redoubled his attempts to bring about a reconciliation (*sulh*), and succeeded where he had failed earlier. Partly as a result of his mediation efforts, the older members of his family realized that he had become more "mature" in prison, and they began to take his ideas more seriously and to give him an equal role in helping to deal with other problems in the household. Similarly, after leaving prison he discovered that his relationship with his friends had changed; significantly, he says that the lessons he had learned in Ansar III made him impatient with friends who wanted to go back to the practices of their youth—using rude language with each other, for example—instead of acting like adults. With his new status as a former prisoner, he found that he was able to influence these friends in ways that were not possible in the past.

## Of Romance and Revolution: Love, Marriage, and the Intifada Generation

Although Isam was generally willing to oblige me when I asked him for specific information about his personal political history, he often tried to nudge my questions about such matters in the direction of the general rather than the specific. Consequently, I found myself face to face with one of the romantic assumptions I had brought with me to Balata: I began to acknowledge, more than a little sheepishly, the possibility that some Palestinian activists might not be eager to share their personal intifada stories with me. By the time I returned to Isam's house for a third interview, I was convinced that for whatever reason—perhaps something in the way I was coming across to him, or perhaps his own weariness of thinking and talking about the uprising—he was not going to "open up" to me. In the end, however, the problem lay with a much more fundamental (and naïve) assumption I had been making: despite my theoretical belief in the need to conduct open-ended interviews, and for all my suspicions about the existing, media-driven public record of the intifada—with its narrow focus on what Janet Varner Gunn calls the "Big News" of repression and resistance[17]—I had still come to the field expecting that young people in Balata would invariably recall this period as a series of highly dramatic, often violent political events, and my interview preparation reflected this expectation.

Isam was hardly wanting for material out of which to construct this type of narrative; at the same time, I don't think that this is what he wanted to talk about. Instead, near the beginning of our third interview, he took my question about how to characterize the *jīl al-intifāda* and used it as a springboard to discuss the issues that were clearly at the front of his mind—romance and marriage. The members of his generation, he argued, are "suffering" from a troubling contradiction: their experience in matters of politics is matched, ironically and perhaps tragically, by their inexperience in matters of love. "Maybe we're successful in political or economic life," he observed, noting the ways in which young people were able to take difficult decisions and to act "beyond their years" during the intifada. "I can talk about all these subjects—I'm twenty-five years old. . . . But I can't express my own feelings" when it comes to dealing with the opposite sex. This situation amounts to what he calls a "return to adolescence" (*ᶜauda lal-murāhiqa*)—an adolescence that was either interrupted or never happened—in the sense that he and his age-mates were suddenly being forced to go back and work through feelings and experiences that were denied them during the politically charged days of the uprising.[18]

The incongruity of physical and political maturity paired with emotional adolescence is directly related to the issue of early marriages (*zawāj badri*), a subject which came up repeatedly during my interviews in Balata. Existing statistical information on marriage patterns in the West Bank and Gaza, while somewhat uneven, indicates a gradual rise in marriage age in the past quarter-century.[19] My first clue that the intifada may have disrupted this pattern came from Ashraf, who outlined for me the tentative results of an undergraduate research project he had done in Balata, documenting a lowering of the average age of marriage in the camp during the uprising. His conclusions fell in line with the published literature on the intifada, in which researchers have argued that the uprising saw a significant, though perhaps temporary, shift in the social relations of marriage, with two related results: more people got married, and more did so at a younger age.[20]

Based as they are on a small number of existing studies, and on what seems to be a critical mass of anecdotal evidence, such claims are more successful in suggesting an empirical trend than they are in answering the more speculative question of why the shift may have taken place. In terms of early marriages, economic factors are undoubtedly central, with the general downturn in employment prospects leading many parents to marry off their daughters as soon as possible, and with the moratorium placed by the intifada leadership on lavish public ceremonies and the use of the *mahr* (bride price) making marriage an affordable option for younger men. As Philippa Strum (1998) notes, however, other marriage trends may be better explained with reference to changes in political culture. The mixing of men and women in political activities, for example, led many young women to reject the idea of arranged marriage and to choose a husband for themselves. Moreover, she adds, the choice of marriage partners was often affected as much by political reputation as by economic considerations, with family members of "martyrs" being seen as more desirable spouses.

Many feminist researchers and activists have tended to analyze the marriage issue by placing a gendered view of the intifada within the longer history of movements for women's equality in Palestine, and by emphasizing the negative consequences of early marriages for young women. Suha Sabbagh (1998), for example, traces the rise in early marriages to a reassertion of patriarchal authority, arguing that fathers arranged early marriages to keep their daughters out of politics and to protect their "virtue." Characterizations of the long-term impact of these marriage trends are more varied, and correlate closely with assessments of the success or failure of the women's movement as a whole. Strum takes a somewhat optimistic view, referring to the widespread involvement of women in the intifada as a "revolution"—albeit one with an uncertain future—and arguing that while the effect of changing marriage patterns on women is "obviously complicated," the real story lies less in the temporary lowering of marriage age than in the increasingly popular acceptance of women's right to education and employment regardless of marital status.[21] In contrast, researchers such as Sabbagh and Islah Jad, who are reluctant to claim too much for the women's movement in light of the setbacks suffered by women in postindependence Algeria and elsewhere, emphasize that early marriages tend to work to the detriment of women, particularly in preventing them from pursuing higher education and careers outside the home.

Within the context of existing scholarship on the intifada, then, discussions of changing marriage patterns tend to be informed primarily by the perspectives of women activists, both young and old, married and unmarried. Against this paradigm, Isam—young, unmarried, and male—offered a perspective on the phenomenon of *zawāj badri* that is strikingly different in emphasis. While he did not deny that parental pressure may have played a role in many intifada marriages, he nonetheless argued that most young people *chose* to get married, in effect, because they *could*—because norms prohibiting the social contact of young men and women were relaxed to allow for the unusual political situation, and because the financial impediments to marriage were significantly reduced. The problem with these marriages, he stressed several times, lay not in their reinforcement of patriarchal modes of authority, but in the motivation of those who entered into them. Traditionally, he said, marriage was about long-term goals such as "stability" (*istiqrār*)—of which there was none during the intifada. Instead, many young people saw marriage as a kind of "sexual experiment," a view which only demonstrated their lack of preparation for being married. For this reason, he concluded, many of the early marriages ended quickly in divorce.

Isam's motivation for lamenting his generation's lack of romantic experience is, as he indicated quite explicitly, a personal one. Having completed his university education and reached what he called "a suitable age for marriage," he said he still felt totally unqualified to meet the "responsibilities" that come with marriage. While claiming that words like "love" were absent during the intifada, he nonetheless went on to narrate his own experience of a vibrant, though ultimately failed, romance which took place in the midst of the uprising. Shortly before his arrest in 1991, he fell in love with a young woman and decided that he wanted to marry her despite the objections of one of his older brothers, who argued that it was wrong for the young woman to visit Isam at his home, as she had been doing occasionally. Other friends warned him that the Israeli security forces might use the relationship as a kind of blackmail against him, but he says they were determined to get married. When I asked Imm Ghassan about the relationship, she emphasized her own role in defending her son's right to marry the woman he loved:

> He [Isam] had a girlfriend, she was studying with him [at the university] before he was in prison, and she loved him and he loved her. I went to ask for her hand, and they said yes, but then he was imprisoned for two years and her father said, "Look, he is in prison for two years, and I want to marry her off." But then I went to talk with the girl and she gave me pictures of her, to give them to Isam.

When she heard of the father's plan to marry his daughter to another man, she went and had an argument with the girl's family, insisting that this other man didn't love the girl, and demanding to know why the father was arranging the marriage. The father, however, stood firm and reiterated that he simply couldn't afford to wait for Isam to get out of prison. After his two years in political detention, Isam emerged to find, to his obvious disappointment, that his intended wife had indeed married someone else.[22] The new husband, Imm Ghassan noted disapprovingly, was a "bastard" who even went so far as to go to the prison on the day of Isam's release so that he could demand that Isam return the pictures of his wife. Undeterred by her inability to help her son turn his intifada romance into marriage, she says she is still confident that he will find a wife soon: "So now, hopefully, when he finds a job, I will try to get him married. . . . Isam is at the university, and there are lots of girls at the university." Isam, for his part, is less certain that his wedding day will come soon, saying that his experience in prison, his concern about failed marriages, and his conversations with friends and neighbors who are married have all convinced him that it is better to wait a while despite his mother's wishes.

Isam's interpretation of intifada marriage patterns, of course, is no less gendered than the testimony offered by the Palestinian women who are cited in feminist studies of the intifada; spoken in an all-male context—a conversation between the two of us, with a male interpreter—his words were clearly based on his knowledge of what young men like himself had experienced. Issues of romance and marriage, I began to see, were popular topics of discussion in his social circle, with friends and relatives routinely asking each other for advice and sharing ideas about proper courses of action. As an example of this subcultural dynamic, Isam described the case of a friend in the camp who insisted on getting married as soon as he had finished his university degree, then came to Isam a few months later and said that he was "bored" with his marriage and wanted to end it. According to Isam, this friend had thought of marriage only as a means to satisfy his "biological needs," and so was shocked to find that he could not cope with the other "needs" associated with married life. At the time of our interview, the friend was still married, but was planning—against Isam's advice—to divorce his wife, and was trying to convince Isam never to get married himself.

In relating the details of such conversations, Isam was pointing to the existence of a discourse on marriage that is "generational" in two closely related ways. Most obviously, it is a discourse *of* generation, associated with a group of young men who were at a similar stage in the life cycle: having shared a range of formative experiences (resistance activities,

political detention) during the intifada, they were reaching what is supposed to be a new stage of life accompanied by new challenges, and they
were attempting to meet these challenges collectively. Their assessment of
intifada marriages, however, is also a discourse *on* generation, in the sense
that they were beginning to analyze openly and critically what it means
to be part of the *jīl al-intifāda*. Indeed, a number of the young men I interviewed in Balata cited the high rate of unsuccessful marriages as one of
the most far-reaching negative consequences of the uprising. It was Isam,
however, whose reading of the situation was the most explicitly generational, drawing a direct link between marriage problems, the specific historical situation of the intifada, and generational identity. Philip Abrams
(1982), echoing Mannheim's work, argues that periods of political upheaval can foster precisely this sort of generational consciousness:

> If a new sociological generation is to emerge . . . the attempt of individu-
> als to construct identity must coincide with major and palpable histori-
> cal experiences in relation to which new meanings can be assembled. . . .
> The social organisation of the life cycle creates moments of more or less
> acute exploration—searching the environment to create a unity of mean-
> ing between self and others. But it is historical events that seem to pro-
> vide the crucial opportunities for constructing new versions of such
> meanings. Such opportunities are seized, in turn, most avidly and imagi-
> natively by those who are most actively in the market for such meanings
> (identities). Hence the peculiar connection between youth (a span of bio-
> logical history) and generations (a span of social history). And the more
> the overall configuration of a society leaves the mode of entry of new in-
> dividuals open to negotiation the more likely it is that those individuals
> will put together a sense of themselves as being historically unlike their
> predecessors. (255)

What is striking about Isam's situation is that throughout his life, the
"mode of entry" Abrams describes seems to have changed more than
once, always subject to the vicissitudes of history. For young men of his
age, the intifada initially provided an alternative way of proving their
manhood and gaining social respect at a time when economic prospects
were increasingly dim. Too young to try their luck as labor migrants, as
many of their older brothers had done, they turned political resistance
into their own rite of passage (Hudson 1994). Buried beneath Isam's
quiet, thoughtful responses to my questions was a kind of angry bitter-

ness deriving from the realization that someone had changed the rules of the game once again, snatching from his grasp the social standing he thought he had earned during the intifada. His testimony suggests a profound sense of generational failure, a general anxiety over the plight of an entire group of young people that is unable or unwilling to move fully into adulthood and take its proper place in society and, by extension, to reproduce itself. It is difficult to separate this concern from the broader historical context in which it was being articulated, namely, a time when the *jīl al-intifāda* was being stripped of the political power it enjoyed during the uprising.

This sense of political marginalization applies equally well to women like Imm Ghassan, who joined their children at the forefront of the anti-occupation struggle in the intifada, but who were watching and waiting for the outcome of political negotiations that seemed far removed from their lives. Imm Ghassan's narration of Isam's troubled personal life also tells us a great deal about the politics of generation in Palestine, particularly the ways in which generational authority is both constituted and negotiated in everyday life. With Isam aged twenty-five and finished with his university degree, she was faced with the erosion of her influence as a parent. Isam, who seemed well aware of his special status as the youngest child in the family, nonetheless wanted to take responsibility for his own life. Imm Ghassan's involvement in Isam's decisions about marriage is indicative of her careful attempts to maintain some control over the reproduction of her family. On the one hand, she had exercised her authority against Isam's brother when Isam wanted to get married before his arrest; on the other hand, she was still trying to marry Isam off even though he said he would prefer to wait. Mother and son, in short, were left trying to strike a balance between parental authority and its complete absence at a time when little else in their social world seemed to be under their control.

## Fixing the Past, Rejecting the Present, (Re)generating the Future

When Isam showed me the photographs of Nizam during my first visit to the family's house, I was struck by the familiarity of the impulse that his gesture suggested. As I have argued elsewhere (Collins 1998), when Palestinians create records of their suffering, such as photographs or other documents of physical violence—records intended in part to be shared with "outsiders" and, by extension, to serve as "evidence" in front of the court of world opinion—they are engaging in a type of "stockpiling" that can be politically counterproductive. This is no small irony, for the effort to uncover and make public the "facts" about Zionism and about the Israeli occupation has long been a cornerstone of the Palestinian liberation struggle. By the 1970s, for example, scholars sympathetic to the Palestinian cause had already begun to respond to this perceived need by researching and documenting a vast array of colonial practices—massacres, land confiscation, destruction of villages, deportations, economic exploitation—in exhaustive detail, while others took the route of compiling huge, encyclopedic volumes of primary and secondary materials related to the conflict. During the intifada, human rights groups documented a pattern of systematic Israeli repression; when combined with the existing journalistic record, this work allows any reader to access the daily chronicle of the uprising in an almost mind-numbing level of detail. This process has only accelerated in recent years, with internet technology providing new ways of disseminating information and images, often in real time.

For all the available information, however, Palestinians still find themselves forced to place their hopes in a political negotiation process to which none of the human rights abuses committed against them are technically relevant, since the terms of the process—terms which the Palestinian leadership, positioning itself against popular Islamic movements and other insurgent social forces, has largely accepted—allow no role for international law.[23] If we follow John B. Thompson's (1984) definition of ideology as designating "the ways in which meaning (or signification) serves to sustain relations of domination" (4), then it seems that while Palestinians who attempt to document their suffering are, on one level, challenging the ideological narratives associated with Zionism and the Israeli state, they are also ironically implicated in another ideological process: the maintenance of an official Palestinian nationalist project that is increasingly undemocratic.

Such a view derives partly from the critical theory of Walter Benjamin, the late German-Jewish philosopher and literary critic whose work provides a provocative rejoinder to those who would uncritically posit memory as a source of resistance. Benjamin, using as his starting point Proust's famous distinction between "voluntary" and "involuntary" memory, highlights the potential complicity of memory (in the form of active preservation of the past) with domination, a process he saw actively at work in the Europe of the 1930s (Benjamin 1968a, 157–158). Voluntary memory—and here Benjamin employs an invented term, *Eingedenken*, which connotes a deliberate act of memorializing—is characterized by the conscious *and always unsuccessful* attempt to preserve or freeze the "experience" of the past through the use of photography, sound recording, print media, or other fixed, concrete forms. Such attempts at preservation, Benjamin argues, actually encourage the "forgetting" of the past by preserving only a kind of "information" that conveys no sense of experience or meaning. In short, attempting to "fix" the past in this way only abets what he saw as the growing hegemony of a form of historical consciousness for which information, rather than experience, is paramount. Furthermore, in a move with provocative implications for national liberation struggles, he suggests that such "stockpiling" is entirely consistent with the most repressive aspects of nationalist thought:

> Our consideration proceeds from the insight that the politicians' stubborn faith in progress, their confidence in their "mass basis," and, finally, their servile integration in an uncontrollable apparatus have been three aspects of the same thing. It seeks to convey an idea of the high price our accustomed thinking will have to pay for a conception of history that avoids any complicity with the thinking to which these politicians continue to adhere.[24]

Seen in this light, Isam and Imm Ghassan's "performance" of Palestinian identity discussed above—a practice which I enabled through my presence and my questions—may also be seen as providing support for what is still the dominant narrative of Palestinian nationalism. Thompson notes that ideology commonly takes a narrative form, justifying asymmetrical relations of power by situating those relations "within a tissue of tales that recapitulate the past and anticipate the future" (11). The narrative advanced by the PLO, and now the PA, exhibits a teleological structure that is common to many anticolonial nationalisms, a structure which "recapitulates the past" in terms of collective victimization and "anticipates the future" in terms of the taking of state power. In this sense, the inspiration behind what I am calling "stockpiling"—particularly with respect to memories of violence—lies less in the past, or even in the present, than in the *future,* a predestined time when what has been suffered can be incorporated retroactively into a narrative of triumph.

Many of the Palestinians I interviewed in Balata, however, demonstrated surprisingly little willingness to believe in the future promised in this dominant narrative. This refusal, I believe, not only signals a collective frustration with the "peace process," but also illuminates the power of such an unsatisfactory situation to produce new kinds of historical consciousness. When we consider Isam and Imm Ghassan's intifada stories as a group—stories of death and defiance, of romance and revolution, of nostalgia and bitterness—what emerges is a picture of two individuals who are each at an important crossroads in terms of their relationship not only to each other and the rest of their family, but also to the national political struggle that has consumed so much of their lives. In many ways, both Isam and Imm Ghassan have often played the roles into which they are cast as loyal Palestinian nationalists—he by fighting the Israeli occupation in the streets, going to prison, and finishing his education, she by bearing, fighting to defend, and being prepared to sacrifice her children. Yet neither has taken on these identities uncritically, in the manner of the wholly "interpellated" subjects who populate many theories of nationalism and ideology. On the contrary, even as they continue to express their support for the goals associated with the nationalist movement (an end to the occupation, a Palestinian state with Jerusalem as its capital, a just solution to the refugee problem), both are careful to maintain a position from which to assess the successes and failures of that movement. This position might best be described as a "local" one, in the sense that the claims advanced by the national leadership are routinely judged against personal experiences and everyday living conditions in the camp. Isam's concern about his generation's "return to adolescence" exemplifies this kind of local critique, in this case of a narrative that romanticizes the heroic exploits of the "children of the stones."

Similarly, Isam expressed a desire to support the PA—at least for lack of a better alternative—but went on to recite a litany of "problems" (including mass arrests of the opposition and the March 1996 raid on An-Najah University by Palestinian security forces) that have marked the post-Oslo period of "limited self-rule." When I asked Imm Ghassan for her opinion of *al-Sulta* (the Authority), she neatly captured the sense of ironic juxtaposition that often results from such a critique: while admitting that her leaders had technically rid Balata of the occupation, she pointed out that there were still Israeli tanks within range of the camp entrance (Balata is located on the edge of Nablus, and hence close to the outer limit of the PA's control), and that the IDF could easily enter the camp at any time—a prediction that proved correct in subsequent years. The PA has little power over the situation, she concluded shrewdly, because "they have already signed the papers [in the peace agreements]." Concerning the future, both she and her son were similarly ambivalent: Imm Ghassan said she is neither optimistic nor pessimistic, while Isam, invoking the famous character created by the Palestinian novelist Emile Habibi, described himself as a "pessoptimist" (*mutashāʾil*), a deliberately ironic fusion of pessimist (*mutashāʾim*) and optimist (*mutafāʾil*). Significantly, neither spoke of the future in terms of concrete, expected events that would constitute the victory of the national struggle.

Here again it is useful to consider Benjamin's writings on memory and history, for it seems that insofar as they are moving away from the nationalist notion of history-as-progress, Isam and Imm Ghassan are now caught between two related, but ultimately opposed alternatives, each of which might be termed "antinationalist." On the one hand, there is Benjamin's (1968c) famous image of the "angel of history"—forever looking backward, yet driven forward by the notion of progress "while the pile of debris before him grows skyward"—in which history appears as endless wreckage piling on itself, going nowhere but simply cycling through the same injustices (257–258). Here memory serves to deny any idea of progress, insisting on an isomorphic relationship between past and present and revealing the future as essentially meaningless. Imm Ghassan's characterization of her life as a story of relentless personal suffering has this sort of cyclical quality, precisely because she provides no end point toward which the story, however tragic, is moving. On the other hand, there is the "quasi-Messianic" view Benjamin aimed to specify, in which memory, according to Peter Osborne (1994), serves not to verify history as progress or as a "pile of debris," but rather to establish a "living relationship" between past and present, and to ensure that the present is viewed from the perspective of a "completed whole." What makes such a view antinationalist, in this context, is that the moment of redemption to which it looks forward is located outside history, or, in other words, it is *imagined*: each present moment, located between a specific past and this imagined future, "carries within it the *perspective* of redemption" (87, emphasis in the original).

The point here is not to turn Isam and Imm Ghassan into critical theorists, or to insist that they have found a way to escape entirely the nationalist categories that still form, in many ways, the boundaries within which most Palestinians conceive of their political universe. Nor is the point to claim that Benjamin's theoretical work easily and unproblematically "explains" the relationship between memory and politics in Palestine. On the contrary, as Osborne notes, Benjamin is often frustratingly noncommittal on the issue of political action, to the point where his dramatic reconception of memory—vividly expressed in terms of "flashes of lightning" and explosive, revolutionary moments—seemingly ceases to have any practical political referent at all and "contracts into a politics of time" (93).

At the same time, however, Benjamin provides us with a means to understand how a shift in an individual's (or a community's) "politics of time" may enable what is one of the most salient elements of Isam and Imm Ghassan's testimony: a fundamental dissatisfaction with the present situation. Our interviews took place at a time they clearly saw as a political low point, a time of stalled peace negotiations punctuated by occasional bursts of violence, closures of the West Bank by the Israeli military, and flurries of meaningless diplomatic activity. In discussing what Palestinians call *al-wade$^c$* (lit., "the situation," referring to the current political and social climate), Isam used the word "unexpected" several times, indicating that this was not the outcome he and others had envisioned when fighting in the intifada. The present juncture, in other words, was looking less like a stage on the way to national liberation and more like a distinct moment unto itself, a kind of unhappy temporal collision that called into question all that had come before it and all that was supposed to come after it.

Such a negative reading, of course, stresses what is *missing* from the present moment; for Benjamin, however, the critique of the present also carries liberatory potential. His "dialectical" reading celebrates the promise of history waiting to be actualized, the possibilities that are unleashed when assumptions about historical inevitability are abandoned and memory emerges as a living process of history-making rather than history-recording. This notion bears an interesting resemblance to Mannheim's characterization of "actual" generations as those age-cohorts that come to carry out the possibilities for change embodied by every emerging generation. Given this connection between memory and generation, and given the centrality of generational categories and identities in intifada discourses, it is not surprising that Isam and Imm Ghassan have responded to the "incompleteness" of the present situation with actions and ideas that suggest an impulse toward *regeneration*.

*Figure 5.* Balata residents in the camp cemetery on a Thursday (the most popular day for visiting the cemetery), May 1997. On this day most of the visitors were women and children, although there were also a few men present. Children are often assigned the task of reading Qur'an verses at the graves of family members. (Heidi Gengenbach)

This is particularly the case with Imm Ghassan, whose experiences of loss and sacrifice are balanced, in her stories, by her attempts to replace those losses in a variety of ways. After Nizam's death, for example, another of her sons decided that he didn't want his wife to have any more children (they already had three daughters), but Imm Ghassan insisted that she wanted *more* grandchildren, and so didn't allow her son to give his wife access to birth control. The wife, who occupies a completely passive role in Imm Ghassan's narration of the story, soon became pregnant and gave birth to twin boys, one of whom was named Nizam. In this way Imm Ghassan was able not only to reassert control over her family's reproduction, but also to regenerate—both literally and symbolically—the family in the aftermath of the loss of Nizam. Some time after our interviews, she took me to visit the camp cemetery (see Figure 5) and showed me the olive tree she had planted, in another powerful gesture of rebirth, next to Nizam's grave.

Once again Imm Ghassan's own stories closely parallel Kanaana's collection of intifada legends, several of which focus, as does the following story about a mother from Nablus, on miraculous events following the death of a son:

> A *shahīd's* mother went to the cemetery to visit the grave of her son. When she got there she saw him together with a group of his *shuhadā*ʾ friends walking toward the mosque to perform their prayers. She called to them, "Come (back) with me!" They answered her, "No! Here we are in the house of ultimate truth, and we are much happier here!"

In this case, the "much happier" afterlife enjoyed by the martyr is similar to Benjamin's imagined moment of redemption: located outside earthly, historical time, it provides a vantage point from which the present appears, as it were, unhappy—or, in Benjamin's terms, incomplete.

Isam's unhappiness with his current situation came out not only in his discussion of romance and marriage, but also in his stated plans for the future, plans which are rooted in the hope of personal regeneration. One of the first things he revealed about himself during our initial interview was his desire to leave home, perhaps to find work in one of the Gulf countries:

> J: Do you have an idea right now what kind of work you'd like to do after you finish [university]?
>
> I: Right now, no. Why? Because when I see the graduates, those who graduated in the same specialization as mine [sociology], there is no work. Or those who are working, they aren't working in their field of specialization. They're doing other kinds of work. . . . Right now, my main goal is to get out of the country.

This comment resonated with something his friend Khaled had told me when he and I were first introduced: after hearing that I wanted to interview members of the intifada generation, he responded half-jokingly that I had better work fast, because in another year there would be no one left to interview—he and all the young men like him would be gone, presumably either in prison, working in the Gulf, or studying somewhere outside the country. I originally assumed that Isam's motivation for wanting to leave was primarily economic, and perhaps it was, but near the end of our final interview he put a rather different spin on the issue. His determination to get out of Balata, he told me, comes from a will to change a situation that has left him emotionally and politically spent, feeling he has "nothing to live for" in Palestine. Only by going away and recharging himself could he put himself in a position to return home and work for such a change.

These images of regeneration suggest that for Isam and his mother, the period of our interviews was, as much as anything, a time of "getting by," a time in which they were engaging in what might be called active waiting. Equally important, they were telling stories—Imm Ghassan giving security officers a piece of her mind, Isam struggling to have his intifada romance recognized by his family—that reflect their attempts to "get by" as much as they reflect the larger structural aspects of Palestinian life. Storytelling, as Benjamin points out in his essay on the work of Nikolai Leskov, is a form that maintains the "communicability of experience" by encouraging the teller to put his or her own stamp on the story: "The storyteller takes what he tells from experience—his own or that reported by others. And he in turn makes it the experience of those who are listening to his tale" (1968b, 87). While stockpiling ironically serves the "forgetting" function discussed above, then, storytelling enables everyday experiences to be preserved in popular memory in a fluid, living form rather than being "fixed" in any absolute sense. Indeed, hermeneutical open-endedness is one of the distinguishing characteristics not only of intifada myths and legends, but also of the personal narratives examined here. An invitation to tell a story, or to listen to one, is thus an invitation to discover the ways in which history—in both senses of that term, as event and as narrative—can be *made* rather than given from above.

The intifada is very much a living event to which Palestinians give meaning every day through stories that explore the conflict between an idealized (albeit tragic) past and an unsatisfying present, the intersection of personal relationships and political history, and the mutual determinations of national, gender, generational, and class identities. Unlike the narratives that tend to dominate the standard histories and political programs associated with the conflict over Israel/Palestine, these personal stories are rooted as much in the family as in the nation. What I have tried to argue here is that as Isam and Imm Ghassan are rethinking the relationship between the past they lived and the future they once envisioned, they are also articulating narratives that disrupt one of the building blocks of nationalist thought: the assumption that the family is a metonym for the national community. To the extent that they are Palestinian nationalists, theirs is a nationalism that is not entirely coincident with subjectivity, and it is hard to imagine that it ever could be. Instead, it is a contested identity which, because of their particular life circumstances, is forced to share cognitive and narrative space with other identities. To put it another way, their stories suggest that the family—a complicated nexus of "local" and national identities—cannot be "nationalized" any more thoroughly than it can be colonized. More broadly, these stories demonstrate that social memory, far from being an uncomplicated amalgam of predictable reactions to historical events, is actively created—in ways which are often profoundly *un*predictable—in the border zones where life history and world history meet and transform one another.

# 4

# The Secret Locations of Memory
## Political Lessons at Home and in Prison

> The discussion of one's own roots seeks to supply the context sur-
> rounding a political birth. The interpretation of the link between
> roots and context is delicate.                    —Luisa Passerini

Telling the story of one's childhood or youth in terms of the
places that inhabit one's memory is a convention with a long history in
the genre of autobiographical writing. An excellent example is Walter
Benjamin's "A Berlin Chronicle," in which the German philosopher
likens his memories of childhood in Berlin to "the ground . . . in which
dead cities lie interred," suggesting that the process of remembering is as
much a spatial, even archaeological exercise as an intellectual one.[1] The
Palestinians I interviewed would agree, although they speak much less
philosophically about the places of their youth. Rather than emphasizing
fleeting, peaceful moments and scenes described in minute detail (Benjamin, for example, recalls "the strip of light under the bedroom door"
on nights when his parents were entertaining guests), they tend to highlight those spaces where the most memorable political events—traumatic,
empowering, exciting—took place.

"I remember myself running, always running," says Hassan. "Always
I remember running and moving [across] the roofs . . . [even now] I can't
go slowly in the streets, even when I'm not throwing stones." Iyad, one
of the oldest of the *shabāb* with whom I spoke (he was twenty-seven at
the time), locates his own political awakening in the years before the intifada, when he and other young men used to go to a playing field
(*malʿab al-shabība*) at the edge of the camp to discuss books the Israeli
authorities had banned and to exchange opinions about stories they had
heard from their parents concerning the dispossession of 1948. In the

self-representations of young people in Balata, then, the mutual articulation of generational and national discourses is revealed in the attempts of the narrators to *locate,* in a spatial sense, the "drama of their youth." After I had done a number of interviews, I began to notice the frequency with which descriptions of these experiences remained tied to certain key sites—most notably prisons, schools, and the streets—where political organizing and resistance were remembered as having been most effective, *and* where generational hierarchies were most open to temporary suspension, disruption, or inversion during the intifada. The first of these sites is one subject of the present chapter; I explore the latter two in chapter 5.

The spatialization of popular memory begins to make sense if we consider the ways in which Israel's occupation of the West Bank and Gaza has been enacted and reproduced through a variety of practices, both direct and indirect, involving the control of public and private spaces. While a thorough analysis of the operation of power under the occupation is beyond the scope of this book, a skeletal outline provides a structural context for understanding the personal narratives with which I am primarily concerned here. Many of the measures through which the state of Israel has maintained the occupation have involved the direct use of force—suppression of demonstrations, torture of political prisoners, destruction of homes—and thus can be encompassed within the realm of domination, or what Michel Foucault (1979) calls "pre-modern" power. At the same time, a broader view of the occupation, particularly its spatial aspects, suggests the operation of more "modern" or "disciplinary" power coexisting quite comfortably with structures of overt domination. As a host of researchers working from Foucault's example have demonstrated, "disciplinary" power is highly spatialized or "capillary," that is, located in and produced through not only (or even primarily) the most visible actions of the state, but also the micropractices of daily life.

In Palestine, growing up under occupation means being regularly observed by soldiers stationed in guard towers and by Israeli settlers living on high ground overlooking Palestinian population centers; in addition, all Palestinians were issued identity cards, knowing they could be arrested if they failed to produce the card when stopped by soldiers for any reason. An elaborate network of collaborators and informants, cultivated and maintained by the Israeli security establishment through economic incentive, moral blackmail, and intimidation added another layer of suspicion and invisible surveillance to everyday social relations. Especially during the intifada, Israeli policy nearly eliminated the distinction between safe spaces and dangerous spaces through midnight raids on Palestinian homes, army incursions into hospitals, and the use of tear gas in a variety of enclosed spaces including schools, mosques, medical facilities, and private homes. Perhaps most totalizing were Israeli actions aimed at preventing Palestinians from moving freely through public space, and, in what amounts to a more "disciplinary" version of the same process, restricting the willingness of Palestinians to risk engaging in such movement in the first place: these actions include extensive use of "administrative detention" (arrest without trial, imposed in renewable six-month sentences); dusk-to-dawn and even twenty-four-hour curfews imposed on entire communities; periodic closures of the entire West Bank and Gaza, either limiting the number of Palestinians allowed to enter Israel or banning all traffic across the borders; and military roadblocks designed to inhibit the flow of people and goods and conduct random security checks.

Given this array of repressive spatial practices, it seems that the politicization of the spaces that are so prominent in young people's narratives is a product not only of Palestinian resistance to Israeli colonial policies, but also of the policies themselves, which ensured that virtually any location could become a site of struggle between occupier and occupied. For young people involved in the intifada, however, claiming particular spaces for political activity was about more than confronting the Israelis; it was also a way of negotiating the rapidly shifting politics of generation. Children and youth, after all, are generally subject to at least two major authorities—adults (parents or other guardians) and the state—and the fact that these two structures of power are not coincident, and often not complementary, can leave young people with a certain amount of leverage. Social movements such as the intifada, or the 1976 Soweto uprising in South Africa, represent cases in which young people succeed not only in claiming a kind of political authority vis-à-vis the state, but also in chipping away at the control typically exercised by their parents, teachers, and other adult authority figures.

In Palestinian society, generational hierarchies are anchored most fundamentally in the family; in terms of space, then, it is the home that must be either redefined or transcended in some way if young people are to play an active role in such a movement. Here again, however, we must consider Passerini's reminder that "memory speaks from today," for in the self-representations of Balata's young people, memories related to the challenging of generational authority within the family and the home are gradually being recast, depersonalized, even filtered out altogether as individual experiences continue to mingle with a changing social and political landscape. This process, in turn, is profoundly affecting the ways in which young people conceptualize and assess the very idea of generational hierarchy.

## Home Stories: Doors, Rooftops, and Secrets

In many of my interviews, I asked young people to reflect on their own political education in the broadest sense, and to identify situations in which they remembered having learned the most about political issues during their younger years. Like Iyad, who recalled hearing stories about the past from his parents but spoke of the playing field as the place where he came to understand the political significance of those stories, most were not inclined to point to their own home environment as a primary site of political awakening. Yet when discussing the intifada, many were also quick to offer stories concerning memorable, sometimes traumatic events that occurred inside the home, particularly the violation of domestic space by Israeli soldiers.

> The soldiers would come and dump out the sugar, the rice, and the oil, all together, whenever they entered any house. . . . The hardest thing was when they came to arrest someone—they would come at 11:00 or 12:00 at night. (Jamila)

> They used to come into the camp to search houses, and they would come at about ten in the evening and stay until ten in the morning. . . . There were about ten times when they entered the camp specifically to search this house, and also my grandfather's house. . . . One time the soldiers came to my grandfather's house, where my aunt was staying because my uncles were in prison. . . . My brother and my sister went over to my grandfather's house, and the army entered the house. My sister was about fourteen years old, and she was wearing a necklace of the map of Palestine. One of the soldiers took it, and she spat on him and hit him. (Hussein)

> On April 14 [1993], at about 5:00 in the morning, I was sleeping of course. I didn't wake up until the soldiers were right over my head. . . .

They demanded that I get up and asked me for my ID. I gave it to them, and they told me I was under arrest. . . . I still had my pajamas on. . . . They handcuffed me, and took me out of the house. (Qassem)

Taken together, these stories speak to what Allen Feldman (1991) calls the "deterritorialization of the sanctuary," that is, the encroachment of state harassment and political violence into areas previously considered safe havens. They also signify the recollection of events that were undeniably formative in a political sense for the young people who experienced or heard about them.

Home stories often called attention to specific "interfaces" (Feldman's term) dividing the house from the world outside or, alternately, enabling passage between the domestic and public spheres. It is useful, I think, to conceptualize these "interfaces" as sites of everyday struggle along multiple axes of power: between Israeli soldiers and Palestinians in general, between soldiers and young activists in particular, and also between these young people and their parents. The rooftops of houses, for example, had the potential to serve the interests of more than one party, depending on the situation, the location of the house, and the degree to which one could occupy the roof while remaining hidden from the view of those in the street below. In some cases, soldiers simply appropriated rooftop space as a way of gaining additional bases for surveillance; Intissar and her family had this experience on a regular basis. Other people, including Intissar's older sister Leila, related stories of residents using the roof for their own purposes:

I remember one time when I was at my uncle's house, and his daughter was engaged to be married. In another week she was going to her new husband's house. There was a young boy there, her youngest brother. . . . There was a curfew, and he was going to take food to someone, so we girls had to go outside to see if there were soldiers around or not. . . . So we went up on the roof to look for soldiers—she watched to the east and I watched to the west. When I looked out to the west, I saw the soldiers, but she didn't see them because she was looking to the other side. When I saw them, I yelled to her, because the day before they had come to her house to take one of her brothers, and so they were very vexed with her, almost like they were looking for something to use against her. They saw her, so I pushed her down the stairs. When I did that, they saw me, and one of them picked up a brick and threw it at my leg. . . . That day sticks in my mind, and I remember it because my leg hurt so much that day, but also because it was the day I saved my cousin's life. And her husband was so happy, because his wife was well when they got married [laughs]! (Leila)

I remember at the beginning, the people had heard about the martyrs in Gaza, and they all came out after Friday prayers, and three were killed. Of course I was young then, so my father prevented me from going out of the house, and everybody else was going out. . . . So I went up to the roof. . . . I still remember the sound of the ambulances and the sound of the bullets and the tear gas. . . . These are things you don't forget. (Hussein)

I didn't participate in [the intifada], in terms of being "wanted" or throwing stones. But I was still threatened, and afraid of the soldiers, like all of us. My parents were afraid for me, and so they locked the door and didn't let us go outside. But we were watching all the events from the roof. . . . We didn't have a lot of friends, we didn't get to know a lot of people, like the young people who liked to throw stones. But still we were able to see the events from the roof. One time my brother and I were up there, by the [water] tank. You can see our house from the main street, and the army was out there. One of the soldiers started to shoot, and he shot right through the tank. This is the event that affected me the most. (Yousef)

Rooftops were clearly a site of struggle between camp residents and the occupying army, but for young people in particular the meaning of the rooftop depended on the degree of one's participation in the intifada's most confrontational activities. In the cases of Leila, Hussein, and Yousef, going up to the roof may have served as an intermediate step between the house and the street, a way of establishing some control over the terms governing their encounters with both repression and resistance. Each, however, had his or her own reasons for taking such a step.

For Leila, the roof was a primary location for spotting soldiers, which she describes as one of the most important activities that women and girls carried out during the uprising; the pride and excitement with which she tells the story of saving her cousin's life calls attention to the risk she sees herself as having taken by going up to the roof. Hussein links his decision to watch the intifada's first day from the roof to his inability—because of his father's prohibition—to go outside; the roof, he implies, was the next best thing for a ten-year-old who wanted to join the *shabāb* in the streets. Yousef, on the other hand, says he was quite content to stay on the roof and watch from a relatively safe distance; in fact, he is the only person I interviewed who openly identifies himself as *not* having participated in the intifada. Yet he also attempts to compensate for this aspect of his personal history by insisting that he was "threatened" like everyone else and implying, through the story of being shot at with his brother on the roof, that he was not entirely averse to putting himself in danger. For activists who were most directly engaged in confrontations with the army, rooftops could also serve as crucial vehicles of escape, since soldiers were often unable or unwilling to chase young people from one roof to another.

Many narratives were also punctuated with references to doors, the primary "interfaces" controlling access to the house. The memory of soldiers beating on the door at all hours of the day and night, for example, appeared in a number of interviews. Abu Nimr recalls how soldiers would knock at the door as a prelude to taking away one or more of his sons to be beaten or detained. Ramzi tells the story of his own arrest:

> They came during the night, on the twenty-first of March—it was Mothers' Day. They beat on the door at 1:00 in the morning . . . and the sound, it was like they were pounding on the door with their legs, the whole patrol. So the whole family came out, old and young. They entered the house and said, "Whose house is this?" My father said, "It's the house of [family's name]." They asked him, "What children do you have?" He said, "I have Asʿad, I have Ramzi"—and when he got to "Ramzi" they stopped him. "Where is he?" He said, "He's in his room," and they said, "Go get him." . . . I gave them my ID and they said, "You have to come with us." The *mukhtār* of the camp was with them, to show them where the house was—sometimes they would come without the *mukhtār,* but our house was not known to them. . . . He told me to say goodbye to my family, so I was saying goodbye to my mother. . . . Then the officer pointed at me and said, "You are not allowed to talk to anybody."

The frequency with which I heard such stories says a great deal about the "deterritorialization of the sanctuary," an experience that was shared by so many camp residents during the intifada, and also testifies to the

existence of certain widely employed narrative devices through which intifada stories are commonly constructed. In this case, the percussive
image of unwanted pounding at the door acts as a kind of signal not only
in the story itself, but also in the telling of the story, announcing a narrative rooted in the powerlessness of those whose home is being invaded
("you are not allowed to talk to anybody").

Doors, however, face in two directions, and in other stories, doors
emerge as highly flexible signifiers marking not the *absence* of power, but
its *production* through a variety of everyday practices:

> When my father heard the sound of bullets outside, he would lock the
> door and say that we were forbidden to go outside. In a lot of houses,
> they were afraid for their children. I know of people who prevented their
> children [from going out], but who went out themselves to throw stones.
> . . . My father didn't do this, but I'm saying I know people who did.
> (Ramzi)

> During the intifada, during all the clashes, there were no houses that
> were locked, because everyone was prepared to welcome a young man
> who was wounded or in trouble. (Jamila)

In some cases, according to Isam, soldiers were even forced into the humiliating situation of having to emulate the escape tactics used by the
*shabāb*. "Sometimes when we were throwing stones [at a soldier], he
would have no place to hide," recalls Isam, "and he would start to knock
on doors" in order to get some protection.

To the extent that rooftops and doors occupy important, often pivotal
locations in these narratives, they do so as signifiers of situations in which
young people discover the possibilities and limits of their own agency vis-
à-vis Israeli soldiers. Equally important, however, is the fact that the appearance of these "interfaces" in personal stories also coincides with
processes of negotiation between parents and children. Given that the
parents are generally the ones who decide whether to lock or unlock the
doors, their place in such stories is obviously a complicated one involving
the protection of their own children (by keeping their doors locked), and
the protection of other people's children who may be in need of sanctuary (by keeping their doors open). It is not surprising, then, to find that
young people tend to remember themselves as alternately being required
by their parents to stay *behind* doors and being dragged *out* of them by

soldiers, thus connecting these points of entry and exit not only with the exercise of parental authority, but also with its erosion or absence.

In analyzing the self-representations of Italians belonging to the generation of 1968, Luisa Passerini (1996) writes of the "ambivalent quality of the paternal figure," suggesting that fathers, both in their actions and in the memories of their children, are at once "affectionate and absent, authoritarian and weak." Mothers, on the other hand, either are missing from the narratives, or else appear as one-dimensional caricatures displaying idealized attributes that leave little to the imagination. Memory, it seems, has done little to smooth out the strongly felt contradictions that inhered in the relations between student activists and their parents; on the contrary, these contradictions loom large as structuring mechanisms in the narratives Passerini discusses.

In my own interviews, I tried to encourage reflection on the complex question of generational authority in a number of ways: by asking how parents reacted to the presence of Israeli soldiers in their homes, particularly when their children were threatened with arrest; by pursuing issues related to parent-child conflicts, as well as attempts to resolve them; and by inquiring as to how much parents knew or did not know about their children's activities in the uprising. In addition, I often asked young people to step back from their own stories to assess how generational dynamics may have changed during the intifada, and to speculate as to whether such changes were temporary or permanent, positive or negative.

In analytical terms, the resulting disjunctures that often appeared between personal memories and more abstract characterizations proved to be a fruitful terrain for understanding the intertwining of generational identities and hierarchies on the one hand, and processes of individual and collective memory formation on the other. Many young people, for example, expressed a sense of ambivalence about their parents' willingness or ability to engage in effective acts of political resistance, citing cases in which fathers were exposed as powerless in the face of soldiers. When I asked Jamila what her parents did when soldiers entered their house in order to arrest one of her brothers, she said, in effect, that this was not a situation in which they felt they could make a stand: "They had no chance—I mean, [the soldiers] came to take him, so they took him."

Such stories diverge sharply from other accounts, found throughout the literature on the intifada, of mothers bravely confronting soldiers in the streets in an attempt to free young men who were being detained. The fact that many of the young people I interviewed referred to these latter actions generically, as constituting one of the most important "roles" of women in the uprising, indicates not only a gendered distinction between parents in the memories of their children (similar to the pattern Passerini notes), but also a recognition that the intifada may have witnessed a literal shrinking of patriarchal authority: the rule of the father extended, at most, to the boundaries of the house. Inside the house, women were subject to the same erosion of authority, at the hands of the occupation, as their husbands; outside the house, women and children alike had much more freedom to act.

Despite telling stories of parental weakness, most of these young people seemed to acknowledge, at least implicitly, the authority of their parents within the home and the inadvisability of challenging that authority directly. As a result, their stories contain a number of references to actions designed to circumvent parental authority, either by leaving the physical space of the house, or by deliberately keeping secrets regarding dangerous political activities. In the former case, there were ample opportunities for young people to find spaces away from their parents where the authority of age was weaker, or even nonexistent. For some, the sheer amount of time spent in these nondomestic sites completely transformed their daily lives, perhaps most drastically in the case of fugitives who were unable even to sleep at home for fear of being captured or killed; consequently, being at home became the exception, and parents had to adjust to this new situation and realize that the rules of the game were changing. For many younger children, however, the very act of leaving the house without permission, even once, was a significant and memorable event.

> There was a day at the end of '87, maybe the beginning of '88, it was during the mid-year school vacation, and there was a strike. My mother and father weren't at home—they had gone to Gaza to visit my grandfather, who was sick—so it was a good chance for me to get out, with my father gone. . . . So I went out and saw what was going on. . . . There was a strike, I don't remember exactly why, and the *shabāb* were waiting for the army, so I stopped and waited with the *shabāb*. . . . My father spent two weeks in Gaza—he couldn't get back because of the situation—so I would go out in the morning and I was free to throw stones or whatever, and then I would return home in the afternoon to be with my brothers. (Ramzi)

We were kids, you know, and kids like to go outside—any child likes to go outside the house. So on days when there was a curfew, our mother or father would tell us, "Don't go out," but sometimes we went anyway. I remember one day when I got really bored and went out, and there were some soldiers walking in the street. I went running home as fast as I could and fell into my mother's lap and cried, and [here she jumps to what happened after the soldiers entered the house in pursuit of her] they asked my parents, "Who let her go outside?" But they didn't let me—I went out *myself.* (Intissar, her emphasis)

As noted above, Ramzi was later arrested after he became a more active participant in the intifada; a self-identified Hamas activist, he spent two years in prison and was released shortly before our interview. Still only twenty, he nonetheless spoke of the intifada's early period as a strikingly different time in his life, a time of youthful and cautious—but determined—exploration, a time when the temporary absence of his father meant a rare chance to avoid the locked door and get "outside the house" (*khārej al-bayt*) when demonstrations were taking place. Intissar's foray into the streets during curfew, while ostensibly more limited spatially and temporally, had the potential to bring serious repercussions onto her family, and in our interview, even at age twenty-three and in her final year at university, she told the story with an air of mischief, her voice speeding up as she related the details of her frantic sprint home and proudly insisted that she had *chosen* to leave the house against her parents' explicit instructions.

For young people who were constantly out of the house because of their involvement in intifada activities, but who also had reason to worry about their parents' approval, subterfuge was often an option. Several narratives, therefore, rely on themes of secrecy and covert disobedience, with moments of revelation—when secrets are exposed—figuring prominently as potential crisis points, or turning points, in the relationship between parents and children. "In a colonized culture, secrecy is an assertion of identity and of symbolic capital," writes Feldman (11). "Pushed to the margins, subaltern groups construct their own margins as fragile insulations from the 'center.' Secrecy is the creation of centers in peripheries deprived of stable anchorages." In this case, secrecy occupies a complex location on the protean border between national and generational identities, with young people "constructing their own margins" with respect to parental authority even as they moved toward the "center" of national political life. Qassem, a Hamas supporter, admits that before being detained, he used to keep his parents in the dark about his activities; consequently, when his initial day in court arrived, his parents were "surprised" and "angry" upon hearing the charges against him. Leila, who spoke of saving her cousin's life on the rooftop, insists that it was sometimes necessary to hide the truth from her mother:

> L: My mom was always worried about me, but I couldn't stop myself. Some people . . . watch things on TV, [but] I wanted to live it and see it for myself. I was always taking CPR classes—if I could help, I was going to help.
>
> J: I've heard other young people say as well that they disobeyed their parents sometimes. When that happened, did they know [what you were doing], or did you try to keep things secret from them?
>
> L: I used to do things, and then come home and tell my mom what I had seen and done.
>
> J: And what was her reaction?
>
> L: *Khalas* [forget it, it's over], she can't do anything [laughs]! But she knows what I did wasn't wrong, she was just worried about me.

In a narrative move I witnessed more than once during my interviews, Leila takes the issue of generational conflict and works it from both sides, making a serious point but stepping away from it at the same time. Her implicit contrast between her parents' generation and her own ("Some people . . . watch things on TV, [but] I wanted to live it") is quickly offset by her contention that she and her mother were really of the same mind.

The issue of secrecy (*sirrīya*) figures most centrally in the self-representation of Ayman, a Fateh activist and son of the aforementioned Abu Nimr. During the first of our three interviews, Ayman's father and one of his uncles came in for part of the conversation, and Ayman was generally cautious in his answers to my questions, making only brief reference (when Abu Nimr was out of the room) to differences of opinion he had had with his father. In the second interview, however, no adults from the family were present, and Ayman spoke at length about his continuing attempts both to keep his political activities secret and, when necessary, to convince his parents of his need to be involved in those activities, which have included organizing other students in his school and participating in street clashes with Israeli soldiers beginning in 1992, when he was in the seventh grade. Secrecy was often essential during the intifada, he said, partly because of the presence of collaborators in the camp, but also because parents were so anxious to "protect" their children. When I asked him how his own attempts at secrecy might have colored his relationship with his parents, he reminded me, in effect, that the beauty of secrecy lay in the possibility of preserving a space for him to engage in resistance activities while allowing his parents to remain content in their ignorance of what he was doing. Because of this secrecy, he says, his relationship with his parents "wasn't affected at all," adding that "even now they don't know about a lot of my activities."

On occasion, however, he was unable to maintain this cloak of secrecy. "There was one time when I took part in a military show in the camp—all the young men and women from Fateh, all the activists and administrative people participated in it," he recalls. Afterward Abu Nimr asked his son why he had joined in such a public event where there might have been spies or collaborators present. "I told him that it was my duty, that I had to," says Ayman. "I can't change who I am." Like Leila, Ayman attempts to walk a fine line when speaking of his parents, admitting that even at the age of eleven or twelve he used to disobey the "orders" Abu Nimr gave him, but also insisting that he has always "respected" his father "completely," regardless of the serious disagreements they may have had. To put it another way, he portrays himself as a loyal, active nationalist who has also tried his best, in his short life, to be a good son. The issue of generation thus permeates the entire narrative, opening up numerous possibilities in terms of emergent political and social identities even as it enables the narrator to smooth over any potential contradictions between patriarchal and nationalist ideologies and the expected behaviors embedded in them.

In terms of his self-representation, then—and as always, it is important to emphasize that this may or may not correspond to the "factuality" of the events and relationships he is describing—we might characterize Ayman as, at most, cautiously rebellious. Even so, his narrative is exceptional among those surveyed here because he does admit a significant degree of conflict or disagreement with his parents, particularly his father. By comparison, other young people tended to downplay even more any elements of generational upheaval or rebellion within their own family when discussing the intifada. At the same time, however, when offering broad-brush assessments of the intifada and its social dynamics, these same young people quite often asserted that the "intifada generation"—that is, people their own age—essentially ran the show during the uprising, achieving levels of authority typically reserved for adults.

This lack of congruity between the personal and the general, I would argue, has much to do with the process of memory itself. As the intifada passes more and more firmly into the realm of the historical, these young people are increasingly inclined to take a more sympathetic view of their parents and, more generally, to deemphasize elements of internal social conflict. Furthermore, in their memories of this formative period, they have compartmentalized the social world in a number of ways. Most importantly for our discussion here, their narratives mark the home as a fundamentally separate space where different rules and expectations apply. Despite the fact that the same primary antagonists—Israeli soldiers—populate stories rooted both inside and outside the home, it seems that the possibility of strongly resisting soldiers in the home was mitigated by the operation of parental authority. As we will see below, insisting on the unique nature of the home and family situation thus enables young people, as they reconstruct the intifada through memory, to focus more attention either on those places where conflict and "negotiation" took place not with parents but with other adults (teachers at school, shopkeepers in the streets), or on places where their interactions with soldiers were active rather than reactive.

## Prison Stories: "During the Intifada . . . the Freest Place in Palestine"

In one of the most insightful articles on the intifada, Julie Peteet (1994) argues that through a remarkable kind of cultural "trick," a determined act of collective hermeneutic reversal, Palestinians under occupation were able to take one of the most visible demonstrations of Israeli power—the public beating of young men—and turn it into a rite of passage, thus conferring social legitimacy and political prestige on what might otherwise appear to be an extremely passive experience of domination and humiliation. "To let bodily violence stand as constitutive of an inferior and submitting social position and subjectivity without interpretation and challenge would be to submit to the dominant performers' meaning," writes Peteet, contending that the popular validation of the beating experience "reverses the social order of meaning and leads to political agency" (45). In this section I argue that a similar achievement marks the stories that young men told me about their prison experiences. While not entirely ignoring the most traumatic aspects of prison life, these narratives offer a vision in which the prison (*sijen*, pl. *sjūn*) emerges as a space of dynamic resistance, personal growth, and education.

Like all personal narratives, these prison stories are constructed through a complex interaction between individuals and the diverse set of existing narratives to which they have access. Defining prison life in terms of the agency of those who are incarcerated, for example, represents a powerful challenge to narratives grounded in the authority of the prison regime, narratives which use "law and order" and "national security" paradigms to reinforce the regime through the endless repetition of images, episodes, and legal categories that stress both the omnipotence and the moral correctness of those who run the prisons. Political prisoners are also well aware of, and inevitably influenced by, the existence of narratives associated with human rights work or with certain nationalist pronouncements aimed at an international audience. In these other, more sympathetic narratives, the repression of prisoners serves as valuable symbolic capital, for to be a political prisoner is to bear, in the most direct and often prolonged way, the impact of Israeli domination, and thus to be emblematic of the suffering of the larger national community. Yet the dominant public narratives of the nationalist movement also validate the role of prisoners as agents of political resistance and examples to Palestinians struggling against the occupation outside the prison walls: UNLU leaflets speak not only of "sons . . . incarcerated in Nazi prisons," but also of prisoners who "imbue us with a constructive revolutionary spirit to escalate the blessed uprising and ignite the fire of confrontation" (Mishal and Aharoni 1994, 77, 152). In terms of the framework discussed in chapter 2, the former prisoners I interviewed preferred to rely much more heavily on discourses of empowerment than on discourses of victimization. Their tendency to skirt the latter suggests that as they gain greater temporal distance from their prison experiences, they are more inclined to gloss over memories that provide reminders of passivity; in doing so, they decenter the notion of the prison as primarily a space of suffering. Equally important, their narratives identify the prison as a separate, bounded space where authority was rooted less in strict generational hierarchies than in the achievement of social status through political activism and experience.

The question of why prison stories figure prominently in the self-representations of so many Palestinians of all ages is largely answerable, of course, with reference to the statistical record. Virtually everyone in the West Bank and Gaza has been directly affected by imprisonment, either their own or that of close friends or family members. As with figures on intifada deaths and injuries, exact information on the numbers of people arrested during the uprising is impossible to obtain and has been the subject of some dispute; nonetheless, even the most conservative estimates—those provided by the IDF—indicate a concerted policy of mass arrest, with some fifty thousand Palestinians in the West Bank and Gaza (out of a total population, at the start of the uprising, of roughly one and a half million) spending time in prisons or detention centers by the end of 1989. Many of these were held and interrogated for days or weeks while awaiting trial in military courts, then either released or sentenced to terms of varying lengths, often after group trials designed to maximize the efficiency of the judicial process while providing a minimum of due process (Al-Haq 1990). Of the approximately nine thousand more who were placed under "administrative detention" (*iʿtiqāl idāri*) during the first two years, many were interned in the notorious Ketziot military detention camp, located in the Negev Desert, and popularly known as "Ansar III."[2] In addition, special facilities such as Ofer Detention Centre—which detainees dubbed "the kindergarten of the intifada"—were set up especially for the holding of young people, since Israeli law permitted the detention of minors as young as twelve.[3]

The vast body of human rights material on the intifada supplements basic legal and statistical information with the stories of individual prisoners, stories that provide vivid, often harrowing illustration of experiences ranging from simple arrest to torture and interrogation. As an effort to document both the quantitative scope of Israel's arrest policy and the most repressive of that policy's associated practices and qualitative effects, this literature is tremendously exhaustive and looms large over any discussion of the issue of prison experiences during the intifada. At the same time, however, this literature is less useful in explaining the complex set of images, assertions, silences, and other cognitive and narrative mechanisms through which my interviewees remembered and described such experiences. How, for example, should we read statements like these?

Ansar III. It was a fantastic experience there. Lots of ages, different ages, professors, teachers, married people, educated [people] . . . and just to say "good morning" to each one, your day will finish, you know? (Hassan)

Everyone had high spirits at that time—even the young children had high spirits. If you were to sit with a child, you would feel that you were sitting with an older man, because the intifada made the child into a man before his time. And just as the rock was their weapon, prison was their school. . . . Whenever someone used to go to jail, even if they were young, they would come out more educated because there were people in prison who gave them lessons about life, about struggle, about patience. . . . So when a person who was fourteen went into prison, he'd come out as though he were twenty-five. (Leila)

There was a young man [a Hamas prisoner] from Nablus, and they put him in the kitchen—the guys from Fateh put him in the kitchen—and a whole group of guys spat on his face, and they were praising Abu Ammar [Yasser Arafat] and insulting Hamas. (Qassem)

During the intifada time, I think the situation was such that the prison was the freest place in Palestine. (Khaled)

If these brief interview excerpts speak to experiences and opinions not typically found in the human rights literature, this disjuncture has much to do with sharply differing narrative situations. When individuals speak with human rights case workers and researchers, they do so largely in response to extremely focused sets of questions rooted in a documentary model of research rather than a narrative model. They also do so, in most cases, with the understanding and expectation that their testimony will serve as evidence with which to indict the Israeli government, at least symbolically, for its policies in suppressing the intifada. My interviews, by contrast, were shaped in part by the subsequent passage of time and by my identity as someone with little access to the circuits of world opinion and government policy, someone who was soliciting memories (*zikrayāt*) rather than affidavits. Even more fundamentally, however, the tendency of young people to deflect attention away from their suffering in prison represents a powerful technique through which they recast, retroactively, their personal and collective political histories in such a way that Israeli actions play a minimal role in the creation and development of Palestin-ian national identity.

Each of the four excerpts quoted above points to one or more ways of understanding how the members of the *jīl al-intifāda,* including those (like Leila) who were never arrested, have begun to transform prison ex-periences into prison memories through an emphasis on the prisoners' ability to make the most of a difficult situation. Both Hassan and Leila echo Isam (see chapter 3) in highlighting the notion that prison provided a kind of social education and personal guidance to many young men. Hassan's comment about the possibility of spending an entire day just greeting the other prisoners in his section (the camp was divided into sec-tions of between two hundred and two hundred fifty detainees) at Ansar III, for example, suggests that for this young man, a refugee who grew up in Jenin, entering the confining walls of the prison was, paradoxically, like entering a much wider social universe. Because Ansar III was used as the primary holding center for thousands of administrative detainees dur-ing the intifada, it was home to men representing a variety of ages, geo-graphic and socioeconomic backgrounds, and political leanings—includ-ing men from villages Hassan had never heard of before. Others I inter-viewed expressed similar sentiments, emphasizing the ways in which being in prison opened their eyes to the diversity of identities and experi-ences in their own society, and taught them important lessons about in-terpersonal relations. These stories were regularly punctuated with refer-ences to the "respect" and "patience" with which prisoners learned to treat each other while sharing long days, weeks, and months in crowded tents and cells.

Prison could also serve as a school (*madrasa*) or university (*jāmiᶜa*), al-lowing prisoners to continue their education (*taᶜlīm*) behind bars. In a strictly formal sense, of course, the mass detention of young Palestinians, when combined with Israel's policy of closing schools and universities as a punitive measure (see chapter 5), effected a fundamental and potentially devastating disruption of the educational process. Several of the *shabāb* I met claimed that the Israeli military deliberately timed arrests in order to maximize this disruption, detaining large numbers of young men shortly before they were to sit for the *tawjīhī* exams required for university ad-mission. Samer, who works in the PA security forces and volunteers at the Palestinian Prisoners' Club, was arrested for the first time at age fourteen or fifteen, then spent three years in prison at the start of the intifada. After being released, he was arrested again, having completed all but one of the exams with good marks. "I think it was timed," he insists, adding that "it wasn't only me—it happened to a lot of people." Aged twenty-five and newly married at the time of our interviews, he was still trying to finish his *tawjīhī* certificate. Two Hamas activists told of similar experiences: Qassem had just graduated from a two-year, postsecondary training school in 1993 when he was arrested as he was preparing to take the comprehensive exam required of all graduates, while Ramzi was in his *tawjīhī* year in school at the time of his detention.

In discussing how their actual time in prison affected their education, interviewees were much more inclined to focus not on the negative aspects—that is, what was taken away from them while in prison—but rather on what they and others like them were able to produce through their own efforts. In some cases, prisoners actually succeeded in creating temporary educational structures to replace schools that were closed or unavailable to them: Majid, who was arrested seven times and spent a total of two years in prison, told me that at one point there were so many students and professors from An-Najah University being held together in Nablus prison that they simply held classes as usual, often receiving credit from the university for the work. In general, however, the absence of formal schooling, combined with the dangerous (in terms of the ubiquity of torture and the presence of informants) and highly politicized atmosphere that prevailed in the prisons, meant that "education" could refer to any number of things. When Nabil speaks of his experience in Megiddo prison, he stresses that even though he was only two months from completing his *tawjīhī* at the time of his arrest, and had been getting good grades in school up to that point, he was nonetheless weighed down by a certain level of ignorance when it came to political matters. "I didn't know things," he recalls. "I didn't know why I was throwing stones at the Israelis." Inside Megiddo, the more experienced detainees taught him about Palestinian history and passed on other information that was vital for getting by in the prison, most notably how to recognize and combat the "games" the *mukhābarāt* (the intelligence services) used during interrogation sessions and how to make use of these techniques when questioning other prisoners suspected of being informants. To this day, he says, when he and his friends reminisce about the intifada, they talk most about their prison experiences.

Other young men also remember detention as a time of learning on a number of fronts, with many "subjects" mingling to form a kind of popular curriculum oriented primarily toward the concerns of everyday prison life, but also toward larger educational goals:

> In the prison, there is more of a system than there is outside. In the morning all the *shabāb* used to have sessions, classes—political classes, about the [political] situation. . . . In the prison you had all types of people—if you were well-educated, then you taught, if you were illiterate, there were special classes for you. . . . Some of the guys used to write pamphlets inside the prison on the political and security situation. . . . We had morning lessons every day except Friday, political sessions from forty-five minutes to an hour each, and then we would have relaxation time in the afternoon. In the evenings we would have administrative sessions to discuss the situation and how to organize life inside the prison. (Ramzi)

> I was ignorant [when I came to prison], but it changed me. We Palestinians think of the prison as a school or a university . . . and when you get out, you are like an expert. . . . Many of the *shabāb* in prison were illiterate [when they came], but they were able to complete their studies, even pursue a doctoral or master's degree while they were in prison because we had programs, lectures, and classes. (Ra'id Amr)[4]

> You learn a lot about social relations, how to get along with people. You see how to find the correct path in life, how to change your life in every way, even how to deal with the *mukhābarāt* and the interrogations. You learn to rely more on yourself, and you almost become a different person. . . . The prison was like a lecture hall—there was a cultural committee that organized sessions, and there were even people who could teach you languages like English or French if you were in prison for a long time. There were professors and doctors who were prisoners, people trained in all different fields. (Hatem)

When I heard these young men talking about turning the prison into a "lecture hall," I was at first surprised to be confronted with the idea that political prisoners might have had the freedom to organize such an effective system of alternative education. Palestinian prisoners held in Israeli jails and detention centers, after all, have very few rights to speak of, and during the intifada even these rights were curtailed significantly.[5] Yet there is ample indication that prison guards and authorities were not always able to produce the docility they desired. A military police officer working in the Ansar II detention center, for example, told an Israeli newspaper in mid-December 1987 about a group of 160 prisoners aged fourteen to twenty-four who apparently could not be "disciplined":

> The prisoners behave as though it was a holiday camp, and think that they are in a kindergarten. Sometimes we tell them to sit with their face to the wall and to keep quiet, and then they start to laugh in our faces and break out into Palestinian songs. They don't respect us any longer.[6]

The insistence of young people in Balata that they had a certain liberty to act while in prison, then, is about more than a retroactive desire to minimize the extent of their own powerlessness; it also tells us something about the actual dynamics of prison life. Khaled's statement that the prison was "the freest place in Palestine" is thus significant in terms of both memory and event, with popular memory representing the meeting place of these two aspects. In the case of political prisoners, writes Feldman (1991), agency is produced through the same repressive practices—physical violence, restrictions on the movement of bodies—that aim to curtail or remove it: "the shrinkage of the space of political enactment corresponds to the expansion of the acting subject" (10). Telling the story of one's imprisonment, then, constitutes "the weaving of a new body through language" and "testifies to the emergence of political agency."

One way to explain the ability of Palestinians to create, in effect, new freedoms inside the prison is to focus on the limitations inherent in the Israeli policy of mass arrest and detention. In the words of a top IDF lawyer, for example, the goal of the administrative detention policy is "to enhance public order and safety by removing the person in question from a location in which he is expected or deemed likely to commit acts damaging thereto" (Yahav 1993, 106). The emphasis, in other words, is spatial and physical: the state attempts to prevent certain actions by separating the actor from the "location" and restricting him or her to the space of the prison, thus accomplishing the "shrinkage" to which Feldman refers. Inside the prison, the focus is much the same, with many punitive and repressive practices—solitary confinement, "counting," removal to separate locations for interrogation (*tahqīq*), temporary bans on family visits—aimed again at controlling the movement of bodies and the actions of individuals in particular spaces.

As Majid commented in the course of a discussion of prison education, however, other areas were more difficult for the authorities to control. "The thing about prison is that you have more time there than you do on the outside," he noted. "Especially in certain prisons, you can have a kind of stability. . . . You can talk about political subjects—about *jihad,* about the intifada." The presence of soldiers or prison guards was rarely a deterrent once one had already been incarcerated and interrogated. As Majid added shrewdly, with what else could they threaten you? One of the responses of the prisoners to *spatial* regulation, then, was to seize control of the *temporal* side of life by taking advantage of the surplus time that was suddenly available to them. Ramzi's description of a typical daily schedule, with morning "political sessions" of forty-five to sixty minutes followed by afternoon rest time and evening "administrative sessions," can thus be read as an attempt to demonstrate a careful, practical approach to time management.

A number of interviewees made reference to the availability of certain books—whether allowed by the authorities or obtained through clandestine efforts—inside the prisons, suggesting that time spent reading contributed directly to the process of political education. Iyad, who returned time and again to his experiences with banned books as he narrated the story of his own political development, recalls smuggling reading materials into prison and hiding them underneath floor tiles in order to prevent guards from finding them. Khaled notes that in certain cases, prison authorities acquiesced to the presence of texts that were actually banned on the outside, such as the constitution of the Fateh movement. (Abdul-Jabbar, who was the interpreter for this interview, laughingly pointed out the irony of the situation: one could be arrested for possessing such a document, yet the only way to read it "legally" was precisely to get arrested!) In some cases, however, it appears that the officially tolerated presence of "political" books was dependent upon the willingness of prisoners to engage in collective action in order to have their reading demands met. Both Iyad and Khaled spoke proudly of the difficult, protracted efforts through which they and other prisoners succeeded in achieving a variety of goals, many of which centered on their right to use their time as they pleased, whether for holding classes and administrative sessions, reading books or newspapers, or visiting with family members.

At the extreme, this collective mobilization took the form of hunger strikes, ranging from brief campaigns concentrated in a single prison to massive, coordinated strikes that garnered international media attention and generated widespread public demonstrations in the Occupied Territories. As in the case of the famous 1981 hunger strike by Republican prisoners in Northern Ireland, which was sparked in part by the British government's decision to construct so-called "H-Blocks" (units designed to separate individual prisoners from one another) as an alternative to the "cages" in which paramilitary detainees had lived collectively up to that point, shifts in the technologies and strategies of incarceration appear to have been crucial motivating factors in the Palestinian strikes of 1991 and 1992.[7] The growing use of solitary confinement, as well as the deaths of several prisoners in interrogation units and isolation wings, led directly to the hunger strike that began in late June 1991, with the closure of solitary confinement facilities reportedly serving as the primary demand of the strikers.[8]

Perhaps because of the failure of the 1991 hunger strike—the strikers later claimed that they ended the action because they were promised reforms that were never implemented—prisoners launched what became the largest strike of the intifada on 27 September 1992, in the midst of the ever-underachieving "peace process." Beginning in Israeli jails and then spreading to the detention centers, the strike at its zenith involved some eight thousand prisoners, including four thousand at Ansar III, and also saw the participation of students from Palestinian universities. In contrast to the previous year, the strikers succeeded in wringing some concessions from prison authorities on "humanitarian" issues, though the practice of solitary confinement itself was not discontinued. Equally important, the protest action captured the attention of the Palestinian public, leading to a decline in interfactional violence and a general "reigniting" of the intifada.[9]

In his study of political violence in Northern Ireland, Feldman writes that hunger strikes are "a dramatic and eloquent form of political expression," one in which prisoners' bodies gain symbolic power in inverse proportion to their declining physical strength. He also draws particular attention, however, to the ways in which such events can be the subject of drastically differing narrative constructions. In the case of the intifada hunger strikes, there is a subtle but important distinction to be made between the stories of journalists, Palestinian nationalist leaders, and human rights activists on the one hand, and those of the strikers themselves on the other. In the wider public narrative, the strikes are generally portrayed as functions of the policies of the Israeli government in general and the actions of administrators, guards, and soldiers at individual prisons and detention centers; those who carry out the strikes are thus inevitably characterized in more *reactive* terms, as responding to provocative actions and intolerable conditions. The brief overview of hunger strikes I have just provided essentially falls into this category, focusing as it does on the structural (or macropolitical) contexts in which the prisoners' actions took place. Once again, however, oral testimony suggests that the operation of memory, and particularly the desire to bracket elements of suffering in one's self-representation, can produce narratives with a significantly different inflection. In the following excerpt, while not removing the structural element from the picture altogether, Hatem places a much greater emphasis on the prisoners' strikes as self-generated and self-organized actions:

> Hunger strikes happened a lot. . . . The system was that after coming out of interrogation, if anyone [i.e., a soldier or guard] hits you, you hit him twice, you don't hit him just once. Or if he curses you, you give him two [curses]. . . . And anyone who doesn't do likewise, you punish him—he'll be ostracized by the rest of the *shabāb*. . . . Sometimes we would [go to the administration and] ask for this or that, and they would stall and stall and stall, so we would make a strike in order to improve our living conditions and so forth. Sometimes they would help us out and give us everything just before the Red Cross came to visit, and then after the visit they would take away the televisions or the radios or whatever, you know what I mean? So . . . we would start a hunger strike. [First] the *shabāb* . . . would start to explain about the practices of the prison administration, what the administration is trying to do. . . . So they [the administration] would start to get really annoyed, and they would try transferring people in order to break the coordination, and they would use solitary confinement—that was the first step. We would do some experimental actions, having intermittent strikes for one or two days as a way of warning the administration. . . . The hunger strikes in prison were voluntary, just like most of the strikes were voluntary. You had to sign a paper pledging that you were prepared to strike. You would be asked for three days [i.e., three times]. . . . The first time you would say "yes," the second time "yes," the third time "yes," and then on the fourth time, if you still wanted to strike, you would sign. . . . Some people were excluded—people over fifty weren't allowed to go on strike, children under sixteen weren't allowed to go on strike, and so on. But

then we would find many of them striking by themselves, in solidarity with the *shabāb*. There was one strike that lasted for seven days, and in some other prisons they went on strike for twenty days or so, and some of the *shabāb* were martyred. . . . Sometimes one of the big generals would come to put down the strike—they would tell [the administration] that they're not allowed to say this or that [i.e., to negotiate with the prisoners], they would change the director of the prison, they would take all sorts of steps to quell the strike.

Among interviewees who spoke about the organization of political activity in prison, Hatem's story is typical to the extent that he spends very little time describing the "practices" (*mumārasāt*) of the penal regime, preferring to explain in more detail exactly how, in his memory, the prisoners were able to exert a significant amount of control within that regime.

In the context of broader self-representations that touch on a wide range of social interactions, these prison stories seem to function as a counterweight to the home stories discussed above, in which young people are much more likely to describe themselves in passive terms vis-à-vis soldiers who invade homes, make demands, and drag family members out the door. It is striking, for example, that in none of my interviews did an individual's description of his prison experiences include any reference to specific soldiers in the way that the prisoners featured in Feldman's book tend to focus on "screws" (prison guards) who were especially sadistic or otherwise memorable. The absence of such characters is not, as one might expect, a product of a prison system in which the operation of power is faceless or distant by design; to the contrary, particularly in the military detention centers, prisoners constantly came face to face with a range of Israelis who represented "the administration" (*al-idāra*). Instead, the character choices embedded in these prison narratives serve as evidence of "emplotment," that is, as signals that a particular kind of *story* is being told.[10] Here, for example, we have a story in which events are driven not by the occupying power, with its superior technologies of domination, but by the occupied.

Whether the act of drawing on one type of narrative to the exclusion of others is a deliberate one is, in many ways, beside the point; what matters here is that the young people I interviewed construct such stories not only from the raw materials of their own experience, but also from available narrative models, and that they seem to do so in similar ways.

Returning to Hatem's story, we find that even when discussing the experience of prolonged interrogation, powerlessness gives way to a "game" in which the playing field appears to be tilted to the prisoner's advantage:

H: Interrogation is the most difficult time for any prisoner. Because of the torture, especially the psychological torture and the physical torture, and also because of the solitary confinement, this is the most difficult time. The symptoms start to affect your behavior later. Let's say you meet someone on the street, just in a normal situation, and maybe he doesn't understand you, or he snaps at you. But if you studied this person, you would find that his behavior isn't in his own hands or within his normal nature. The circumstances that he has experienced [i.e., the torture and interrogation] have put him in a bad mood, have made him deal with other people in a vicious way. Even in his own house, you'll find that his way of dealing with his wife and his children has changed.

M: [Here Mohammed joins the conversation] He's aggressive?

H: He's not aggressive exactly, but he's violent—how can I say this? We're talking about someone who has been under a lot of pressure. He has a problem, he's been under pressure, OK? And he can't deal with any kind of injustice.

J: How often were you interrogated?

H: Twice.

J: How long did it last?

H: The first interrogation time was fifty-five days. The second time was about eighteen days—but then I made a deal because I didn't have any objection to their conditions. . . . And this is the way it is with a lot of second-time prisoners who have experience in dealing with the *mukhābarāt*. The *mukhābarāt* check to see what path you've chosen, they look at your file to find out if you were an organizer, if you were an activist, or something like that—and then they treat you accordingly. . . .

M: And the deal that was reached, it was between you and them, or . . ?

H: Right. . . . They tell you, "Look, we know you have information that you're not going to give us—even if we make you sit under interrogation forever, you're not going to give it to us." They talk to you about freedom.

M: They do this openly?

H: Yes. So they say, "Here is your lawyer," and there is a negotiation

with him—between the *mukhābarāt* and your lawyer. You negotiate in a room that's different from the courtroom, and the judge
never comes in—during that period it's just for the *mukhābarāt* and
the prisoners. So the negotiation starts. . . . I told them that I only
wanted eight months, and not a day more. They said five years, and I
told them any more [than eight months], I won't confess. . . . Finally
we settled on eight months, and I had to admit to a statement, of
course—this is so you can reach an agreement. I said, "Fine," the
*mukhābarāt* went away, he [the lawyer] told me, "You're getting
eight months," and then we went to the judge and he told me, "Eight
months." So I knew the sentence before I left the courtroom.

M: What was this paper you had to sign?

H: Charges against me—they said they had witnesses for them. It's really
like a game.

In this excerpt, Hatem's recognition that he is inevitably going to be
sentenced represents an implicit admission of the regime's power; at the
same time, by highlighting his success in receiving the exact sentence he
"wanted," he insists that he (and others like him, for he adds that "lots
of people made deals") was the one in control of a situation that took
the form of "negotiations" (*mufāwadāt*) rather than the straightforward
passing of a sentence (*hukum*).

Hatem's account of the sentencing "game" is also significant for the
way it blunts the impact of his description of interrogation and torture
(*taʿzīb*). To be sure, he does place a great deal of importance on the way
these experiences imprinted him in fundamental, potentially lasting ways.
Yet the sharp transition he makes in midsentence ("the second time was
about eighteen days—but then I made a deal") effectively redirects the
narrative, focusing attention on practical personal achievements rather
than physical and psychological torment. This move illustrates a broader
pattern, in which interviewees regularly emphasize what they and other
prisoners were able to accomplish while in prison, leaving organizational
failures and negative effects either marginalized or unspoken.

Ra'id Amr of the Prisoners' Club, for example, declares firmly that
most of the protests prisoners and detainees launched, including hunger
strikes, were "successful" in the sense that they led to the realization of
the protesters' demands. Other available information on these actions,
however, suggests that even in the case of demands regarding everyday
living conditions (e.g., better food, access to newspapers or radios, longer

family visits), prisoners often won only temporary reforms, or else prom-ises of changes that never materialized. As for more explicitly "political" demands, such as the closure of solitary confinement units or the outright release of political prisoners, strikes and other protests appear to have had even less of an impact on Israeli policy.

By focusing in his mind on cases when demands were met—usually, he says, because there was a high level of coordination between prisoners held in different facilities—Ra'id is able to minimize elements of the protest campaigns that might easily be characterized as failures (or, alter-nately, as successes for the prison authorities). In addition, he is careful to downplay the longer-term effects of imprisonment in general, and torture and interrogation in particular. In our first meeting, I asked him about the issue of psychological consequences and he responded, in effect, that such problems were rare and that the issue of helping former prisoners find employment was a much greater priority for the Prisoners' Club. When I pushed him on this question during our second meeting, he modified this position slightly, saying that people who had served long sentences (twenty or thirty years) often have psychological difficulties readjusting to social life outside the prison. Despite the efforts of some nongov-ernmental organizations, he said, not enough help is available for such individuals.

The dearth of formal institutions and facilities designed to deal with these kinds of psychological problems—for example, the small number of psychiatrists in many parts of the West Bank and Gaza—is closely related to the reticence Ra'id demonstrated in our conversations when the sub-ject of these problems came up. According to Jamila, who works in a small center for the disabled in Balata camp, Palestinians tend to be re-luctant to admit that they or someone in their family may be suffering from psychological difficulties. As a result, she and her coworkers had re-cently launched an informal campaign of public education, going into people's homes and encouraging families to take advantage of available services for treating mental health problems. In the case of prisoners, the cultural attitudes and personal fears to which Jamila referred may color political perceptions as well, reinforcing the notion of prisoners as na-tional heroes and lessening the impact of victimization discourses that might, in other circumstances, be politically useful.

Indeed, both in popular discourses and in personal narratives, prison appears as the great leveler, subordinating structural identities such as age, class, and refugee status to identities rooted in the individual's own political choices and experiences. With respect to the issue of generation, then, it is important to distinguish the prison from the sites discussed in the next chapter (schools and the street), for it would be inaccurate to speak of prisons in terms of generational *inversion,* in the sense of young people sometimes replacing their elders as the primary authorities. Several former prisoners I interviewed, for example, argued that "respect" (*ihtirām*) for older men was alive and well in the prison, perhaps even more than on the outside. Hatem recalls the way in which the *shabāb* used to act as "nurses" for some of the older prisoners who had difficulty caring for themselves: "You might have ten or twenty guys working together to take care of him, treating him like he was their father." At the same time, neither is the generational order of the prison, as described in the self-representations examined here, identical to the "traditional" order of the larger society. Leila's comment that prison effectively turned boys into men speaks to the fluidity of generational identities, suggesting that having gone through similar experiences of activism and/or incarceration, young and old alike could have a similar status within the prison.

One of the most important mechanisms for gaining, or losing, this status concerned the "giving" of information during interrogation. Hassan recalls that when soldiers came to arrest him, his mother said "Hassan, after eighteen days we will see you"—meaning, in his words, "You will enter prison, you will give nothing and [come] back, as a victory" following what was typically an eighteen-day interrogation period. If he had "given" information, he insists, it would have been impossible to hide the fact, and he would have been reminded of his failing immediately after his release:

H: When you gave information [to] your enemy and you're released, a few people, they will come [to greet you]. . . . When you gave nothing, thousands of people from different areas, even from different cities, come to say hello—Palestinians' special words that we have in the intifada, "You're a strong person" and "You're brave."

J: I don't understand—how did people know whether you told anything or not? How did they know whether you have given any information?

H: When I am in prison, [I am] not alone—[there are] lots of people around me, Palestinian prisoners, and they know exactly that I gave

something or not—not [in] each case, but in general they can recognize. . . . They will discover you one day—if not today, tomorrow, if
not tomorrow, after, you know?

*J*: Did you have friends from Jenin who were in prison who gave into
the pressure and told things?

*H*: Yeah, sure. . . . I mean, I have a friend—I don't like to tell his name—
who was in prison, and he gave information about others, what they
did, and said, "I did nothing—I didn't give any information." And I
discovered later that he gave the police all the information about
these people. . . . I told him directly, "You'll discover later, soon, that
you're guilty, and you'll make your future black because you did
something wrong . . . to others. Even if you told the police about you
[i.e., if you only gave information about yourself], it's easier . . . [but]
if you did the opposite, you'll be a very bad person and people, they
will not respect [you]." And this is something very important: if you
give information, and people know about it, you'll stay in prison
longer. If you do not, they will release you, because you have nothing
to tell them.

In Hassan's view, achieving the privileged status that can come with having been a political prisoner is contingent on one's ability to make the
right choices while in custody; the political stigma attached to the person
who "gave" information observes no distinctions related to preexisting
social standing, including age. It is perhaps most accurate, then, to say
that markers of social status such as age and economic class ceased to
have the same meaning inside the prison (or that they ceased to matter in
the same way that they often did on the outside), overshadowed as they
were by personal qualities and choices such as courage, endurance, and
political identification. If we return to Qassem's statement quoted at the
start of this section, for example, we see that even in a story that highlights dissension and the exercise of force and intimidation between prisoners, it is not a case of the old ruling over the young, nor vice versa—all
of those involved in the confrontation, he says, were "*shabāb*"—nor of
the wealthy dominating the poor, but rather of one group of prisoners
staking a claim to authority on the basis of factional affiliation.

# 5

## The Testing Grounds of Memory

*Social Inversion at School and in the Streets*

To be a child in Gaza is to be enticed by its streets, incited by the graffiti on every wall and irritated by the Israeli soldiers patrolling on foot or in their jeeps through your own territory. . . . There he is, waiting just for you. This is where you can avenge your father's humiliation. . . . In the psychological sense, throwing stones is a form of recognizing and identifying the problem, a very crucial step in the making of the Intifada child.
                                                                    —Eyad Sarraj

Young people are usually students, and so they are more free to be active. Because there were lots of curfews and strikes here, often there was no school, so most of the activists were students. . . . The word "children" [*atfāl*] means something different for us than it does for you—for you, a sixteen-year-old boy is a "child," but for us, if someone is ten years old, he is a *shab*, alright?
                                                                    —Samer, former political prisoner

The kind of hermeneutic reversal discussed in the previous chapter, in which interviewees reformulated the prison as a space of political action and personal growth, is largely absent from narratives focusing on the school (*madrasa*) and the street (*shāre*c). The difference, I argue, lies in the nature of the spaces involved. As we have seen, attempts by Palestinians to stress empowering aspects of the prison experience are partly explainable as reactions to the widely held assumption that Israeli prisons and detention centers were inevitably places of direct, totalizing repression and thus of victimization. In the schools, however, Israeli control was for the most part indirect: while instances of soldiers actually attacking students inside school buildings did increase during the uprising,

Israeli policy generally took the form of censoring the Jordanian and Egyptian curricula used in the West Bank and Gaza respectively, and discouraging "political" activities within the schools through the threat of school closures, sanctions against teachers, and other punitive measures. In the street, where television cameras frequently captured images of Palestinian demonstrators triumphantly marching, displaying the national flag, and defiantly throwing stones at soldiers who often appeared to be on the defensive, the Israeli occupation was never able to articulate a convincing narrative of its own omnipotence. Consequently, the meaning of the encounter between occupier and occupied in the schools and the streets is less fixed, more immediately open to multiple interpretations, and less in need of redefinition.

At first glance, it may seem incongruous to treat these two sites as similar social locations; after all, are schools not designed in part to keep young people *off* the street and out of trouble? During the intifada, however, the physical and experiential boundaries separating school from street became much more porous, to the point where either space could easily function as an extension of the other. Like the prison, schools and streets appear in young people's narratives as spaces of political awakening and mobilization, and thus as spaces for the creation of political agency. At the same time, however, school and street memories are marked by a number of significant differences with important implications for our understanding of the relationship between generation, narrative, and nationalism. In remembrances of the prisons and detention centers, for example, agency derives from the "shrinkage" of space, leaving prisoners able to act collectively and decisively on an admittedly limited range of issues. In school and street stories, by contrast, agency is produced when young people expand and transform a much more elastic and public space, thereby maximizing their ability to affect the wider political situation.

With respect to the issue of generation, whereas the particular situation prisoners faced necessitated a kind of determined intergenerational cooperation in the interest of self-imposed unity and discipline, schools and streets provided an opportunity for young people to try out certain "adult" roles, even if this meant challenging teachers, school administrators, and other authority figures. As a result, these spaces essentially became testing grounds not only for new strategies of resistance, but also for new identities forged within a particularly fluid political context.

## The Assault on Palestinian Education

In order to understand the relationship between school and street during the intifada, it is necessary to examine briefly both the structural effects of Israeli policy on Palestinian education, and also the ways in which the intifada sparked new debates within Palestinian society about the relationship between education and broader processes of socialization, political action, and nation building. On 3 February 1988, the Israeli Civil Administration issued an order closing all West Bank schools, approximately twelve hundred in all, preventing over three hundred thousand students from attending classes. Schools were gradually reopened for a brief period in early June, but during the following weeks, authorities pursued a policy of periodic and selective closures affecting dozens of schools before unilaterally ending the school year on 21 July, a month earlier than the normal calendar allowed. The 1988–89 and 1989–90 academic years were similarly wracked by interruptions, resulting in students moving from one grade to the next despite having completed only a fraction of the required curriculum. In addition to lowering academic standards in general and increasing the chances that younger students would fail to achieve basic literacy, the situation also reportedly led to poor performances by secondary school students on the *tawjīhī* exam and, in some cases, to widespread cheating by students who knew that failure on the exam would bar them from higher education and from a range of desirable career paths.

Israel's policy of closing schools led in short order to two important consequences, both of which were arguably unintended. First, in the words of one analyst, the policy represented an ironic situation in which "the Israeli state apparatus turned against itself," effecting a "liquidation" of a major structural element of its rule in the West Bank (Bargouti 1991, 113). In place of an education system that had long been under foreign (British, Jordanian-Egyptian, Israeli) domination, Palestinians developed a range of alternatives, including underground classes held in private homes, churches, mosques, and other locations. Israeli authorities responded by banning all "popular committees" (*lijān shaʿbiyya*), including those designed to organize grassroots education efforts, and began a policy of raiding clandestine classrooms throughout the West Bank and arresting students and instructors alike, effectively criminalizing the practice of education as such (Birzeit University 1989). Given the prevailing political situation, efforts at clandestine schooling necessarily took an ad hoc form and obviously could not have constituted a fully realized, independent educational system. But their initial successes signaled the potential crumbling of the old structure and may have helped fuel later Israeli decisions to reopen the schools. Second, the initial order to close the schools en masse, while purportedly aimed at reducing the incidence of political "disturbances," had a boomerang effect: temporarily eliminating the school as a mobilizational *space* simply gave students additional mobilizational *time*. Equally important, students found themselves better able to take advantage of a more expansive location for political organizing and resistance—the streets. In the later years of the intifada, when schools were more often open, these students brought the seasoning they had gained in the streets (and in prison) to class with them, making the boundary between school and the outside world less of an absolute barrier than a revolving door.

Given the high value traditionally placed on education within Palestinian society, Israeli attempts to criminalize education and to use school closures as a form of collective punishment represent not only a calculated counterinsurgency effort, but also a full-scale cultural assault launched at the level of the national imaginary. In a practical sense, Palestinian educators and students responded to this assault by redoubling their efforts to preserve the integrity of their existing educational institutions, particularly the universities, which were more independent in terms of their curricula (though no more immune to military closure) than the primary and secondary schools. In a broader sense, however, the educational crisis that accompanied the intifada also sparked a critical examination of exactly what kind of pedagogical philosophy was at work in those institutions. Looking back at the history of Palestinian education from the British Mandate through the expansion of externally funded higher education in the 1970s, educator Munir Fasheh (1989) argues that Palestinians have been too slow to criticize the "colonialist" foundations of their educational system, and thus unable to recognize fully what is excluded by the "ideological environment" in which they have found themselves while struggling for national liberation. A more desirable alternative, he suggests, is a "praxis"-oriented model championed by Paolo Freire and others, in which "concrete conditions, reflection, and action [are] in constant interplay." In the intifada, he sees the possibility of such an alternative beginning to emerge, if only by laying bare the contradictions of the old system:

*Al-intifada* produced irreparable cracks in the old facade of myths and convictions covering almost all aspects of life. In education, for example, those myths include: the myth that education can take place only in special places (usually called schools and universities); the myth that the educational process consists mainly of rigid syllabi, fixed textbooks, and courses, and tests, and grades; the myth that learning is equivalent to formal education, and that schools and universities have the right to monopolize the definition of what constitutes learning; the myth that learning can be measured through tests; and the myth that the best form of education is a full-time course of study that cuts students off from producing anything for many years (560).

Fasheh's questioning of the idea that "education can take place only in special places" is significant, and speaks to the importance of political action, most particularly the action of young people in the streets, in enabling the kind of critique he is putting forward. In other words, changes in popular ideas about education arose not only because schools were periodically closed by the Israeli authorities—thereby necessitating the development of clandestine educational practices—but also because many students found themselves unwilling to distinguish between the more abstract "learning" processes that traditionally took place inside the school building and the political activities and social change in which they were participating in the streets.

Fasheh clearly recognizes the extent to which the issue of generational identity is implicated in these kinds of educational shifts, and he makes an explicit distinction between students and their elders in terms of the ability to link words and actions. "One significant fact about Palestinian education today is the painful discovery that the youth no longer need us (I am referring to people working in educational institutions, and to other similar hegemonic intellectuals) to acquire knowledge; neither do they need us to understand and to act," he writes. "In addition, their expressions and articulations are more dynamic and relevant: they express ceaseless activities. Our expression, in comparison, is for the most part a dead product: a piece in a final and rigid form" (545). In linking the emergence of a new generation with the revival of language—its reconnection with a world of "ceaseless activities"—he echoes Ghassan Kanafani's 1968 essay on "blind language" (Kanafani 1990). Both writers employ the rhetorical mode of heroism, suggesting that in a time of rapid social change, the rhythm of generational change also speeds up and youth are able to point out, through their actions, the flaws and inconsistencies of "old" ways of thinking, and to take an active role in bringing about a radically different future. Yet where Kanafani laments the Arab world's inability to tap the potential of the younger generation after the 1967 defeat, Fasheh also borrows from the rhetoric of empowerment to emphasize that with the coming of the intifada, the replacement of one generation by the next has already begun: with their "ceaseless activities," the young are actualizing their own potential—"thinking while actually doing"—rather than waiting for their elders to hand over power.

The notion of young people revolutionizing a moribund or authoritarian educational system and, by extension, breathing new life into the national liberation struggle, is one of the most influential "public narratives" available to young people as they assess the significance of their own formal schooling and its relationship to their political education. Equally important is the idea of education as a crucial mark of national pride and building block of Palestinian identity. According to this more "official" nationalist narrative, education (particularly insofar as it is identified with the achievement of "scientific" and technological knowledge) is the key not only to survival in a diasporic existence, but also to national potency, development, and, eventually, independence; consequently, the mass denial of educational rights that occurred during the intifada represents nothing short of a national catastrophe. A third "public narrative" that may color the self-representations of young people accepts Fasheh's premise that students were empowered vis-à-vis their teachers during the intifada, but reads this process in terms of "growing up too fast" and suggests that generational upheaval, when combined with Israel's repression of Palestinian education, may have created a "lost generation" whose members are both uneducated (in the formal sense) and unwilling to accept any authority but their own. The empowerment of young people, in other words, carries with it the potential of social breakdown: in the words of one psychologist, the intifada "sowed the seeds of confrontation at school, in the family and in society at large" (Mansour 1996, 299).[1]

## School Stories: "The Headmaster Started to Negotiate"

The idea of "confrontation" between teachers and students at school is present in the stories of a number of young Balata residents, though often in muted form. Many interviewees spoke of the declining authority of the teacher (ʾ*ustāz*/ʾ*ustāza*) and school headmaster (*mudīr al-madrasa*), suggesting that the intifada marked a turning point in the ability of both to wield absolute authority at school, and that this change is linked to wider social dynamics.

> At the beginning of the intifada, a shift happened in our society. Take the school headmaster, for example—it used to be that the headmaster ruled over the students, and the students would treat him with a kind of respect and so forth. You would see that they were afraid of him, and it was the same thing with the teacher. But then [in the intifada] you might have a ten-year-old or twelve-year-old kid who would stop the car of the headmaster in the street and search it carefully . . . not out of revenge, but as a way of demonstrating that in the streets, we are the ones in charge. . . . You see, throughout Arab society it's the old who dictate to the young, but during the intifada, the child started to control everything in the street. (Hatem)

On one level, the kind of incident to which Hatem is referring here is a simple, almost mundane example from the vast lore of the intifada, one that appears in other narratives as well.[2] To leave it at that, however, would be to miss the profound sense of social inversion at work in the story. The notion of a young student having the power to stop the headmaster's car and force him to be searched takes on added significance when we consider that the verb Hatem uses to describe the headmaster's pre-intifada authority (*yithakkam*) connotes the *arbitrary* exercise of power by someone who does not need to consult with those who are being ruled or judged. In a narrative sense, then, the contrast between intifada and pre-intifada dynamics works in much the same way as the famous biblical tale of David and Goliath, perhaps the ultimate story of generational inversion. Hatem's story speaks to the ways in which the availability of such metaphors extends to memories of intra-Palestinian dynamics, providing a ready device through which these memories can be "emplotted."

When schools were open during the intifada, students struggled with their teachers and headmasters over a number of issues ranging from grades and homework assignments to requirements concerning attendance and school uniforms. At the extreme, stories of students "taking over" schools and exercising occasionally violent intimidation and retribution against teachers seen as representative of "authority" in general, or of the political status quo, have found their place in public narratives of the intifada period. The typically anonymous nature of reported events—the "*shabāb*" taking part are rarely identified—only adds to the aura of mystery and danger surrounding such stories (Mansour 1996; Yair and Khatab 1995). During a group interview with three men who teach in Nablus secondary schools, for example, I heard accounts of students routinely disobeying their teachers, cheating on exams, and bullying headmasters into reversing failing grades. Yet in the self-representations of young Balata residents such as Ayman, stories of violent conflict and social breakdown are generally eschewed in favor of memories that focus on how the practical exigencies of political organizing entered the classroom during the uprising, sparking a sort of low-key war of position between student activists and school authorities over when classes should be suspended in favor of political demonstrations in the streets. Ayman spoke of a hypothetical seventh grader who is arrested, then returns after two years, and becomes a political leader in the school:

> He will coordinate with a group outside the school, or with those [activists] responsible for the school, and they will decide to make a suspension [*taᶜlīq*] of classes—without the knowledge of the teachers or the headmaster. And the students would go out. . . . Authority definitely changed, and this had its positive and negative sides, but I think things should be done with the knowledge of the headmaster, or the teacher. . . . The positive thing is that the young people are more enthusiastic than the teacher or other older people. They will go out to make a protest [*ihtijāj*], and the teacher will say, "Why are you protesting?" because maybe he is afraid for the students. . . . But the student wants to go out and lead the demonstration. (Ayman)

As noted earlier, I interviewed Ayman as he was completing his final year of secondary school, where he had served as one of the "responsible" (*masʾūl*) activists of whom he spoke in the excerpt just quoted. He has few clear memories of the time before the intifada, and thus no period against which to compare the kinds of generational dynamics he describes. Yet even though school-based activism has obviously played a central role in the development of his political identity, he firmly offers a normative qualification to his discussion of this activism, arguing for the necessity of "coordination" between students, teachers, and headmasters.

Hatem, by contrast, draws on his memories of pre-intifada days in order to emphasize the significance, for him, of the shifts in generational authority that accompanied the uprising:

> Even in the schools, the headmaster used to come into the classroom or call for me so that maybe we could negotiate about whether we should go out [i.e., for a demonstration], or what we should do. He would speak with the coordinating committee [of the students], which was recognized by the school. When the students wanted to go out [i.e., for a demonstration] or something, and he would speak with the coordinating committee. . . . The headmaster started to *negotiate*—he would come to the committee that was organizing things, and he would negotiate with them. This never used to happen before. (emphasis added)

As he did when speaking of his interactions with the intelligence officers in prison, Hatem uses the verb *tafāwada* (to negotiate) here, suggesting that much as the collective action of prisoners during the intifada revealed the cracks in Israel's penal regime, the organizational activities of students in the schools effectively gave the lie to assumptions about the educational administration's unquestioned authority.

On the surface, Ayman and Hatem are speaking about similar events, yet when placed in the context of their personal histories and broader political opinions, these school stories can be seen as the products of two sharply differing narrative strategies. Ayman, an ardent Fateh supporter, views the coming of the PA as the most important accomplishment of the intifada and insists that the national leadership is doing its best under difficult circumstances. As we saw in the discussion of secrecy in chapter 4, the way Ayman recounts his personal memories is consistent with this view, striking a balance between challenging authority and remaining within the boundaries of the "official" nationalist project. Hatem, five years older than Ayman, is a former Fateh supporter who joined the Palestinian army, but quit after ten months because of his profound dissatisfaction with the PA, which he accuses of "betraying" the goals of the intifada. Having given up, in effect, the privileges that his former Fateh activism may have held out for him—he was working for an Israeli dairy company when I met him—he is much more inclined to emphasize the possible connections between all the "authorities" he has confronted, whether Palestinian or Israeli.

The fact that schools became a site of negotiation and contestation between students, teachers, and administrators posed a difficult challenge for those young people who see themselves as good students yet who also wish to affirm their nationalist credentials. "I used to go to school every day [before the intifada], I didn't miss a day, " recalls Samira, who later received her bachelor's degree from An-Najah University. In assessing the impact of the first prolonged school closure, she insists that while many students suffered as teachers rushed to get through the required material during a truncated school year, she was able to succeed because she studied hard at home during the closure ("I was always at the top of my class") and because she was too young to take part in anti-Israeli demonstrations. When we discussed the development of the intifada, however, she admitted that she and other girls her age (she was thirteen when the uprising began) soon began to get involved in these activities, and suggested that the initial impediments to political activity were related less to age than to the intersection of gender and education. Unlike boys, she says, girls had few opportunities to gather as a group outside the school; as a result, she and her friends took advantage of the reopening of the schools to organize themselves in the classroom first before going out to protest.

In a follow-up interview, when we returned to the issue of generational authority, Samira suggested that the tension between education and politics in the schools reflected a basic contradiction between the goals of students and teachers, respectively, with the former wanting to go outside for demonstrations and the latter wanting to keep things calm and continue with the normal educational process. Both sides, she said diplomatically, needed to work harder to maintain the necessary amount of "respect" for the other. Though expressed as a general assessment of intifada dynamics, this point also functions as an expression of Samira's own personal dilemma regarding how to reconcile the multiple strands—young woman, serious student, political activist—of her own identity. This dilemma speaks to the uncertainty of the historical moment in which our conversations took place.

## Street Stories: Producing "Youthful Veterans"

Even when they put a post-intifada gloss on their memories of school-based activism, however, many interviewees testified to the breakdown of

the line between school and street. In their narratives, these two social locations appear not as entirely distinct spaces, but rather as overlapping elements in a larger, highly integrated political field in which they, along
with Israeli troops, were the primary actors. Like the narrator in Ghassan
Kanafani's story "The Child Goes to the Camp," a man who recalls the
"drama" of his youth in the years after 1948 by repeatedly reminding the
reader that "it was a time of hostilities" (1984, 62–68), these young people speak of the intifada as a time when school and street, in effect, were
forced to invade each other. In their stories, one gets a sense of how this
collapsing of boundaries helped democratize a political subculture that
had been previously open only to dedicated activists associated with particular factions. As mass demonstrations became a regular feature of the
formal educational experience—or, in the case of school closures, an alternative to it—participation in this subculture became available, by definition, to almost anyone of school-going age. Echoing Samer's statement
quoted at the start of this chapter, Majid argues that students were the
real "strength" of the intifada—but adds that once young people began
to see that they were relatively free to act, they became too "proud" and
decided that if they could stand up to the occupation, they had no reason
to show respect for their teachers. While his perspective is undoubtedly
affected as much by his current status as a teacher as by his memory of
being a student during the intifada, he nicely summarizes the way in
which the process of political awakening was enabled, for many young
people, by the realization that the school and the street could serve as similar places of empowerment. Intissar suggests a further element of this
student subculture, namely, the development of camaraderie and the operation of a kind of peer pressure:

> On certain occasions, like Land Day for example, it was known that the
> students would go to the schools, but wouldn't go into the classroom.
> Then they would leave the school—practically the whole school would
> go out—and they would burn tires, and then the army would come. . . .
> I remember one time when we were sitting in the class, when the teacher
> was giving a lecture, and suddenly we heard bullets everywhere and
> everyone was screaming, so we went out [to make a demonstration].

As we have seen above, Intissar is quick to call attention to her own capacity for taking political risks, as when she helped protect her cousin on

the rooftop or went outside during curfew. Here, however, she gives no indication that she was a leader in organizing demonstrations; instead, she recalls these events as someone who was essentially watching them unfold even as the crowd was sweeping her along.

"[E]ngagement with an authoritarian state engenders a political precocity, produces youthful veterans," writes Colin Bundy (1987, 321), citing the ways in which youth activists in Cape Town—also taking advantage of schools as key organizational sites—learned and practiced a kind of "street sociology" and "pavement politics" during the turbulent 1980s in South Africa. Likewise for members of the "intifada generation," it was the streets, more than any other location, that constituted the primary canvas on which to fashion a new culture of insurgency through a variety of practices whose seemingly quotidian nature, derived from their sheer repetition and the duration of the uprising, often belied the danger associated with them. During the course of a typical intifada day, a young Balata resident might engage in any number of such practices, many of which became signature elements of the resistance movement, including throwing stones, spraying graffiti, distributing underground leaflets, acting as lookouts, enforcing commercial strikes, taking part in marches and other demonstrations, investigating the activities of collaborators, and organizing neighborhood committees.[3]

Though none of these activities, it should be noted, were restricted to young people, it was the young who generally possessed the requisite qualities necessary to carry them out on a mass basis: surplus time, physical stamina, and a knowledge of the streets that allowed them, for example, to disappear easily and move quickly between houses.[4] In facing the Israeli occupation forces, then, they were "defending their own territory," as psychologist Eyad Sarraj put it to me during a discussion of why so many young people were willing to risk their lives during the intifada. Younger interviewees said much the same thing, regularly emphasizing the special relationship that refugee camp children, in particular, have with streets that function not only as thoroughfare and marketplace, but also as playground and battlefield.

In terms of "street sociology," the intifada provided an opportunity for young people not only to forge stronger personal ties with their agemates, but also to discover the potential limitations of generational solidarity in the face of other, crosscutting social structures and identities such as class, gender, and political affiliation. The fact that not all young

people participated in the intifada in the same way—and that some refused to participate at all—is perhaps the most obvious indicator of these
limitations. The process through which I came to interview Yousef, who
identifies himself as having not taken part in the uprising, illustrates one
way in which such tensions play themselves out within the "intifada generation." When I heard that one of the university students living in Birzeit
village was from Balata camp, I immediately asked Ghassan, a student
who had offered to serve as an interpreter for interviews in the Birzeit
area, if we could set up a conversation with Yousef. He agreed to help facilitate the interview, but told me, in effect, that I would be wasting my
time by talking with Yousef, suggesting that the latter was somehow less
qualified to speak about the intifada. The problem, of course, lay not
with Yousef's inability to provide a legitimate perspective on the issue—
for he had much to say about his memories of his youth in Balata—but
rather with his failure to conform to Ghassan's idea of acceptable political behavior.

The issue of nonparticipation in the intifada proved to be a difficult,
but ultimately fruitful topic in a number of my interviews. On one level,
direct questions about varying levels of participation by individuals and
groups were generally met with defensive responses insisting that "everyone" (usually with the exception of collaborators) took part in the uprising; my presence, in other words, served as an opportunity to repair
cracks in the social fabric, at least symbolically, through the determined
repetition of a powerful "public narrative" of heroic, unified national resistance. That many interviewees nonetheless believed this narrative to
be "false" became clear at other points in the conversations, when questions of participation arose in a more indirect fashion in the context of
discussions about particular social groups. Here it was the issue of social
class in general, and the potentially divisive intersection of class and
generational consciousness in particular, that provoked the most open
and emotional expressions of opinion concerning those viewed as non-
participants.

> The rich have gotten richer and the poor have gotten poorer. . . . And the
> intifada was launched by the poor, in the old city and the central city,
> and what is that? That's the poor area. . . . A lot of the rich families just
> sent their children outside the country for a year or two. Meanwhile,
> there were probably a hundred martyrs from the city center in Nablus

[that is, the poorest area of the city], and the longest areas of curfew were in the city center, even longer than in the camp. (Khaled)

The people were brought much closer together [during the intifada], but the rich people kept themselves far away while the rest of us were trying to help each other. . . . There were some people from the upper classes who didn't do anything, who sent their children away or even left themselves, left the country. (Hussein)

In these two excerpts, what might be identified as a general class-based resentment of the wealthy emerges in a very specific context: in descriptions of how the *children* of the wealthy were able to live qualitatively different lives during the intifada.[5] None of these wealthier children, insists Khaled, had to take the same personal risks that he and others like him took; on the contrary, they were able to avoid the suffering of the prison and the dangers of the streets, and to continue their education outside the country in schools that were not subject to arbitrary closure. In a spatial sense, to use Hussein's imagery, they were able to separate themselves from their own society at a time of political turmoil. Ironically, of course, the "advantages" these children enjoyed are also tied precisely to the fact that they did *not* experience the same processes of political awakening we are discussing here, in the same locations, as did poorer refugee youth such as Khaled and Hussein.

Other commentators have noted the ways in which complex social changes that accompanied the intifada included significant, if temporary, shifts in gender relations.[6] For young people, these changes included increased opportunities to interact with members of the opposite sex, either in the context of doing "political work" or in unplanned situations where such interaction could facilitate personal safety. Among the countless myths, legends, and other stories that make up the folklore of the uprising, for example, is the story of the young man, fleeing from the army, who is given sanctuary by a woman who hides the fugitive by having him get into bed with her sleeping daughter, thoroughly fooling the soldiers who come to search the house but find only "a man sleeping with his wife."[7]

In the memories of several young people in Balata, the interface between school and the streets was one area where the boundaries of "traditional" gender relations could be explored and tested. As eighteen-year-old Hussein points out, the separation of boys and girls in school was a potential obstacle to effective political organizing, an obstacle that some of his fellow students were able to overcome—though perhaps not, he hints, for purely nationalist reasons. Some boys, he said laughingly, were "specialists" (*mitkhassesīn*) in acting as liaisons with the girls' schools, eagerly volunteering to cross the gender divide in order to announce a suspension of classes or other protest activity in front of their female counterparts. While clearly labeling such actions as "wrong" with respect to norms governing gender relations, he went on to argue that coordination between leadership cadres among the male and female students was often essential, and admitted that in certain "urgent" situations, he had gone into one of the girls' schools himself to read a statement from the intifada leadership. In his testimony, then, the question of how to characterize the interaction between boys and girls remains open, illustrating that the "political" actions of young people like himself cannot be viewed in isolation from the ever-changing norms of school culture, or from the unusual historical context in which those actions took place.

As we saw in the case of relations between parents and children, these emerging shifts in gender relations are also narrated, in part, in terms of Israeli attempts to harness Palestinian social dynamics to the process of counterinsurgency. According to Intissar, soldiers were well aware of the ways in which young men sometimes carried out political actions with a dual purpose: both to resist the occupation and to impress young women. In this light, soldiers' humiliation of the young men in public—that is, in view of young women—could serve as a dual punishment:

> I: I remember one time when my maternal cousin came from studying in Jordan. When he came, all his friends came to the house to greet him because they hadn't seen him for a long time—he was gone for four years because of his studies. Then the soldiers came into the house. They took all the men outside, lined them up against the wall, and made them take their clothes off. . . . I also remember when we used to go to school and the soldiers, in order to vex the students . . . they would see four or five young men walking together and say, for example, "You, come here! You, come here!" So two or three of the boys would come, and they [the soldiers] would take their books and throw them on the ground, throw everything on the ground. Then they would stand them up against the wall and beat them with their sticks. . . . And after that the boys would be really embarrassed, because there were girls and other people watching.

    *J*: You think they did that on purpose because they knew that other stu-
    dents were watching?

    *I*: Yes, they were trying to do that [laughs].

Intissar's laughter—shared with Muna, who was the interpreter for the interview—suggests that the soldiers' attempt to embarrass the boys was at least partially successful, and again indicates the operation of a youth subculture that is neither monolithic nor completely coincident with the operation of the intifada's mass political activity.

If the "street sociology" of class, gender, and generation helped educate young people about the complexity of their own identities, the "pavement politics" of the intifada gave them the chance to try out the micropractices of political action in the social space that arguably allowed them the greatest freedom to operate. As we saw in chapter 2, the activities of young people in the streets led to the development of alarmist discourses among many adult observers (e.g., fears of *shabāb* "stoning anything that moves") and, in the extreme, concerns about "the destruction of society." Yet for young people themselves, memories of actions taken in the streets assume a considerably less cataclysmic and more mundane form, often almost matter-of-fact, focusing on the specificities of practices that became routinized during the uprising despite their dangerous nature.

> I was living in the old city in Jenin. The city is divided into places—south, north, like this. We divided the city into parts, and each part is, let me say . . . some people there are young, or especially educated, and they agreed to do something, to make a demonstration. They get together, and they agree what time they have to start, and where, and how, you know, how to divide each other, where you have to stand, and something like that. . . . Sometimes we would say goodbye to each other—[because] maybe we will not see [each other again]—and that happened, you know. I remember a guy, we shook hands, he gave me something . . . and then I heard that this person was killed, but at least I saw him before dying. And we're sitting in the center of this place . . . and talking together and, you know, it's kind of to encourage each other and to be strong, to make the soldiers afraid, even [though] we are not equal—they have guns, weapons, gas, everything, you know, and we have nothing except stones and our determination. And we started, we got wheels [i.e., tires], big stones, rocks, and these kind of things, and

the soldiers would come from lots of directions and start shooting and gas and it started, you know. (Hassan)

Well, I am with Hamas, so I used to work through their organization, not alone. We divided ourselves into groups, and on a given day one group would prepare for an escalation, another group would write graffiti, and others would do other actions. So whatever my group was doing, I would take part. Sometimes we would get ready for an escalation by gathering tires in the morning, and other times we would confront the army by throwing stones, or we would distribute leaflets or write graffiti. (Qassem)

I was ready to participate according to the situation, as it was necessary. For example, when someone was martyred, there would be a demonstration, and I would participate in the demonstration. If the soldiers showed up at the demonstration, I would join in throwing stones at them. Or if there was a need to write on the walls to announce something in particular, or to call for activities against the occupation, I would write on the walls with the *shabāb*. (Salim)

Here we have three young men of similar age with three different relationships to the process of political action as it unfolded during the intifada. Hassan identifies the uprising as "a unique stage" in his life, and comes closest to identifying himself as a leader of the uprising; in his stories of street actions, one gets the sense of a movement that absolutely took over his life, at least for a time. Qassem's emphasis is on his identity as a loyal Hamas activist, carrying out whatever actions were required of him by the faction that he continues to support. Salim, who among all the interviewees was the least reluctant to speak with me "on the record" despite the fact that I saw him regularly when eating at his restaurant, does not see himself as an activist per se and refuses to link himself with any particular group or faction. In each case, however, we see that the narrative architecture of their memories does not permit any artificial separation between one type of action and another; instead, memories of all these practices flow freely into and out of one another, and the picture thus fashioned is one of a flexible, situational political culture in which one did what was "necessary," in Salim's words, according to the needs of a given time and place.

During the interviews, I struggled constantly with my desire to balance a respect for the integrity of this narrative architecture on the one hand, and the researcher's need to make admittedly artificial distinctions between various practices on the other. Inevitably, my ear was particularly open to any descriptions of street actions that suggested the weakening of generational hierarchies, the operation of generational consciousness, or the possibility of social inversion. Once again it was Hatem, former political prisoner and erstwhile employee of the Palestinian army, whose testimony shed important light on the generational dynamics of street activism, particularly with respect to the enforcing of commercial strikes. The two major Palestinian rebellions of the twentieth century—the 1936–39 revolt and the intifada—each began with a commercial strike, and scholarly accounts in each case suggest that some element of coercion was necessary to convince merchants to observe the strike. Yet we know very little about the experiences of the *shabāb* generally credited with carrying out the instances of coercion that may have occurred.

Hatem's testimony, then, is instructive not only when placed in the context of his prison and school stories, but also as an unusual contribution to a sociological and historical literature in which young activists have been largely voiceless.

> *J*: When the schools were closed, what did you do with all your time?
>
> *H*: Well, most of the students were out in the streets, of course. Any patrol that would pass by, they would throw stones at it. If there was a decision taken to close the shops, they would close the shops, or put up barricades. . . .
>
> *J*: So it was the job of the young people to make sure that the shops were closed.
>
> *H*: Right. They are the ones who are building the intifada, the ones who were throwing stones, making sure the shops were closed, whatever. They were involved in everything. They made sure the strikes went according to plan.
>
> *J*: Would you say that those young people, like yourself, were the leaders?
>
> *H*: About the leadership of the intifada—the intifada was collective, so the leadership wasn't just one person, or two, or three. . . . The decisions were made collectively. . . . So whoever participated in those decisions—whether it was one, two, three, four, ten—if they agreed to abide by those decisions, they were leaders, OK? The generation was

unified, so that even if one person made a decision, it could be considered a collective decision.

M: Let me ask the same question again. . . . Would those young people be considered the effective, active leadership of the intifada?

H: Yes, they were effectively the leaders—they took the decisions, and they carried them out. I mean, if a fifteen-year-old can close the shops, or make an escalation in Balata, or Nablus, or wherever, then he has to be considered a leader. And there are one hundred thousand more just like him.

J: Did you ever have to force any of those shopkeepers to close their shops?

H: Yes, that did happen sometimes.

J: They wanted to keep their shops open?

H: Well, at times some of them asked for an extension for a certain amount of time because of work they had to do. Sometimes you would try to understand their situation and to give them the extra time, but sometimes you had to force them all to close. This excluded pharmacies and bakeries, of course.

J: Was that difficult? A lot of those shop owners were obviously older people—was it ever, I don't know, awkward or embarrassing for a young person to have to do that?

H: Sure, and one or two times I just left. But at the same time, these are collective decisions. . . . He didn't want the embarrassment—and it really was embarrassing. . . . [I told him] "I don't want to close everyone except for you," and so he had to make himself understand the situation.

J: Did the soldiers ever come into the camp and try to force the shopkeepers to open the shops?

H: Sure, that happened a lot. But when it happened, the shopkeepers would respond to *us,* not to the soldiers.

Just as he characterized his relationships with the *mukhābarāt* in prison and with the headmaster at school in terms of negotiation, then, Hatem remembers his days of enforcing truncated commercial hours as a time of empowerment, but also as a time marked by the need to respect the ever-changing rules governing these social interactions. On the one hand, his insistence that fifteen-year-olds had the power to shut down the commercial district of a large city recalls his image of the child stopping and searching the headmaster's car, once again suggesting a powerful, symbolic inversion of generational authority. On the other hand, he is careful to stress that he and other young activists did not exercise their newfound authority as strike-enforcers arbitrarily (as he says headmasters did before the intifada), but rather with discretion and a willingness to bend the rules when necessary.

Given the dubious, occasionally vicious reputation sometimes attached to these activists by many older observers during the intifada—the term *shabāb* could be quite double-edged, suggesting menace as well as heroism—Hatem's description of the enforcement of commercial strikes can be read as a determined balancing act mounted in response to an existing "public narrative." While not denying the possibility of intimidation ("sometimes you had to force them all to close"), he attempts to prove that if he and others like him acted "beyond their years" during the intifada, they did so not as irresponsible youth, but rather through determined effort and collective decision making, as the mature conscience of the nation.

Khaled, who spoke of prisons in terms of the "freedom" they ironically provided during the intifada, makes a similarly nuanced point concerning the increasing involvement of young people in dispute resolution, a social function traditionally reserved for older men. During the intifada, he says, the elders often ended up asking young activists for help, sometimes asking them to use force. "Like we say, when there is no law, the only law is the law of the *shabāb* . . . and that's a problem," he admits, perhaps referring to the sometimes violent score-settling that took place at various points during the uprising (Hunter 1993; Robinson 1997). Yet the bulk of his remarks portray young people as matching, even exceeding, the capabilities of their elders in mediating deep social conflicts. Again we see how the rearrangement of generational authority is embedded in popular memory: the valorization of the young contains within it an implicit critique of the old.

To consider the stories of political awakening and social inversion in chapters 4 and 5 is to open oneself to both the spatialization and the generation of popular memory. To be sure, these self-representations are stories about particular places—home, prison, school, and the streets—that loom large in the narrators' individual and collective memories. At the same time, they are stories told by people who see themselves as not only marked, as a generation, by their location in historical time; but also as having transcended the boundaries and social implications of age even as they tried, with some success, to break the hold of foreign occupation. They are stories, in other words, that attempt to explain how it is possible to claim that a ten-year-old boy could be a *shab,* or even an adult, during the intifada; and they accomplish this explanation by insisting, through vivid illustration, that certain places and circumstances made such a transformation possible.

In bringing together the many stories examined here, as well as the social analysis embedded within them—for the young people quoted here are indeed critics as well as narrators—it is useful to imagine a sort of spatial continuum on which to plot the four major sites I have highlighted. On one end we have the home, on the other prison and the streets, with the school occupying an intermediary position. In terms of generation in the narrow, biological sense, the home for Palestinians is traditionally a place where age matters; not surprisingly, it is clear that young people recall the home as the place where they enjoyed the least amount of freedom and authority. The presence of parental control, combined with the disruptions of domestic space by Israeli soldiers, yielded memories that are often strikingly passive, narrated as if by someone physically unable to respond (Qassem: "I didn't wake up until the soldiers were right over my head . . . they told me I was under arrest."). As we move toward the other end of the spectrum, we find spaces that are both more dangerous and more productive of agency, spaces in which the loosening or transformation of generational structures is closely related to the articulation of memories highlighting negotiation, activism, and, at the extreme, the "law of the *shabāb.*"

The generally passive character of home stories, like the insistence of so many narrators that they learned their political lessons *outside* the home, can be explained in terms of the continuing fusion of age (a biological category) and generation (a social category) within that space. By contrast, stories rooted in prison, in the streets, and to a lesser extent the school suggest a decoupling of age from generation, such that age itself became increasingly irrelevant as an indicator of one's ability to act, to be trusted with political responsibility, and to exert authority in a variety of social situations. If these young people possess a kind of generational consciousness, they do so because they have linked their collective identity less to their age and more to the historical experiences and memories of political action that they share. This process of separating age from generation is crucial, for in these self-representations a young person could claim social and political *authority* to the extent that such a separation took place: a student could legitimately stop and search his headmaster's car precisely insofar as the former's age could be "forgotten" (or its significance minimized) and his "adult" status confirmed.

These stories, then, illustrate the malleability of generational identities, particularly in times of political turmoil and consequent social upheaval. Ironically, as artifacts of memory, they also testify to the fleeting nature of generational identities in another, more historical sense, for as remembered events recede into the past, the drama of one's youth, however positively and energetically it is recalled and narrated, emerges as a temporary stage (Hassan: "at that time I was young and full of energy.") Such a realization has far-reaching implications for the whole range of emotions and experiences associated with this drama in the first place. If the operative assumption of popular memory research is that "memory speaks from today," then we should not be surprised to find that among young Palestinians evaluations of the intifada are changing in response to present circumstances, with the result that the range of possible evaluations is widening. As we will see in the remainder of the book, this includes asking critical questions about the very project for which, in their eyes, they and other members of the *jīl al-intifāda* have sacrificed so much.

# 6

## "In the Beginning . . . but Afterward . . ."
### *Moral Chronologies and Reassessments of the Intifada*

An individual's claim in telling his or her story will often be both
to consistency and change, both to coherence and development.
Narrators thus establish that they are both the same person they
always were, and a different person, too. Thus stories change both
with the quantity of time (the amount of experience the speaker
had accumulated) and with the quality of time (the aspects which
she or he will want to stress at the time of the telling). . . . At what
time in the life cycle the story is told is, however, a crucial factor in
its shape.
　　　　　　　　　　　　　　　　　　　　　　—Alessandro Portelli

It's so hard to understand
Why the world is your oyster but your future's a clam
It's got you in its grip before you're born
It's done with the use of a dice and a board
They let you think you're king, but you're really a pawn
　　　　　　　　　　　　　　　　　　　　　　　　—Paul Weller

　　　In conducting popular memory research, I often found that
my own desire to explore the "subjective" recesses of memory seemed
to conflict with the expectations many interviewees brought to the conversation. These expectations, I think, were rooted in the assumption—
mistaken perhaps, but entirely understandable—that despite my stated
interest in intifada stories, I must *really* be interested in getting "information," in finding out the "facts." Ashraf, the young sociology student
who introduced me to the Abu-Hawila family, was the person most

openly uncomfortable with what was, to him, a contradiction between his own inclinations toward "scientific" research projects and my tendency to ask what must have seemed like very *un*scientific questions about memory. At the end of our first interview, he unexpectedly broke off our conversation, saying he wanted to offer a "commentary" (*taᶜalīq*) on my research. The three of us (Ashraf, Mohammed, and I) then had the following exchange:

> A: You're looking for memories of the *shabāb* from the intifada at a time when they are becoming more independent in their personality and their way of thinking . . . and this causes a kind of interference.
>
> J: You think this affects the way that they remember.
>
> A: You have a new situation now with the [Palestinian National] Authority.
>
> M: But Ashraf, what he's talking about now are *your* memories of the intifada time, OK? You're twenty-four years old now, right?
>
> A: Yes, twenty-four.
>
> M: He's asking you, these memories are from a time when you were sixteen, and then another eight years passed, right? Now you're twenty-four years old, so of course you've changed—you're not Ashraf the sixteen-year-old boy, you're a more educated Ashraf who has a B.A., who has his own independent opinion and so forth. . . . So does this awareness actually make you reflect on your memories from when you were sixteen? Does it influence them?
>
> A: Of course it influences them.
>
> J: For me, that's one of the things that makes this interesting.
>
> A: OK, but memories are just history.
>
> M: [Laughing] Do you agree with him?
>
> J: Maybe, maybe. When I think about memory, I think about it in terms of the relationship between the past and the present.
>
> A: The past is past, and there isn't anyone who has the ability to return yesterday to us, much less ten years ago. It's better to think about the future.

Ashraf's obvious frustration with my queries may have signaled a desire to close the door on a past marked, in his mind, by tragedy and by the failure of the intifada to achieve its goals. It also signaled that he was quite aware of what I was trying to do with my research: the injunction to "think about the future" and to leave "history" where it belongs ("The past is past") can be read as an attempt to shore up the kind of progressive, linear narratives associated with nationalist projects in general against a conceptual framework that cannot help but disturb such narratives.

Yet Ashraf can hardly be characterized as an uncritical follower of his own mainstream nationalist leadership; on the contrary, as we will see below, he adamantly insists that the leadership was responsible for "aborting" the intifada. Equally important, in reminding me that the "youth" of the intifada years are now "grown up," he was recognizing and pointing to what is, in effect, the most basic condition of possibility for popular memory research: the simple passage of time. "Life histories and personal tales," notes Alessandro Portelli (1991, 60), "depend on time, if for nothing else, because they undergo additions and subtractions with each day of the narrator's life." This constant metamorphosis represents the latter half of the dual process—consistency and change—referred to in Portelli's statement quoted at the start of this chapter, and is eloquently expressed in Mohammed's insistent question to Ashraf ("you're a different person than when you were sixteen . . . right?").

In this case, however, the years between the events and their narration also take on an important *generational* meaning, for the members of the "intifada generation" have passed, in those years, from one stage of the life-course to another. The very fact of having completed secondary school, or having passed the age when it is typically completed, has a number of basic implications for these individuals: the growing need to make money, for themselves and/or to help support their larger family; the chance to extend one's education at a university or vocational college; the possibility (or impossibility, depending on one's political leanings) of working for the Palestinian Authority (PA); and the looming issue of marriage. Moreover, the Gulf War, the end of the intifada, the Oslo "peace process," and the creation of the PA have all contributed to a gradual distancing of these young people, in many of their minds, from the position they once occupied as activists with the ability to make history. In short, as the narrators themselves have changed, the world has also changed around them.

This chapter, then, examines what happens to memory when popular mobilization gives way to the logic of political negotiation and state building, and when the generational solidarities of "youth" give way to the economic and social pressures of "adulthood." Specifically, I argue that the post-Oslo period has seen a growing fragmentation of the intifada generation, both in the sense of individuals feeling increasingly ambivalent (even conflicted) about national political issues, and in the sense of the entire generation being divided within and against itself. The narrative effects of this fragmentation are most telling, I suggest, when self-representations turn to memories of the intifada's implosion, to post facto assessments and reassessments of the uprising as a whole, and to evaluations of the "peace process" and the performance of the PA.

Given that the "intifada generation" is in many ways an artificial category to begin with—a composite product of the various rhetorical modes discussed in chapter 2—it is tempting to argue that this fragmentation simply represents the point at which the fiction of a unified "generation" is finally revealed. In a strictly sociological sense, there is much to recommend such a view, if only because a variety of cross-cutting identities and structural factors (class and gender divisions, access to education, political loyalties) have always joined age in exerting powerful, sometimes contradictory pulls on young people in the past as well as in the post-intifada period. At the same time, the notion of *jīl al-intifāda*, as a distinct social category representing a dynamic synthesis of biological and historical identity, continues to have relevance for many Palestinians of all ages, not only for its descriptive utility but also in terms of its embeddedness in the overlapping architectures of official and popular memory.

In a narrative and experiential sense, then, the threat or growing reality of generational fragmentation is also saturated with meaning, particularly insofar as it marks a dividing line between two distinct periods of personal, collective, and national history. In the early intifada stories of many of these young people, deeply felt notions of generational unity—sometimes overlapping with or even subsumed within national unity, but never coincident with it—are clearly identifiable; generation, in other words, is one of the most important devices through which memories of that period are structured. As a result, discussions of subsequent events and analysis of the current situation stand in even sharper relief: instead of excitement and pride, for example, these more contemporary narratives are tinged with regret and detachment, and in place of stories rooted in collective action, we find stories reflecting a relative sense of personal isolation.

*Generational Fragmentation*

The September 1996 clashes in the West Bank and Gaza illustrated one of the central ways in which the intifada generation had already begun to divide along one important axis, namely, between those who work for the PA and those who are more free to continue independent political activities (see chapter 7). The process of fragmentation, however, goes well beyond this particular phenomenon to encompass emerging dynamics in the areas of education, employment, gender roles, and political affiliation. Any attempt to fix the current status of the intifada generation in a taxonomic fashion is obviously limited by the shifting nature of these dynamics: changes in the political or economic climate directly affect the social location of countless individuals and, by extension, the collective profile of young Palestinians in general.

Nonetheless, I have found it heuristically useful to think of the young people I interviewed as divided into four major "generation units," a term Karl Mannheim (1952, 304) uses to describe "groups within the same actual generation which work up the material of their common experience in different specific ways." The first group, those whom I call *soldiers,* belonged to the thousands of Palestinians employed in the various branches of the PA's security apparatus, ranging from traffic police to the most secretive intelligence services.[1] The second group, the *activists,* were still involved in political action on a regular basis, but were not formally affiliated with the PA. Third are the *students,* who were focused primarily on pursuing their education, in some cases after undergoing a period or periods of political detention. Finally, I have labeled the last group *spectators* to indicate those who had retreated from politics and were either working (but not for the PA) or looking for work. Table 2 represents a snapshot of these "generation units," graphically locating the twenty-one young men and women at the core of my interview cohort in terms of both their stated political affiliation and their location, at the time of our interviews, in one of the four categories I have identified. It is important to emphasize that these categories are not mutually exclusive, particularly with respect to the line separating activists from students.

When we move beyond the individual level, however, we begin to see how the post-intifada years have acted as a kind of sociohistorical centrifuge, loosening bonds of friendship, political camaraderie, even the most fundamental relations of biological kinship. Three sets of examples

TABLE 2
*"Generation Units" within Interview Cohort*

|  | Soldiers | Activists | Students | Spectators |
|---|---|---|---|---|
| Pro-PNA/Fateh | Nabil<br>Samer | Ayman<br>Iyad | Hussein | Issa<br>Samira<br>Khaled<br>Hatem |
| Opposition | None | Ramzi | Yousef<br>Ghassan<br>Majid | Hassan<br>Isam<br>Qassem |
| Independent | None | None | Ashraf<br>Intissar | Jamila<br>Salim<br>Leila |

will help illustrate some of the patterns that emerge from the arrangement of Table 2 while also suggesting how the process of fragmentation was unfolding in early 1997 in the lives of these twenty-one young Palestinians. First, the most dramatic shifts have arguably occurred among those who have historically supported Fateh and who are now scattered through all four categories. Samer, for example, was working for ʾamen wiqāʾi (the Preventive Security Forces or PSF, popularly known simply as al-wiqāʾi), the intelligence arm of the PA. Recently married to a young schoolteacher, he appeared to enjoy a relatively prosperous and stable economic situation when compared with the others in the group. Hatem, as we have seen in the previous chapter, was given the opportunity to be a soldier, but gave up his position in the army out of political frustration and became a noticeably disgruntled spectator. He and Samer were good friends who had shared a long history of political activity, but because of the different paths they have taken, their time together was increasingly spent in half-joking, half-serious argument. Iyad was working as an organizer within the Fateh movement, operating under what might be called the ideological umbrella of the PA. Though he was a university student, he was notoriously uncommitted to his studies and was well known in the camp for his frenetic schedule of political activities. Khaled, on the other hand, spent his days languishing unhappily in his family's shop and spoke bitterly of how his years of dedication to Fateh and the national cause had not brought him the material benefits of association with the PA.

In contrast to these Fateh supporters, individuals identified with the political opposition (either Hamas or the leftist factions) tend to be concentrated, not surprisingly, on the right side of the chart. For some, such as Isam and Hassan, the move from past "activist" to present "student" or "spectator" is related to dissatisfaction with the results of the intifada, and to the continuing inability of the Left to mount a serious challenge to Fateh's dominance of secular national politics. Of the remaining five, four have a history of activism within the Islamic movements, and one (Yousef) explicitly identified himself as politically inactive but indirectly expressed support for Hamas. Given the regular crackdowns on Hamas in the post-intifada years, it is difficult to assess the self-representations of individuals such as Ghassan, Majid, or Qassem; they may, in fact, be activists who chose to emphasize other elements of their identities for reasons of personal security or political expediency. Even if this is the case, however, the fact that some activists (such as Iyad and other Fateh supporters) were able to discuss their political work openly while others were not is an indicator of one type of generational fragmentation, in this case abetted by a coincidence of political interest among the major parties to the "peace process."

A third pattern found among these members of the "intifada generation" concerns the gradual retreat of women from the political arena, a process that began during the later stages of the intifada and has continued since the arrival of the PA (Abdo 1999). None of the four women in the group was a political organizer during the uprising, but all participated in various types of collective action ranging from medical relief work to demonstrations and street reconnaissance. Each in her own way identified herself as having taken advantage of what sociologists call a favorable "political opportunity structure," making careful but determined efforts to get involved in the intifada when circumstances permitted it. In such stories, the intifada emerges as an unusual historical moment affording openings for political action that were comparatively rare during earlier periods. The post-intifada situations of these four women, by contrast, are one indication of how the passing of this moment has forced many young women to put their energies elsewhere: Jamila was dealing with the uprising's aftereffects at Balata's center for the disabled, while Intissar was studying commerce at the university, and Leila was working as a hairdresser.

## Moral Chronologies of the Intifada

Oral testimony concerning the periodization of the intifada has much in common with existing scholarly narratives, particularly when the testimony comes from those young people who are inclined, perhaps because of their university training, to take a more analytical perspective on the uprising. What sets most personal narratives apart, however, is the presence of two additional elements that are often filtered out or hidden in the accounts of academic observers: ambiguity and moral judgment. The major source of ambiguity can be found in the temporal context of the interviews themselves—a time of profound uncertainty, on a personal and national level, for many of these young people. Given the meandering, often disappointing path of the "peace process," the continuing political detention of friends and relatives, and the seemingly perpetual economic instability facing Balata residents, many found it difficult to speak confidently about the intifada; it was as if all the cognitive pillars on which they had built their understanding of the uprising were shaking, if not crumbling altogether. With this in mind, it might seem strange to find the same young people continuing to make strident moral judgments about the intifada. It is possible, however, to see this component of their narratives as arising from some of the very ambiguities and contradictions that have crept into their memories in recent years. Indeed, one of the most powerful and effective ways of dealing with such contradictions—for example, between remembered goals and observed results—is to integrate them into a new narrative whose tone is explicitly ethical and judgmental, thereby creating a frame of reference within which the contradictions "make sense."

The dominant existing narrative of the intifada to which these young people have access, of course, is the official nationalist narrative in which the uprising appears as a crucial stage in the long but steady ascent to statehood. Many of the assumptions, categories, and collective longings embedded in this official narrative are indeed present in the stories examined here, particularly those of young people who are sympathetic to Fateh and the PA. Samer, for example, firmly disputes the notion that the uprising was in any way a revolt against the "outside" leadership of the PLO.[2] Yet taken as a group, these personal narratives suggest what I call a *moral chronology* of the intifada that is rooted in a markedly different interpretive framework from the linear, triumphant story associated with official nationalism.

The outlines of this alternative chronology often emerged when interviewees employed the language of contrast, attempting to show how much the end of the uprising differed from its beginning. Generally eschewing precise, calendrical markers, these young people instead relied

TABLE 3
*Critical Intifada Chronologies*

| | In the beginning . . . | . . . but afterward |
|---|---|---|
| Major events | The intifada begins | Fall of USSR |
| | | Gulf War |
| | | "peace process" |
| | | U.S. hegemony |
| Nature of political leadership | Everyone was a leader | PLO "interference" |
| | Women and youth | PA arrives |
| | UNLU | factional disputes |
| | popular committees | "outside forces" |
| Motivations for political action | Selflessness | Selfishness |
| | Pure nationalism | Money |
| | Liberation | Political influence |
| | Dignity | Revenge |
| Resistance tactics | Stonethrowing | Armed attacks |
| | Molotov cocktails | Suicide bombings |
| Relationship of narrator to events | Participation | Observation |
| Descriptors used in interviews | "a real intifada" | "we have no option" |
| | "victorious" | "tranquilizer injection" |
| | "outbreak" | "abortion" |

heavily on pairs of phrases such as *"fil-bidāya . . . w baᶜdayn"* ("in the beginning . . . but afterward"), discursive signals whose significance in the context of their self-representations was as much evaluative as temporal. Particular events and processes identified in interviews, in other words, were invested with meaning less through their exact location in time than through their placement in a narrative universe built on the deliberate juxtaposition of opposing elements.

To say that any of these interviews contained a fully articulated chronology (in the strictest sense) of the intifada, then, would be both inaccurate and beside the point; as Portelli (1991, 63) notes, "Historians may be interested in reconstructing the past; narrators are interested in projecting an image." To the extent that such a moral chronology exists in the stories of these young Palestinians, it is undoubtedly a "national" narrative, but clearly *not* a narrative of steady progress and inevitable national triumph. Instead of a "sociological organism moving calendrically through homogeneous, empty time" (Anderson 1991, 26), the nation appears here as a community winding its way along a tortuous, often downward path from "the beginning" of the uprising through later periods of decline, corruption, and loss of collective will. Table 3 illustrates a number of different axes on which this basic contrast operated in the interviews, including shifts in personal motivation (from selfless to selfish), tactics of resistance (from stonethrowing and Molotov cocktails to armed attacks and suicide bombings), and figurative terminology (from the intifada as "outbreak" to the peace negotiations as "tranquilizer" or "abortion"). It is important to point out that this is a composite picture created from observations scattered throughout the interviews; no single self-representation contained all elements of the whole. At the same time, the testimony reflected in the diagram is remarkably consistent, if diffuse, in terms of the kind of story it tells: on each level, later developments are contrasted sharply, and almost always negatively, with the early period which Nabil suggestively called "a *real* intifada" (*intifāda haqiqiyya*).

Equally important, this alternative chronology cannot be separated from the issue of generational identity, for all the descriptive and normative elements in the chart are set against the backdrop of the narrators' own movement from youth to adulthood. It is significant, for example, that several interviewees defined the "intifada generation" with specific reference to the *beginning* of the intifada, thereby linking their own political influence as youth with a particular stage of the uprising. Nabil, for example, collapsed age and political prominence in arguing that the "children of the stones" (his preferred term) are those who were aged fourteen to seventeen when the uprising started. In general, then, we might say that within the universe of meaning constructed in this moral chronology, youth is identified with many of the elements located on the left side of Table 3, including mass politics, purity of intention, active involvement in events, democratic forms of resistance, and local (or "inside") authenticity. Becoming an adult, on the other hand, is connected with elite politics, selfishness, passive observation of events, specialized forms of resistance, and the relocation of political authenticity and authority in the hands of the formerly exiled ("outside") national leadership.

In many of my early interviews, I made a habit of asking young people what they could recall about life before the intifada, particularly the economic situation (*al-wadeᶜ al-iqtisadiyya*) of their family and the camp as a whole. The youngest members of the group remembered little from pre-intifada days, but among the rest there was general agreement that the situation was relatively good at that time, largely because so many people in the camp were able to work in Israel. As I continued interviewing other residents, I began to notice that responses to this line of questioning were becoming more and more insistent, to the point where some young men went out of their way to stake out a position on the issue before I explicitly asked about it. People in Balata, I realized, were reacting not only to the question itself, but to the implication lurking within the question—the idea that economic deprivation might have been a *motivation* for political action; moreover, it seemed that at least some of them were comparing notes about their conversations with me.

During my first interview with Hatem, for example, I asked him if he had learned anything about Israelis while in prison. In the middle of his response, he suddenly shifted gears, perhaps sensing an opportunity to preempt questions about economics by emphasizing other factors:

> You know, the intifada wasn't—I mean, at the time of the intifada, the economic situation was good. . . . So the intifada didn't happen because of economic difficulties or something like that—it was the result of injustice [*zulum*]. . . . It didn't come from the economic side or from living conditions—just the opposite. Living conditions, as far as money goes, were very good, OK? It came from the psychological side.

Hatem's emphatic statement is consistent with what many Balata residents told me: that while the camp may not be a prosperous area, it saw a drastic worsening of material conditions *after* the start of the intifada, not before it. In such narratives, the collective ability to engage in resistance activities thus becomes even more heroic, for the struggle continued in spite of the severe economic hardship that resulted from prolonged curfews and the closure of the Israeli labor market.

In many interviews, young people employed the language of contrast when discussing the role of "money" (*masāri*) in the intifada, taking the offensive against questions (asked or implied) about economic issues by speaking of money not as a motivating factor for action (through its absence), but rather as a potentially divisive factor working against the unity of the people. Here the role of the exiled PLO, headquartered in Tunis at the start of the uprising, emerged as a source of significant controversy, generating angry denunciations and awkward moments in the conversations. Samer, in keeping with his contention that tensions between the "inside" and the "outside" were minimal during the intifada, argues that the PLO played a thoroughly positive role in the movement through its ability to offer various kinds of "support" (*diᶜam*), including financial support, to those struggling on the "inside." In this view, however, he is in a small minority even when compared with other PA supporters. Nabil, the other soldier in the group, singles out the PLO's financial involvement as the factor that marked, in effect, the end of the "beginning" of the intifada:

> J: What was the PLO's role in the uprising?
> N: The PLO interfered in the uprising after about six months . . . and this was the greatest mistake of the intifada.
> M: Because they introduced money?
> N: Right. But the feelings of the guy who is confronting the Israeli patrol or Israeli soldier, they were patriotic feelings, activist feelings. . . . He wasn't doing it because of money. . . . At that time we were three brothers. The one who was martyred when he was eleven, he was about nine [when the intifada started], and the oldest, he was about thirteen. . . . At that time it was a real intifada, not an intifada for money.

Nabil was also careful to distance himself from these very dynamics, demonstrating the kind of depersonalization we saw in chapter 5:

> J: You said that the PLO didn't really have a role in the uprising for the first six months, but after that, it started to influence it with money, is that [right]?
> N: It *supported* the intifada. Not influence—*support*.
> J: OK. And when you say support, you mean that they were providing money to people to help people get by because of the situation, because of the conditions?
> N: Right. . . . The PLO would send money to the local leaders, and then the money was distributed, first of all to the poor people. And for intifada activities, to pay for uniforms, spray paint for graffiti, leaflets.
> J: All this sounds to me like it was probably very important in helping to keep the uprising going, so why do you think it was a mistake?
> N: Well, let's say I am in the streets, facing the occupation. There were some people who used to say that this person, he is not throwing stones because of the nation. Because the most money went to the families that were the most active. . . . But I'm not fighting for the money—I'm doing it for my land, to get rid of the occupation.
> J: Did they also—did they specifically give money to families who had someone who was a martyr?
> N: There was some support for martyrs' families and for people who

were wounded. But it was informal support, not official . . . not like a monthly salary. The support was under the table.[3]

J: But everyone in the camp was aware of who was getting money and who wasn't, for example—or was it not that clear?

N: No, it wasn't well known . . . it was a very secretive process.

J: [But] you also said that sometimes people would accuse other people of being active only because of the money. So they must've known who was getting money.

N: At the end of the eighties, maybe around ninety or ninety-two, there were special monthly salaries [for the martyrs' families].

M: Official salaries?

N: Official. . . . You would go to Amman [to get the money].

J: Did this affect your family?

N: Yes, until now.

J: Were there people who ever accused you, for example, of throwing stones for the money, because you had a brother who was martyred?

N: Never—the ones who were accused were . . . the leaders on the inside. This is one of the negative sides of the intifada.

The insistence that "money" only entered the equation after a specified period of time (in this case, after six months) serves to reinforce the picture of the preceding period as a time when motives were less suspect, a time when the ongoing process of collective struggle eclipsed any thought of personal gain. The "mistake" of the PLO leadership, then, lay in its attempt to tinker with, or exert more influence over, a locally generated movement rooted in the uncorrupted spirit of "pure" national feeling.

Hussein, a student and Fateh supporter, echoes Nabil's reading of the situation but gives events a slightly different twist, absolving the PLO of direct responsibility for the negative influence of money on the intifada. His testimony, nonetheless, creates a familiar moral chronology:

J: What exactly do you think was the role of the PLO outside in the intifada?

H: Support.

J: What kind of support?

H: Financial support, support for the families of martyrs, for people under curfew, all types [of support]. The PLO encouraged the continuation of the intifada . . . and this led to the assassination of Abu Jihad.

J: OK, about the PLO and the support that they gave, the money that they gave, I've heard from other people that that caused some problems here, that some people were jealous or were upset about who was getting money. Is that something that you were aware of?

H: That's right. But this happened after the deportations, after Husam Khader and the other leaders were deported at the start of the intifada. . . . After that, others [i.e., other leaders] came, and every one of them wanted something [for himself]. Of course the occupation had a lot to do with causing problems between people. All the honorable people were in prison. So you had collaborators, people who were paid by the occupation, maybe people who were less honest, and when the support came in [from the outside], they would keep a share for themselves.

In this case the moral contrast has to do with both factional and generational identities: the man Hussein identifies by name as being more "honest" in his handling of financial matters, Husam Khader, was closely affiliated with Shabiba, the Fateh youth movement, before his deportation in January 1988. After his return, Khader was one of three Balata residents elected to the first Palestinian Legislative Council in early 1996; a widely popular figure in the camp, he became a vocal critic of the PA and a forceful advocate for the rights of refugees in the years since his election. Given his credentials as a lifelong Fateh organizer, Khader's antagonistic relationship with the Fateh-dominated Authority is significant and speaks to a wider rift that has developed between younger, "inside" activists—those who "paid their dues" in the streets and the interrogation cells during the intifada—and the older, "outside" leadership that returned from exile in the wake of the uprising.

In Hussein's testimony, however, this political division remains unspoken: rather than directly criticize the national leadership, he focuses on the admirable qualities of the young Fateh leaders who, he says, were "loved" by everyone in the camp. On the other end of his moral spectrum, he remains vague as to the identity of the people who subsequently were put in charge of distributing PLO funds and others who contributed to the "decline" of the intifada, referring to them only generically as "collaborators" and "rude" people. When these people started to take control of the situation, he recalls, "it felt like we [had] lost something very important."

Similar assessments appear in the self-representations of the spectators, but here the blame for the moral backsliding—whether in the form of money or other "outside interference"—falls even more directly at the doorstep of the PLO. Khaled, the disgruntled Fateh activist, provided a quiet but sarcastic example of this sentiment when I asked him to define the role of the PLO in the intifada. Laughing, he replied (in English), "Only financing!" The outside leadership, he said, tried to control the situation through financial means and political directives, but was only partially successful because local leaders would often ignore some of the orders that came in from outside. PLO attempts to influence the uprising, in other words, only succeeded in sowing the seeds of disunity within the movement. Hassan and Isam, former and current PFLP supporters respectively, identified some of the internal social problems which resulted:

H: The revolution is started by the courageous, exploited by opportunists, and its fruits are harvested by cowards.[4] If I'm speaking about the intifada, I can say that there are people who sacrificed, those who had real beliefs. And the opportunists, they are the ones who came along a bit later, who had their own interests, and they abused our sacrifices. And the cowards—we're seeing them today.

J: And the people who started the intifada, did they also have economic interests? Was that part of their motivation for protesting and sacrificing and so forth?

H: In general, no. They were simple people . . . but [the intifada] gave them a chance to do something, to sacrifice and struggle. . . . [Later] you had the exploiters, some of whom were collaborators, and people with their own political and economic interests, and this caused problems between factions. . . . There was stealing, for example. . . . And this weakened the intifada and took away our unity.

At first, all of us were struggling together . . . and anytime someone would see the [Israeli] army, you would automatically try to do something. I remember one such event that just happened by chance: I was with a group of guys, and I had an apple in my hand. Automatically I looked on the ground, but there weren't any stones, so I took the apple and threw it at the patrol. What I mean to say is, there was something, some kind of motivation, that came from inside us. But then money entered in a big way and came between people, and it caused people to look around them and think about someone, "Why is he getting more than I am? Didn't I do as much as he did? Maybe I even did more than him." And this was the major internal factor that really troubled the intifada. (Isam)

Unlike Hussein, both Hassan and Isam are quite willing to trace such developments back to the actions of the national leadership. "They don't have the ability to invest the intifada. . . . These kinds of people, they never see a real budget. Most of them, they have companies—they are rich people," says Hassan, his chosen imagery perhaps a function of the accounting degree he received at university. Isam argues that as time went by, the allowances the PLO had traditionally sent to help meet the expenses of full-time activists and young people who were on the run from the Israeli security forces began to find their way into the pockets of people who were not even involved in resisting the occupation.

Like so many of their age-mates, Hassan and Isam both speak of "money" as having *entered* the equation from outside, bringing jealous feelings and selfish attitudes to the surface and leading ultimately to the growth of factional disputes that sometimes turned violent. The memory of such conflicts was particularly troubling for Leila, who said she favored the "unity" of all political groupings:

L: Some of the factions are still against peace, and so we're afraid that this is going to have negative effects on the peace process.

J: Do you support any of the factions in particular?

L: I'm in favor of unity. The religion is one, the language is one, the identity is one, so I'm not with any of the factions.

J: Did the fact that there are different factions—did that cause problems during the intifada? Were there problems between the factions?

L: No, because each one took its own decisions and carried out its own decisions. But there were times when outside forces would come in and make things happen [i.e., cause problems] between the factions. We've all seen this kind of trouble between two of the factions.

J: Do you remember any incident in particular that you can talk about as an example?

L: Toward the end of the intifada in Gaza, there was something between Hamas and Fateh, a clash between them. But I think it was caused by outside forces. There were even some people who died from both factions.

J: The differences between factions in the camp here—did they ever become violent?

L: Only in Gaza. The problem in Gaza was a big problem. . . . Maybe some small incidents happened here, but soon afterward the factions would return to normal. But the incident that happened in Gaza . . . there were people shooting each other. Those who wanted to cause this trouble succeeded.

The incident to which she was referring—a November 1994 shoot-out between PA police and Hamas activists that left at least twelve people dead and roughly two hundred wounded—provoked a great deal of shock and anxious discussion throughout the West Bank and Gaza, briefly raising fears of a Palestinian civil war. Significantly, Leila said nothing about the PA's role in the battle, preferring to label it a case of unnamed "outside forces" (*harakat kharijiyya*) exacerbating factional infighting.[5]

Through her own description of the event, Leila constructs two overlapping comparisons that allow her to distance such a difficult chapter in her nation's recent history from her own experience and from the positive qualities she wishes to associate with the intifada. First, she locates the outbreak of factional infighting—a form of political activity that is largely associated with certain groups of young men—at the end of the uprising, implicitly contrasting this period with an earlier time when, in her words, "all the people" participated in resistance activities. In addition, the fact that the clash took place in Gaza allows her to make the claim that Balata did not see such deadly breakdowns of national unity—and she identifies Balata, not Gaza, as the place where the intifada began. In her reckoning, serious internal dissension did not arrive until the uprising spread outward from Balata, and until "outside forces" began to impinge on the efforts of Palestinians on the "inside."

## Suicide Attacks: Revenge and Stages of Resistance

Needless to say, the outlines of such moral chronologies are not always immediately clear; on the contrary, one often finds hints of contrast lurking below the surface of personal narratives or embedded within characterizations that might appear to be more value-neutral. This is the case with the issue of armed actions, particularly suicide operations (*ʿamaliyyāt intihariyya*) such as the bombings that Hamas and Islamic Jihad activists carried out at various points during the Israeli-Palestinian peace negotiations. For many young people in Balata, the mention of these bombings, some of which occurred during the months when I was conducting the interviews, elicits noticeably ambivalent reactions that rarely take the form of outright condemnation or unmitigated support. Of all the interviewees who spoke about suicide attacks, for example, only two offered what we might characterize as straightforward defenses of those attacks as logical steps in a process of escalating resistance, although they did so from very different political positions—one (Majid) an ardent Hamas supporter, the other (Ashraf) an independent:

M: At the beginning of the intifada, the people weren't prepared to arm themselves, so they were obliged to use whatever was available to them. And the thing that was most abundantly available to them at that time was . . . the stone. But throwing stones didn't satisfy people's needs in clashes . . . and they had to invent something quickly. . . . So they started using gas bottles. And you don't need a lot of knowledge or experience [to make one]—anyone can get the gasoline or kerosene, and any available bottle, and you throw it. But because of the violence of the occupation against our people, the people started to think about ways of arming themselves to respond. . . . After a while they started to get automatic weapons.

J: Well, I guess the next question would be, when did suicide actions become an option for Palestinians during the intifada, and how would you assess the importance of those actions in the intifada?

M: First of all, no suicide operation ever happened except as revenge for Israeli attacks on civilians . . . especially the massacre at the Ibrahimi mosque.[6] After that, people decided that they had to respond.

J: When you think about the actions that were carried out in the intifada and before the Oslo agreements, how do you evaluate the success or lack of success of those actions in terms of what they were trying to achieve—in other words, what was the effect of the actions?

M: First, to be fair, these actions did force [the Israelis] to turn their attention to finding a solution, regardless of whether this is a suitable solution or not. The second issue is that these actions stopped the killings by the Israelis, because they knew there would be a response from the Palestinians. And another issue is that it showed the strength of the Islamic movement in Palestine, and it showed that the military option is the most useful option against the occupation.

J: Is it possible for you to characterize each [of the stages of the in-
   tifada]—in other words, what made them different from the others?

A: In the beginning the actions were direct and sharp. The first year was
   a time of disorder, and that gave it a chance to continue. Then the
   United National Command began to control it through leaflets—it
   started to give the people directions concerning which actions would
   happen each month. In the second phase it was controlled by the
   United National Command and by the PLO. This is when the armed
   actions started.

J: What's your personal feeling about armed actions? Do you make a
   distinction between those against soldiers and those against civilians,
   or do you see them all as part of the same category, and what's your
   personal feeling about it?

A: That question isn't relevant to studying the intifada memories of
   young people—it's very personal, this question.

J: What I'm trying to get at is, when the change occurred in the intifada,
   and armed actions started to occur, what I would like to know is how
   you felt about that change. In other words, in a strategic sense, do
   you feel like it was a smart course of action for the intifada to take?

A: Everything always goes in stages. . . . And the Palestinian people are
   launching a revolution *(thawra)*. They are not playing with the Israelis—they are aiming toward *liberation* from the Israelis. And the
   Israelis, they used too many men in the mass intifada demonstrations—they used rock-launchers, hot water, live bullets, economic
   sieges. They killed children. . . . As I said, we are in a revolution, not
   a football match.

Of the two, Majid was the more insistent in his defense of suicide actions;
as a Hamas activist, he clearly saw our conversations as an opportunity
to emphasize the vanguard role of the Islamic movements in developing
new forms of resistance, and to combat what he views as Western mis-
conceptions about the motivation behind such actions. Rejecting the notion that hunger or "hatred of humanity" are driving suicide bombers, he
argues that the primary factor is the loss of "dignity" *(karāma)* that comes
with living under occupation. To an extent, Ashraf echoes this interpretation: his contention that "we are in a revolution, not a football match"
is an implicit critique of outside observers (like myself) to whom he im-
putes a willingness to support certain types of resistance but not others.

The kinds of justifications these two young men offered may not allow them to circumvent fully the dominant paradigm of "terrorism" through which suicide bombings are generally viewed in the West. Yet it is clear that the need to allay the concerns of uncomfortable outside observers on this issue, as on the question of Palestinian support for Iraq during the Gulf War, is not a major preoccupation for them (though it may be for their leaders). One may suspect that this is one of those situations which Jean-Paul Sartre had in mind when he wrote about "the moment of the boomerang" in his famous preface to Frantz Fanon's *The Wretched of the Earth*.[7] Indeed, both Majid and Ashraf discuss ʿamaliyyāt intihariyya in a way that suggests a Fanonian reading of the political situation in which Palestinians, as a colonized people, have found themselves.

In this respect, two major points emerge from their testimony: the absolute necessity of violence as a response to the violence of the colonizer-occupier, and the idea that liberation struggles are animated by a particular historical logic that plays itself out in definite, successive stages (marāhel, sing. marhala). The conviction that acts of Israeli repression must be answered at all costs—or that "accounts" must be "settled," to use Portelli's terminology—recalls Hatem's description of the "system" political prisoners developed, in which any prisoner receiving a beating or a curse from a guard was required to repay the abuse twice or face being shunned by his fellow detainees (see chapter 4). Ashraf's insistence that "everything always comes in stages" provides additional support to this kind of argument, intimating that the development of increasingly violent forms of resistance operates according to a predetermined schema and implicitly linking the intifada with the many anticolonial struggles that have preceded it.

The reason I have highlighted the admittedly exceptional examples of Majid and Ashraf here is that in discussing suicide attacks, they use narrative building blocks that are also available to other Palestinians whose personal view of these attacks may be somewhat less unqualified. For these individuals, invoking the notion of "stages" or speaking about revenge provides a way to smooth out their own ambivalence and to minimize disagreements within the national community over issues of political strategy. Leila, for example, argues that suicide actions were "wrong" and contrary to the goal of "building" the nation; yet this assertion is tempered by her claim that the bomb, as the successor to the stone and the Molotov cocktail, was what brought the Israeli government to the negotiating table. Similarly, Nabil suggests that the bombings should be viewed as a tactic of political or military resistance differing only in method or degree from other tactics used in the uprising. But his endorsement of the more violent actions is less than wholehearted in tone:

N: In the beginning it was big, mass actions. . . . The first stage was the period of stones, and the second stage was the period of incendiary bottles. And the third stage, of course, was the suicide operations.

J: How do you feel about those changes? Do you think those were positive at the time in terms of strategy and how effective they were?

N: Well, they led to what we have now.

M: They led to the peace process?

N: That's right.

J: When do you think the intifada ended?

N: By the end of the Gulf War.

J: When that happened, when the intifada ended, did you feel like it was appropriate, an appropriate time for it to end, or did you feel disappointed?

N: The end of the Gulf War, it really hurt the morale of the people. It didn't destroy the intifada, but it caused it to shrink.

J: Do you think it would've been better for it to continue?

N: I don't know. If the intifada had continued, we would've had a lot more martyrs. . . . We weren't strong enough to stand up to the Israelis.

J: The intifada led to the peace process—do you consider it to be a success, the intifada?

N: I didn't say that [the intifada] ended—it shrank. But it led to the peace process . . . and after the defeat of Iraq, we have no option but the peace process.

As a self-conscious member of the "intifada generation" who has experienced the full arsenal of Israeli repression during the uprising, Nabil is reluctant to criticize actions that inflicted losses on the enemy. As a PA soldier, he is unlikely to express overt support for actions that damaged the "peace process" in which the Authority is so heavily invested. Characterizing the bombings as one of several "natural" stages leading to "peace" and political autonomy allows him to avoid both extremes. Yet he is hardly celebratory in his description of how the nation has reached this historic juncture: for him, ultimately, "peace" was imposed by "outside forces," not won through the efforts of people like himself. In this sense,

Nabil's is a strikingly disempowered narrative, one which suggests that he also wants to close off the thought of questioning the wisdom of past decisions: things happened the way they did because they had to happen that way.

On the most literal level, Nabil's interpretations of political events might appear contradictory—this is, after all, the same young man who made an impassioned defense of the "intifada generation," insisting that its role in the national political struggle was not finished. On the level of narrative strategies, however, we might say that he is dealing from both ends of the deck, giving the bombings a new meaning by integrating them into a more generally accepted story of national liberation even as he hides those events within the same story, and invoking the "party line" even as he undermines it by saying that "we have no option" but to negotiate. His personal fragmentation came to the fore during an informal conversation following our first interview, when Nabil, Mohammed, and I were joined by a friend of Mohammed's who works as a teacher for UNRWA. The friend accused Nabil of being unwilling, because of his position in the army, to speak badly of the PA. During the same conversation, Nabil started to make a critical comment about the Authority, then abruptly said to Mohammed, "Don't translate this!"

The notion of revenge (*intiqām*) reappears in the narratives of two other interviewees who seem to share Nabil's cautious reading of suicide attacks. Ayman diplomatically softens his own apparent disagreement with such attacks by arguing that we must take into account not only the religious convictions of Islamic activists who carry them out, but also the violence to which they are responding. "You know, the Israeli army invaded southern Lebanon, and then we had the massacres at Sabra and Shatila, and there is Deir Yassin," he points out, spanning several decades in his references. "And here we had the Hebron massacre, when the settler from Qiryat Arba killed sixty people, and we had the al-Aqsa massacre."[8] In the face of such a litany of violence, he says, he can understand the feelings of suicide bombers, even when their actions result in the deaths of children. Hatem is more explicit in his criticism of suicide operations, but he also picks up on the idea of revenge—or, in his words, sending the Israelis a message:

J: What do you think was the role of the suicide operations in the intifada, as a strategy?

H: The suicide operations . . . had positive sides, and even more negative

sides. They started after the Oslo agreement and the Hebron massacre. You know, the Hebron massacre was the reason for those operations—they started right after that.

J: Could you give me some examples of the positive and negative?

H: As far as the positive side, they made it clear to the Israelis that anytime they commit a massacre, like the Hebron massacre, they will
find these operations as a response . . . . That's one side, but there's
another side. On the negative side, there is the pressure that it puts on
our workers [that is, those who work in Israel], because economically
we are very dependent on Israel. . . . And also the tourism side—you
know, all the buses going to Petra and wherever—this affects the
economy of the towns, the tourist towns like Jerusalem and Bethlehem, and this has a negative impact on us.

These comments suggest that for individuals who may have personal
reservations about the use of suicide attacks, drawing on the idea of revenge enables them to smooth out their own ambivalence by shifting the
terms of debate, foregrounding *Israeli* actions as both prior to and infinitely less justified than the Palestinian response. Revenge discourse, to
put it another way, serves as reassurance that even when the bombings are
called into question on moral grounds, or in terms of their negative (in
Hatem's view, exclusively economic) effects on Palestinians, it is ultimately the Israelis who must bear the responsibility.

These discussions of ʿ*amaliyyāt intihariyya* also suggest the operation
of another moral chronology with respect to the intifada's development
over time. Ironically, embedded within this chronology we find an implicit critique of the very notion of progressive stages that so many of the
narrators advance. The shift in tactics from stonethrowing to suicide attacks—whether viewed as a "natural" process or as a response to Israeli
violence—is nonetheless a shift in which each "stage" moves further
away from mass actions and closer to highly specialized forms of resistance, for while almost anyone can throw a stone (or, to recall Isam's
story, an apple), very few carry weapons and even fewer become suicide
bombers. This shift is reflected in both the structures and the articulation
of memory: the more specialized the action, the more removed it is from
the actual experience of the narrator, such that the difference between
mass actions at the beginning of the intifada on the one hand, and suicide actions at the end of the intifada on the other, is the difference between events *experienced* and events *observed*. The ambivalent feelings

of individuals such as Leila or Nabil, in other words, may derive from the conviction that the later actions are less "democratic" than the earlier ones.

### Endings: Natural Causes or Political "Abortion"?

The presence of moral chronologies is equally clear when we examine the kinds of explanations that young people offer for when and why the intifada ended, and it is here that the generational fragmentation discussed above is most apparent. Once again it is the dominant "public narrative" of Palestinian nationalism that provides an important backdrop against which to view this fragmentation and its manifestation in personal narratives. In speeches marking his arrival in Gaza in July 1994, PLO Chairman Yasser Arafat put his personal stamp on the passing of the intifada when he exhorted residents to join him in moving from resistance to nation building. Yet from the perspective of "official" nationalism, the intifada had clearly ended even before the PA's creation. As Graham Usher (1995) notes, Arafat followed the signing of the initial Oslo peace agreement in 1993 with a speech calling for a "return to ordinary life" in the West Bank and Gaza:

> The edict was in line with the PLO leader's "letter of recognition," and was generally understood to mean the cessation of all military operations against Israeli targets. Less clear at the time was that the call amounted to the abandonment of any strategy of nationalist mobilisation or resistance in the territories, with Fatah cadres "inside" relegated to mounting a "holding operation" until the PLO leadership returned. From now on, the only game in town would be the PLO/Israeli negotiations on self-rule.[9] (15)

Thus we can say that the various Oslo agreements—the texts which provided for the establishment of the PA—required the narrative cessation of the intifada; there could be no overlap, in a chronological sense, between the uprising and the PA's arrival. The intifada, however, had no "official" ending. The Oslo accords refer ostensibly to a larger historical conflict to which the PLO, as the recognized national leadership of the Palestinian people, is the relevant party from the Palestinian side. The intifada, however, had its own leadership which, while not unrelated to the PLO, nonetheless constituted a distinct body with a narrower constituency: Palestinians inside the West Bank and Gaza. The Israeli government, in other words, never sat down to negotiate with the leadership of the intifada as such; consequently, the field was left open for the PLO/PA, initially working through a number of prominent political figures from the Occupied Territories, to join a negotiation process in which the end of the intifada would be an undeclared *fait accompli*. All this, of course, is a function of the unusual political situation prevailing in Israel/Palestine, where political agreements appear to be enshrining, rather than reversing, many of the effects of settler-colonialism. Viewed in this light, the "end" of the intifada had little in common with the classic moment of decolonization, where the withdrawal of the colonial power coincides with the granting (or taking, depending on one's political persuasion) of formal independence.

For a soldier such as Nabil, whose personal investment in the intifada is hard to overestimate, the thought of possible PLO/PA complicity in the uprising's demise is obviously cause for concern. It is in this light, I believe, that we should read Nabil's insistence that the "shrinking" of the intifada can be traced to the Gulf War, for such an interpretation allows him simultaneously to defend the integrity of the uprising (by lamenting its retreat at the hands of macropolitical forces) and to deflect criticism away from his employer. Others in Balata are less inclined to smooth over the contradictions of the post-Oslo period, partly because these contradictions are literally a visible aspect of everyday life. In December 1995, when Israeli forces finally pulled out of "autonomous" Nablus, residents suddenly saw uniformed Palestinian police patrolling streets peppered with national flags and pictures of Arafat; just over a year later, when I began my interviews in Balata, there were days when you could still see Israeli tanks—a regular feature of the landscape since the September 1996 clashes—stationed just outside the borders of the city. "The occupation is just five hundred meters away," observed Majid wryly as we looked out of the second-floor window of his family's home in early April 1997; other residents told me that during periods of political escalation in 1996–97, they were convinced that the Israeli troops were going to enter the "autonomous" area in full force and invade the camp.

This state of perpetual uncertainty opens up a range of narrative possibilities in terms of how to interpret the end of the intifada, possibilities available not only to ordinary Palestinians, but also to their leaders. During a visit to Nablus and Balata on 31 August 1996, for example, Arafat criticized the intransigence of the right-wing Netanyahu government in Israel and suggested that the intifada could be resumed. "One of our options is to return to the intifada," he told an audience at a Nablus school; "We are the ones who waged the longest uprising in the twentieth century," he declared in Balata. "I don't have a magic wand, but I have the children of the uprising."[10] On the one hand, by invoking the possibility of the intifada's "return," he confirmed that the uprising had indeed ended, or at least that it had been put on hold. At the same time, by carefully figuring the nation as a unified community (*"we* are the ones who waged . . .") under his leadership and control (*"I* have the children of the uprising"), he implied that the suspension or ending of the intifada had also been a decision of the national leadership, not a function of internal or external factors beyond its control.

In terms of personal narratives, the absence of formal closure in the intifada's political trajectory enables at least three distinct interpretations, the first of which is that the intifada is not over at all. With Hamas as the main focus of opposition to the PA and the "peace process," it is not surprising that Majid, who identifies Hamas as the "spearhead" of the Palestinian liberation struggle, takes such a position. In his view, the intifada is a timeless movement, undeterred by short-term setbacks and unbounded by the intermediate decisions of political leaders:

J: Do you think the intifada has ended?

M: The intifada won't end until we have a just solution for the Palestinian people. Maybe it will shrink, but will it end completely? No.

J: What kind of solution do you see as fair and just?

M: A just solution allows me to have a normal life on my land, to practice my sovereignty in the way that I choose.

J: Do you think that this—the kind of solution you are talking about— is possible? Is it something that could happen in your lifetime?

M: I hope so, yes. . . . And I really believe it's inevitable that someday it will come true, and that my family will be able to return to our land in Jaffa. I still have the papers [i.e., the land documents] with me.

In this way the Oslo agreements, conventionally viewed as signaling the replacement of mass mobilization by political negotiation, are refigured as *unsuccessful* attempts to short-circuit an inevitable historical process— recall the "stages" discussed above—of which Hamas is the vanguard.

A second, more common interpretation is that the intifada ended, appropriately and "naturally," as a direct result of the "peace process." All the interviewees who subscribe to this view are affiliated with Fateh; none are members of the group I have categorized as "spectators." As we have seen with the example of Nabil, this kind of interpretation does not necessarily constitute a deliberate, unambiguous replication of the official story. Even Samer, the Preventive Security officer, argues that the "fruits" (*thimār*) of the post-intifada period have not materialized for most Palestinians, and his explanation for this failure—that the Israeli side is not committed to peace—raises the unspoken question of whether the intifada could or should have continued. Given that his identity is so closely bound up with the PA, his support for the diplomatic path the PA has pursued comes across as a surprisingly lukewarm endorsement rooted in the conviction that the intifada's conclusion was imposed rather than freely chosen.

In order to find anything approximating the triumphant narrative associated with "official" nationalism, we have to move to the two youngest members of the group, both of whom identify the Oslo agreements and the PA's arrival as having definitively ended the intifada. Ayman refers to the existence of the PA as the "greatest accomplishment" of the uprising, while Hussein strongly disagrees with the notion that the leadership may have "betrayed" the people by going down the path of negotiation. Relative age is a significant factor here: while both of these young men remember the events of late 1987, neither became seriously involved in political activities until somewhat later, making them less invested in the initial period of mass mobilization than many others in the group and therefore less likely to construct a moral chronology in which the beginning of the intifada serves as an idealized benchmark.

Ayman and Hussein's level of assurance about the suitability of the intifada's conclusion—or, to look at it another way, the absence of ambivalence or cynicism in their stories—suggests an emerging political division between older and younger members of the "intifada generation," as well as what amounts to a temporary economic division within that generation between those who do not yet have to worry about making a living (because they are still in school and depending on their families) and those who do. For the spectators, the passing of the intifada into history is anything but an unproblematic occurrence; on the contrary, it is a tragic, even catastrophic shift involving the forcible intervention of "outside powers" (named or unnamed), and it requires a lengthy and often highly emotional explanation. Typical of this group is Salim, the restaurant employee and political independent who was so cautious about talking with me. In the middle of our second interview, he broke his pattern of brief, measured responses when asked about the fate of the intifada:

> J: I wanted to ask you if you think that the intifada is over. Has it finished?
>
> S: All the indications are that it is finished.
>
> J: When do you think it stopped?
>
> S: By the beginning of the Oslo agreements.
>
> J: You think that the peace process caused the end of the intifada?
>
> S: It's the peace *drama,* not the peace process, which ended the intifada.

When I asked him why he described the ongoing peace negotiations as a "drama" (*masrahīya*), he explained that during the Oslo process, the PLO, with Israel's support, led the people into "chaos," essentially distracting them with diplomatic posturing while it abandoned long-standing principles like "freedom, liberation of all the land, and the dignity of the people." Here it is helpful to know that in addition to his restaurant job, Salim is an amateur actor who was working on a local theater project at the time of our interview; by using the term *masrahīya,* he was following the outlines of an existing critique of the post-Oslo period, but translating it into what was, for him, a more familiar idiom. Adding another powerful image, he concluded that the effect of Oslo was equivalent to the politicians administering a "tranquilizer injection" through which the people—metaphorically drugged as well as entertained by the "drama"—were manipulated into forgetting their past and believing that negotiations with Israel were the only viable course of action.

Ashraf, also a spectator whose involvement in resistance activities has been fairly limited, is equally firm in denouncing the role of the national leadership in the intifada's demise, and like Salim, he frames his view in a way that closely reflects his personal circumstances and self-identification. As we have seen above, he has a fondness for speaking about "stages" and for offering political opinions couched in a semi-detached, analytical style. Of all the young people I interviewed, for example, he was the only one who took notes during my questions, often pausing to collect his thoughts before answering and then pausing again in the middle of his response to make sure I was following his point. Our conversations, I remember thinking at the time, had the feel of a final oral exam for a sociology course, an exam in which the roles of teacher and pupil were sometimes reversed:

*J:* What about the political process? Many people say that the peace process was a direct result of the intifada, that the intifada led to Madrid, Oslo, the coming of the Authority, all these things. On which side would you place all of that in terms of achievements or failures?

*A:* Failure. [Laughs. In English:] You know why?

*J:* Tell me why!

*A:* When the intifada was at a crossroads . . . they signed these ridiculous agreements, like Oslo . . . and this stupid mistake ended the intifada. . . . I know the Palestinian people are distinguished by having all these Ph.D. holders in political affairs—but we need people who know something about strategy, who understand politics and action.

*J:* What's the lesson, then, that you learn from that? Is there a lesson in the intifada? Should it have continued longer, for example?

*A:* Let me give you an example here. Let's take pregnancy—it goes for nine months, and then the child [comes]. Well, the intifada didn't make it from the beginning to its conclusion. . . . It was an abortion—an abortion right in the middle of it.

*J:* OK, you've talked several times about stages, about how things have to go in stages and about how the intifada went through different stages. If it was aborted, what are the other stages you think it would need to go through? Does that makes sense? In other words, you're saying the intifada was stopped prematurely. So if it had not been stopped, or if it had continued, what other stages would be . . .

*M:* Would take place?

*J:* Right.

*A:* If we are to talk about the continuation of the intifada, about other stages . . . the Israelis themselves would have to ask to sit with the Palestinians [i.e., to negotiate].

Strictly speaking, Ashraf's point here is no different from Salim's: that the PLO made a grave mistake when it decided to exchange the intifada for a place at the negotiating table. The imagery Ashraf chooses, however, is considerably more violent, containing accusations that are unmistakable: the intifada ended not by accident, and not because Israel succeeded in subduing it, but rather because the PLO deliberately terminated the "pregnancy" (*hamel*) before the "child" could be delivered. On one level, he is activating the symbolic link between biology (or "generation") and nationalism, or between biography and national identity: the intifada represents the (tragically unfinished) birth pangs of the nation.[11] On another level, the figurative language of pregnancy and abortion provides a way for Ashraf to distance himself, as analyst and critic, from the processes about which he is speaking. Yet this very language also implicates him as a member of the "intifada generation," for what he describes as the uprising's "natural" growth parallels his own generation's journey to maturity. In this context, the "abortion" (*ijhād*) of the intifada is a doubly powerful act, not only killing a political struggle but also effecting a widespread arrest in the proper development of the *jīl al-intifāda*.

Isam articulates most explicitly this notion of generational failure, although he argues that it was the process of political action itself rather than its eclipse in favor of the "peace process" that left him and others like him unable to complete their transition to adulthood (see chapter 3). Nonetheless, on the issue of the intifada's conclusion, Isam joins Salim and Ashraf in formulating a clear moral chronology. In direct contrast to his statement that the initial mass participation in the intifada was motivated by "something from inside us," he posits an "outside," international dimension to the uprising's demise, seeing the "peace process" as part of a larger *pax americana* imposed on the Middle East—a development in which many Arab leaders, to the detriment of their people, are complicit:

J: When would you locate the end of the intifada?
I: Well, I was arrested in '91. . . . I remember that it was the time of the Gulf War and the breakdown of the intifada. There are a number of reasons for it, not just one, but in my view it started with the Gulf War, with the defeat of Iraq, and the Arab countries turning [i.e., turning on us]. And we didn't expect this—even though it's well known that the Arab regimes suppress their own people, we didn't expect that it would be like this. We were relying on the Arab masses. . . . Also the fall of the Soviet Union and the end of socialism contributed to the defeat of the Palestinians, along with the ascendance

of imperialism to the top of the pyramid [i.e., as the dominant power in the world].

J: When it started to decline like this . . . how did you feel about that?

I: I can't even describe my feelings at that time. . . . When the Authority came, we were happy, but there was also sadness—feelings you can't describe in only one way.

The triumph of U.S. imperialism, as it functions in Isam's narrative, effectively completes a process which began with the apple he threw at the Israeli patrol: from this action, the ultimate example of individual resourcefulness and locally generated resistance tactics, initiative gradually moved outward until, in the end, the most global and alien of political forces imposed a deeply unsatisfying outcome. While the villain may be different—he doesn't directly blame the PLO—the language of contrast operates in much the same way as in the other narratives examined here: the circumstances of the intifada's ending produce mixed feelings, including a sense of disappointment or nostalgia for what was lost in the process.

In the self-representations of these various "spectators," then, we find explanations for the disappearance of the intifada that turn on the actions of the national leadership as well as other "outside" forces. We also find a combination of narrative styles, ranging from emotional, rapid-fire delivery (Salim) to detached, almost didactic analysis (Ashraf), to a combination of both (Isam). Perhaps the richest assessment, however, comes from Hassan, who weaves all these threads into an emphatic moral chronology that is at once personal and analytical, blaming the intifada's demise on multiple factors. On the international front, he joins Isam in decrying the influence of American machinations on the Middle East:

After the Gulf War, you know, they are talking about a new international system, and it means a new—in my opinion—a new occupation, but in a different way. And sure, the United States now, they are the gods of the world, they control every part of this world, and we are one of those parts. . . . I'm sure they told Israel that we have to find a solution, which is not good for us [i.e., the Palestinians] at all. . . . I always considered that this kind of solution is like a cupboard—it's like, if the Palestinians start, they will lead others. We are the gate, actually, for the Arab countries—if they enter our gate it means goodbye for these kinds of countries. . . . I think it's a policy made from the U.S. side. They never—they always fight for Israel. I don't like to talk about this too much, but at least there is an idea that there is a plan for the Middle East, and we are part of this plan, and what is happening now, it's a result of the Gulf War, you know? The United States, they are bad for lots of things in other countries . . . and I knew that before, but they proved that in the Gulf War. They're talking about human rights, they're talking about freedom, and they're just talking, writing this in the papers, no more.

According to Hassan, it is this postwar international system—George Bush's famous "New World Order"—that forced the Palestinians to negotiate from a position of weakness and to draw the Arab states into the "cupboard" of negotiations. Yet for all his talk of global "plans" orchestrated by the United States, he emphasizes that the end of the intifada was largely self-inflicted, a product of the Palestinian leadership's decision to usurp the authority of the movement, asking people inside the West Bank and Gaza to follow the direction of PLO-approved leaders who suddenly began coming out of the woodwork:

J: When do you think the intifada ended?

H: Ended? It's a difficult question. When our leaders started controlling the intifada—do this, do that, you know? Give this, don't give that. . . . Because in our history always, unfortunately, we lacked for a real leadership, and if there is a strong leadership, it means strong action. . . . But when the people who—I've never heard about them, in Jordan, in Lebanon, started showing other people all over the world, actually tried to invest the intifada for them, not for us, the people here. . . . It's simple—they killed the intifada. They never helped the intifada. When you start giving people money and start controlling things and start putting people in positions—they killed the intifada. They put people in the wrong places, and you know, these places do not belong to these people, to these kinds of people. Lots of leaders, I [had] never heard about them, and they consider themselves that they are leaders, and I [had] never heard about these people. Strange.

J: How did you feel when that started to happen?

H: You know, I was disappointed, really. Especially when we lost lots of dear people, lots of people arrested, lots of people injured, lots of people [who] suffered. We deserved more. And they led the intifada the wrong way . . . and we paid for that. We are the victims.

These leaders, he says, included not only PLO officials on the "outside," but also local leaders, such as Hanan Ashrawi, who functioned as representatives of the Palestinians living under occupation during the initial phases of the "peace process." Recalling Ashraf's image of the intifada as an aborted pregnancy, Hassan insists that these leaders "prevented" the uprising from reaching its logical conclusion; if they had "stayed away," he says, the intifada might have been able to produce a stronger negotiating position for the Palestinian side: "I'm sure the results would have been better than this. . . . Because I never dreamed about autonomy. We refused it in 1978, and we accept [it] in 1994, OK, and the first agreement was better than now, which is incredible!" Here it is useful to recall his assertion, quoted above, that "rich people" weakened the uprising by putting their own "interests" ahead of the nation's.

## Generation and Class: *"The Harvest Is Always for the Rich"*

> In the native's eagerness, the fact that he openly brandishes the threat of violence proves that he is conscious of the unusual character of the contemporary situation and that he means to profit by it. But, still on the level of immediate experience, the native . . . is most acutely aware of all the things he does not possess. The masses by a sort of (if we may say so) child-like process of reasoning convince themselves that they have been robbed of all these things. That is why in certain underdeveloped countries the masses forge ahead very quickly, and realize two or three years after independence that they have been frustrated, that "it wasn't worth while" fighting, and that nothing could really change.
>
> —Frantz Fanon

We have seen above how interviewees such as Hatem sometimes went out of their way to claim that the intifada in general had little to do with economics, and that their participation in particular was not motivated by "selfish" economic concerns. The arrival of the PA, however, placed the issue of economic status in an entirely new light for these young people, for the Authority—the major entry point for international assistance coming into the West Bank and Gaza—had the power to create jobs and, more generally, to distribute political and economic "rewards." That it has done so in a highly selective manner is not unexpected, especially given Arafat's history of maintaining power through the careful use of political patronage. What is most interesting in this context is that because of the changing post-Oslo realities, the language of class is finding its way back into the narratives of the same young people who insist, in other contexts, that personal economic goals have no relevance to discussions of the intifada.

While Balata has never been a classless community, the particular kind of relative privilege and deprivation that has emerged under the PA does not sit well with camp residents who tend to remember the past, including the intifada, in terms of circumstances that were shared rather than fought over. Part of what is at issue here is the shifting political meaning attached to labor. In the past, when jobs in Israel were widely available, working on the "other side" could only be justified if the work were divorced from its political context. Such a feat is more difficult under the PA: not only are many appointments transparently political, but the work itself is also seen as *national* work—one is building the nation, defending the nation, or (in the eyes of some) betraying the nation.

The self-representations of young people reveal complicated, sometimes contradictory attempts to come to grips with this new reality. On the one hand, as I have already noted, many are reluctant to find fault with individuals (especially friends and neighbors) who are benefiting from the PA's presence; on the other hand, for those who are not benefiting, self-assessments often involve bitter denunciations and reassessments of the sort that Fanon (in the passage quoted above) had in mind when writing about postindependence disillusion. Fanon's entire analysis of the dynamics of national liberation, of course, is animated by his conviction that decolonization—typically the moment when the nationalist elite takes over from the colonial power—is only the beginning of the struggle for the "masses." Given the general thrust of his argument, which operates on the assumption that national liberation programs can never deliver all that they promise, his description of popular dissatisfaction as "child-like" is strangely dismissive. His choice of imagery, however, is also suggestive if read against the grain, precisely because it raises the possibility of a link between generational identity and critical energy. The post-Oslo dilemma of the "intifada generation" indicates that young people are in a particularly suitable structural position to sense, and react to, the failures of national liberation—not because they are burdened by a "child-like process of reasoning," but because they have the highest national expectations *and* the highest personal expectations.

In many ways, the class-based analysis offered in the self-representations examined here can be boiled down to a conviction that the intifada should have yielded material results, and that these results should have been distributed evenly to all those who participated, suffered, and sacrificed during that intense period of political struggle. The realization that things have not worked out this way is perhaps the most painful, immediate evidence of generational fragmentation. Khaled, who spoke so scathingly about how "rich" people in Nablus sent their children away during the intifada (see chapter 5), summed up his feelings about the growing inequalities around him by telling me, with an air of resignation, that "the harvest is always for the rich" (*al-hasād dāyman lal-aghniya*). His metaphor is, in an important sense, a generational one that recalls Hassan's quotation of Chairman Mao and Ashraf's description of the intifada as having been "aborted" by the national leadership. Yet whereas the latter image calls to mind only unnatural death—the premature stoppage of the growth process—Khaled's choice of words suggests an even more troubling possibility, namely, that the process really did continue to its logical conclusion. To speak of the current period as a "harvest for the rich" implies that there *are* "fruits" to be picked, but that these fruits are not being given to those who deserve them. For Khaled, this reality was brought home when he applied for a scholarship (through the PA) to go to North Africa to continue his postgraduate studies. He was chosen to receive one of the scholarships, he told me, but at the last minute several names, including his, were removed from the list to make room for individuals who had close connections to the Authority.

In Khaled's narrative, economic frustration mingles freely with a kind of populist insistence that the "fruits" of the intifada and the "peace process" are not simply economic goods to be traded in an unequal marketplace, but rather political goods that have a national significance. Even as he complains that he has not reaped any of the post-intifada "harvest," he insists that "we never fought for positions, or to become rich," thus hinting that those who have received such "positions" (*manāseb*) are opportunists with motives less pure than his own. Hatem seems to concur with Khaled's general analysis of the situation, but is perhaps in a stronger position to make the point, given that he *did* receive a "position" (in the PA army), but chose to give it up for what he describes as political reasons:

*H*: I was in the army, the National Security, [for] ten months.

*J*: Why did you join?

H: Because I needed the work.

J: And what are the things that convinced you to get out?

H: Everything I believed in, I found out they were against it. . . . And there was a kind of discrimination against people from the inside. In the army, let's say you're one of the newcomers from the outside, and you make a mistake—they don't do anything to you. But if you're from the inside, they'll make you pay.

J: When you say their practices were against your beliefs, what do you mean?

H: Well, how can I say this? The most important thing for them, the most important thing, their first priority, is the security of Israel. It's the most important thing for them. Their behaviors aren't like our behaviors, their interests aren't like our interests, their way of thinking is different from our way of thinking .

J: You said last time . . . that you didn't fight in the intifada for Oslo, [that] what you have now is not what you had hoped for. Some people say the intifada was betrayed by the Palestinian leadership. What do you think about that?

H: That's right—it was sold.

J: Do you think it's over, or could the intifada continue?

H: The intifada, right now, has basically ended. But it could start up again at any time.

J: This betrayal of the intifada, is this why you think people are less willing to sacrifice now?

H: No.

J: Because you said last time that everyone was willing to sacrifice during the intifada, but now, not so much. So, why?

H: Because they didn't reap the fruits of the intifada. . . . And the practices of the Authority—let's say there's a *shab* who had a lot of responsibility during the intifada, and they just make him a soldier or something like that . . . and then they promote someone who was a collaborator with Israel. This makes people frustrated. . . . What I mean is, they killed the spirit of struggle.

For Hatem, then, the economic "fruits" come laden with political conditions by which he is not willing to abide. Earlier in the same interview, he argued that the PA is in fact making a concerted effort, under Israeli pressure, to dismantle the local Fateh cadres staffed by young men like himself. Recognizing that his own employment was likely a result of this effort, he dismisses the "positions" created for these seasoned activists as "marginal" (*hāmishī*) in terms of their importance within the larger security apparatus, insisting that the "good" jobs—those with real responsibility, a good salary, and the potential for advancement—have been reserved for "outside" people and others who did not pay their dues during the intifada.

Other young people treat the issue of economic justice more cautiously, displacing whatever personal concerns they have onto other individuals and groups who are often described in deliberate generalities. Majid's comment about the "steadfastness" of Palestinian merchants in the face of what he sees as the PA's unfair taxation policies fits into this category; the Authority, he suggests, is taking advantage of shopkeepers' willingness to pay high taxes out of a sense of national duty. Qassem agrees that the PA is exploiting the people: his favorite example is the April 1997 teachers' strike, when the Authority used its security apparatus to put down the protest by teachers who were organizing in order to improve their wages.[12]

For Intissar, a student and a political independent, the problem is at once personal and more general, for it is refugees like herself who are paying the steepest price for the failures of the "peace process":

J: How do you feel about what's happened here since the end of the intifada?

I: Well, we're in a transition period now, and maybe there are some small changes, but internally, for the people, there isn't anything. What has happened? Take the refugees, for example. We're refugees, and what have they done for us? Nothing. . . . If you go and ask a small child, "Where are you from?" he will tell you, "I live here . . . but I am from Jaffa. I'm not from here." This feeling is especially strong in the camps. The camps are saying, "What is this peace? What has it done for us? Nothing! It hasn't done anything. We're all alone."

J: Is life in the city, in the camp, much different because the soldiers aren't here any more?

I: Maybe it's a little better . . . but even when they left, they didn't really leave. Just over here, they're building a road so that they can come in here at any time . . . even into the city of Nablus, so nothing has changed. Just the other day I heard that they came in the middle of the night and arrested someone. . . . And as far as the economic situation goes in the camp, the majority of the workers still work in Israel, so what has changed about the economic situation? Nothing.

*J:* Most of those people still can't go back to work in Israel, isn't that right?

*I:* Right. There is no work after what happened [referring to suicide bombings].

*J:* What about the leadership of the Authority? How do you feel about them? Do you trust them as leaders?

*I:* Everything is at the beginning, and of course there are mistakes because nothing is perfect at the beginning. There are some weak points, but it's a start.

*J:* The economic situation here—you say that it's really bad right now, that people don't have jobs and so forth. Do you think that affects their political views?

*I:* Of course, because politics and economy are connected—this is natural.

Though it may not come across in this written transcription, there is a marked difference in Intissar's manner of speaking between the beginning and the end of the excerpt quoted here. Her response to the question about the PA leadership is flat, almost lifeless, suggesting a kind of reluctant defensiveness. When talking about refugees, she is infinitely more animated, her answers to her own rhetorical questions repeatedly punctuated by the emphatic phrase *"wala ishi!"* ("Nothing!"). The future of refugees, both those living inside Palestine and those in the diaspora, is one of the most contentious of the so-called "final status" issues in the negotiations between Israel and the PA. For a young Balata resident like Intissar—in her final year of university, preparing to enter the job market—the precarious situation of refugees is of the utmost immediacy. Her critique of the "peace process" encapsulates a fear that is deeply rooted in the experience and consciousness of an entire generation of camp dwellers: the realization that while they may not always be young, they may always be refugees, and the suspicion that because of this, they may always be poor.

These emerging discourses of class, then, testify both to the shifting and increasingly diversified concerns of Balata's young people as they move through the life cycle, and to the apparent staying power of many of the factors that drew them together, as an "actual generation," during the intifada. As their testimony indicates, such discourses are not always articulated directly: no one, for example, openly admits that they expected the intifada to lead to upward mobility. The frequent projection of economic motivations and analysis onto others (merchants, teachers) demonstrates the continuing influence of a nationalist narrative which holds that the goals of the nation and the true nationalist are motivated only by a concern for political justice and the redressing of historical grievances. At the same time, insofar as that narrative attempts to blunt the power of demands and social cleavages rooted in non-national identities, its inherent limitations are revealed by the articulation of class-based grievances. Indeed, these meditations on economic inequality provide an important clue to understanding the other discourses examined in this chapter, namely, those which construct "moral chronologies" and those which involve attempts to "move the goalposts" of the intifada. In each case, we find young people expressing what amounts to a deep dissatisfaction not with nationalism or nationality per se, but rather with the fact that the *narrative* of nationalism—a narrative built on references to progress, justice, and victory—has been derailed, rendered unrealizable by events that they themselves have witnessed on the heels of the intifada.

There are two points to be made here with respect to the particular kinds of dissatisfaction expressed in these personal narratives. On one level, these young people are reacting to the fact that the nationalist movement, whose leaders are the custodians of the dominant nationalist narrative, has failed to deliver on specific political promises which are assumed to have material analogues in the lives of ordinary people—a very familiar problem in the history of decolonization. On another level, however, some of their concerns (e.g., Hatem's passionate claim that the security forces are primarily interested in protecting Israel) are related to aspects of the Palestinian situation which appear to indicate that despite the claims of the national leadership, Palestine is not undergoing a process of decolonization at all. The reassessments and critiques offered by these members of the "intifada generation," in other words, are products simultaneously of factors common to many nationalist and other social movements, and of the peculiar dilemmas and contradictions facing Palestinians as a new century begins.

It is perhaps appropriate here to return to the two observations quoted at the start of this chapter, for they provide important keys to the generational aspect of these personal narratives. Alessandro Portelli invites us to consider the ways in which self-representations are inevitably colored and given much of their often dynamic nature by the struggles of individuals to maintain a sense of self that is at once changing and unchanging, a self that continues to reflect the influence of foundational events and principles even as it adapts to ever-shifting historical circumstances. His contention that "[a]t what time in the life cycle the story is told is . . . a crucial factor in its shape" likewise reminds us that such individual struggles are always informed, to a greater or lesser extent, by the generational identity of the teller. If the conceptual bases of popular memory research insist that narratives are overdetermined by the historical moment in which they are produced and articulated, then it is also the case that age (or, in Portelli's terms, a particular stage in the life cycle) is an important part of this "historical moment." The excerpt from Paul Weller's "When You're Young" offers a powerful reading of one such stage, the onset of adulthood, when the recognition of shrinking economic chances and growing personal responsibilities can trigger profound feelings of betrayal and disillusion on the part of individuals who see their youth as having been spent, in large part, anticipating and fighting for social change. Taken together, these two quotations help reveal the present moment, for the "intifada generation," as a time when the two elements that converge to produce generational solidarity—age and history—are both undergoing important transitions that are fundamentally unfinished. The consequent frustrations created in the lives of young people go a long way toward explaining why their self-representations are also unfinished, lacking in narrative closure.

As I noted earlier, the narratives treated in this chapter also suggest that what has happened in recent years is a growing fragmentation of the *jīl al-intifāda* into something approximating Mannheim's "generation units." It is crucial to remember here that these various "units" represent different ways of giving meaning to a set of experiences that continues to be, and always will be, shared by the members of this generation. This fragmentation is thus closely related to the passage of time—the "drama" to which Mannheim pointed was, after all, the "drama of their *youth*"—in the sense that as the temporal gap between the "drama" and its remembrance continues to grow, previous feelings of generational unity are ever more likely to be affected by variations in personal circumstances and by varying narrative responses to the differences between "then" and "now." In such a context, it is hard to imagine that the current situation could be as productive of generational unity for the young people I interviewed as was the intifada itself. To be sure, their narratives still contain appeals to values and goals perceived as unifying all young people (even all Palestinians): fairness, justice, the "liberation of Palestine." The same narratives, however, also demonstrate that it is getting harder for them to sustain this perception in the face of mounting evidence that the "harvest" of the intifada is not being shared equitably. For the time being, the possibilities of generational solidarity and generational fragmentation appear to be coexisting uneasily not only in the daily lives of these young people, but also, increasingly, in their memories.

## Moving the Goalposts: Reassessments of the Intifada

All this testimony, of course, takes on additional meaning in light of subsequent events, including the reemergence of Ariel Sharon, the second intifada, the isolation of Yasser Arafat, and the second U.S. war on Iraq. At the time of the interviews, however, another full-scale uprising in the West Bank was not on the horizon. As Palestinians looked back on the first intifada, they were confronting a dilemma that faces most social movements: the sharp disjuncture between initially stated goals and achieved results. That the goals of the intifada were both understood and widely shared by Palestinians in the West Bank and Gaza is suggested by the near-unanimity with which interviewees responded when I asked them to identify what these goals (*ahdāf*) had been:

> *Hussein*: Complete liberation—all of Palestine, not just the West Bank and Gaza Strip.
> *Issa*: To express refusal of the occupation and anger at what happened in Gaza, and to have our independent state.
> *Jamila*: The goal was the liberation of our land, as with any people living under occupation. And as refugees, we had the hope of returning [to our homes].
> *Samer*: The main goal was to get rid of the occupation and to have an independent state—there were no other goals.
> *Ayman*: The liberation of Palestine.
> *Hatem*: The main goal was the withdrawal of the occupation.
> *Nabil*: The goal was liberation and victory. . . . All of Palestine, including al-Aqsa—to fly the flag over al-Aqsa.

> *Hassan*: To get freedom, first of all, and then to make a state and to have Jerusalem as its capital, and to travel, to live a normal life.
>
> *Intissar*: Of course [the goal] was freedom and the exit of the occupation from here.
>
> *Khaled*: It was like a liberation war—for freedom, for justice, for dignity, all of which we lost under the occupation. But the main goal was freedom.

Not surprisingly, these responses closely parallel the goals the UNLU had advanced publicly on behalf of the movement, goals repeated regularly by Palestinian leaders ever since. In a similar way, the political results of the intifada—the "peace process," the granting of "limited self-rule" to Palestinians, the creation of the PA—are not a subject of dispute. One thing that unites the interviewees across various lines of division, then, is that as they go about the process of constructing and reconstructing intifada memories and placing these memories within broader narratives of identity, all are confronted with what amounts to a political shortfall: the failure, so far, of the nation to achieve the fundamental goals that animated the uprising.

As early as 1995, Salim Tamari argued that while Palestinian intellectuals had begun to undertake a "rethinking of Palestinian consciousness" with respect to earlier periods of the nation's history, there was a glaring need for a "proper critique . . . regarding the character of the intifada itself" (10–12). Such a systematic critique, the outlines of which appear in Tamari's earlier commentaries on the uprising (1990; 1991a), is not to be found in the self-representations of the young people I interviewed, nor is it to be expected given their obvious investment in the "drama of their youth." Instead, with the intifada essentially off-limits, their critical energies are instead turned in other directions. In the forceful assessments of the spectators, for example, we have already seen that one response to the gap between goals and results is to condemn the results, placing the blame squarely on the national leadership for failing to remain true to its goals. Hatem, for example, describes the PLO as having "sold" the intifada; he thus adds his own distinctive metaphor to the gallery that includes Salim's "peace drama" and Ashraf's "abortion." In the following interview excerpts, Khaled pointedly notes that from his perspective, the major goal and the major failure of the uprising are one and the same:

*J*: In your mind, what were the goals of the intifada when it started?

*K*: It was like a liberation war—for freedom, for justice, for dignity, all of which we lost under the occupation. But the main goal was freedom.

*J*: Are there ways in which you think the intifada failed to achieve certain goals? What do you think were some of the shortcomings of the intifada?

*K*: Freedom—we failed in this respect.

For those who are less comfortable with this kind of open critique, yet who are equally aware of the fact that the "liberation of Palestine" has not arrived, there are at least three possible narrative responses. The first is to revise one's own claims about what the goals of the uprising were in the first place, such that the achieved results appear to match more closely what was envisioned from the beginning. The second is to argue that the goals changed along the way, with new concerns supplanting outcomes once seen as central to the struggle. A third response is to focus on other negative effects of the uprising (on education, for example) or to emphasize more immediate personal goals, thereby shifting the energy of the critique away from the question of ultimate political successes and failures and toward areas that can be addressed more easily even in the absence of political "liberation." Each of these responses represents a kind of narrative defense mechanism, an attempt to "move the goalposts." They are reactions to a present moment that is fundamentally unsatisfactory—a present that appears "incomplete" from the perspective of the future once promised in the past but not delivered. As such, they are examples of a process that is one of the building blocks of popular memory: the practice of resolving, recasting, or displacing observed and experienced contradictions through the construction of new stories and identities, and the strategic alteration of old ones.

Issa is an excellent example of an individual who takes the first of these approaches. Consistent with his tendency to avoid direct criticism of the PA, he tries to make the best of the current situation by shifting the terms of reference. His statement that the intifada was launched "to express refusal of the occupation and anger at what happened in Gaza, and to have our independent state," came in the first of our two interviews, in response to a direct question about the goals of the uprising. Toward the end of the subsequent conversation, however, he offered a different view:

I asked him whether there were things that the intifada had failed to accomplish, and he replied that the "main goal" of the uprising had been to "let the world hear our voice," and that this goal had been realized completely. Here Issa works backward from the present in order to claim that one of the identifiable achievements of the uprising had been, in fact, the nation's primary objective all along.

This is not, however, simply a case of looking at the past through conveniently rose-colored glasses; it is also an intervention in the present, specifically in a highly charged political battle between the PA and its opponents. Issa pointedly insists that the positive attention the intifada received was a result of stonethrowing, whereas suicide attacks did little to advance the goals of the movement. Though he does not explicitly identify the political forces behind each type of action, the implication is clear: the tactics of the Islamic movements threatened to undermine the public relations gains the masses had won, gains which have been reaped largely by the faction he supports. In revising his description of the intifada's goals, then, he takes what might appear to be a defensive move and turns it into a mechanism for celebration and indirect political accusation, suggesting that the uprising—narratively refigured as a preliminary stage on the road to liberation rather than the immediate catalyst for liberation itself—succeeded *despite* the efforts of the Islamic movements to lead it in a self-defeating direction.

In contrast to Issa, Intissar and Jamila take a more independent position, stepping back and observing that over the years of the intifada, "the people" (*al-nās*) made regular adjustments in their own expectations. Clearly these changes in popular goals are not unrelated to changes in the way the national leadership articulated its own goals and strategies during the shift from mass revolt to political negotiation. Intissar, for example, echoed the sentiments of many when she identified "freedom" and an end to the occupation as the goals of the uprising; later, however, she noted that "the feelings of the people changed in many ways by the end of the intifada." When I prodded her to specify some of these changes, she offered an explanation that can be read in a number of ways. As the number of martyrs continued to climb and the politicians began negotiating, she said, "peace became the goal." Perhaps being deliberately noncommittal in her assessment, she allows for the possibility that when the leaders replaced the rhetoric of "liberation" with the language of "peace," the people had no choice but to follow; but she also leaves room for the interpretation that in the end, "peace" (in the sense of the absence of daily, violent clashes with Israeli troops) was more important than the achievement of a particular political arrangement—or, to look at it from another perspective, that the Israeli state, through its repression of the uprising, succeeded in reaching a point beyond which Palestinians were not willing to go.

Jamila speaks of a similar shift in national goals, but her narrative is more explicitly judgmental. During our two conversations, she addressed the issue of goals three times, each time raising her level of critical distance from events and popular attitudes:

Statement 1: The goal was the liberation of our land, as with any people living under occupation. And as refugees, we had the hope of returning [to our homes].

Statement 2: At the beginning of the intifada . . . everyone was like one hand. There had been days [i.e., before the intifada] when someone from the city wouldn't even talk to someone from the camp. But in the intifada years, or at the beginning at least, everyone was like one hand. That was the first stage. In the second stage, there were a lot of political and economic changes . . . and we don't know if it's better or not.

Statement 3: [Responding to a question about her earlier statement that the people were like "one hand" at the start of the intifada:] Those relationships still exist, but [people's] concerns are different now. At the beginning, there was one goal, but now, after they said that we have peace, everybody has their own business.

It is not difficult to imagine that her construction of a moral chronology here—juxtaposing earlier unity with later selfishness—may derive from the conviction that in terms of official priorities, popular mobilization has been shunted aside in favor of more lucrative types of "business." Yet like Intissar, she suggests that to place the blame squarely on political leaders may be a convenient move that doesn't tally with observed social dynamics, for it is also "the people" who are unwilling to remain true to their original goals. Thus these narratives expose cracks in two kinds of nationalist myths, calling into question the celebratory pronouncements of political elites while also attempting to give the lie to uncritical, populist readings in which leaders, seen as ultimately loyal only to their own interests, end up "betraying" the eternally unwavering goals of the people.

Jamila's own "business," as noted above, involves working with individuals who suffer from physical and psychological disabilities as a result of the intifada. This work is, in effect, a practical counterpart to the third type of "moving the goalposts": ignoring or minimizing the issue of political outcomes and turning one's attention to what might be called internal problems. Like many of the young people I interviewed, Jamila responded to a question about the intifada's "failures" not by foregrounding the disappointments of the "peace process" (though she doesn't discount these entirely), but rather by pointing to troublesome social and economic aftereffects, particularly in the area of education: the disruption and neglect of schooling, she says, was the "most important" negative effect of the uprising. In the same vein, Hussein argues that the decision to put activism over education was the greatest "mistake" of the "intifada generation," a mistake whose long-term implications are now coming into focus as they confront a job market in which a *tawjīhī* certificate is a minimum requirement for many positions.

Once again it is helpful here to return to Portelli's reminder quoted at the start of this chapter ("At what point in the life cycle the story is told is, however, a crucial factor in its shape"), for these narratives of reassessment are arguably the product of a particular moment in the collective life of the "intifada generation," a time when many are finding themselves increasingly concerned with the most "traditional" of values: work, education, family. Even Ayman, an activist who generally extols the virtues of confronting the Israelis as he did in the September clashes, speaks of education in a way that suggests that he is beginning to make a similar reassessment. In discussing the many verbal battles he had with his father during the intifada, he recalls that Abu Nimr used to try to convince him that education and "science" could also be used as weapons against the enemy, that Palestinians could combat Israel by becoming an "educated people" (*shaᶜb mitᶜallem*). Why, Abu Nimr wanted to know, couldn't his son choose "science" (*ᶜilem*) instead of "stones" (*hijāra*)? At that point, says Ayman, he simply told his father that the "military" side of the battle was more important. In the context of a struggle for national liberation, he insists, one must be prepared to sacrifice everything — including education — for the sake of the cause. Nonetheless, when asked about the intifada's failures, he puts education at the top of the list — an admission, albeit an indirect one, that perhaps his father was right all along.

What we see here is a kind of displacement, a narrative substitution in which these young people are testifying to their increasing distance from the former field of political action, but also attempting to redefine the kinds of activities that constitute political action. Narrators who make this sort of move are implicitly responding to the argument that Jamila makes concerning the reemergence of selfishness in the aftermath of the intifada by insisting that to focus on one's own education (or any other personal goals) is, in fact, to engage in another form of what Palestinians call "national work" (*ʿamal watani*). In chapter 3 we saw this dynamic at work in Isam's explanation as to why he is so desperate to leave Palestine—not to abandon the national struggle altogether, but to "recharge" himself so that he can return at a later time to continue his political activity. Samira, who married in 1997, notes that people are now most concerned with feeling "secure" and "stable," with having a "prosperous life." Such a suggestion would have been anathema during the intifada, with its emphasis on individual and collective sacrifice.

The assumption behind the displacement I am describing, of course, is that effective political action is either impossible, inadvisable, or simply useless. In this sense, the interpretations that emerged during the interviews are closely related to the actions that many Palestinians are taking in their own lives as they try to adjust to the realities of the post-Oslo situation. In the years following the establishment of the PA, for example, there was much discussion in Palestine about how politics was becoming "professionalized," and how the reserves of popular energy that had once gone into the intifada were being directed toward other spheres of activity—needing, in effect, somewhere to go. It is in light of this bifurcation that we can read the exponential growth in the number of local nongovernmental organizations (NGOs) in recent years,[13] the burgeoning debates about "civil society" among Palestinian intellectuals,[14] and the phenomenal amount of independent research (socioeconomic surveys, unofficial "peace plans," public opinion polls, "thought papers") being done in local think tanks and universities. It is difficult to escape the conclusion that much of this activity is rooted in the same sentiment that is driving Balata's young people to throw themselves back into education and the search for "stability": the hope that all their efforts will, at some point in the future, come to have a more direct impact on the political process.

To put it another way, the frenzy of nongovernmental activity in Palestine as a whole can be read as a larger, national response to the dilemma which young men such as Khaled and Hussein have voiced:

> J: What do you think needs to be done in order to achieve freedom then?
>
> K: There is nothing to do. . . . We have enemies coming from two directions—one inside us and between us,[15] and the Israelis.
>
> J: In terms of freedom, do you feel there is freedom here to talk about politics?
>
> K: [In English:] Yes, there is freedom to talk—whatever you want, you can talk—but who is listening?

> J: Personally speaking, at this point, how much do you think you are willing to sacrifice for what you consider to be the goals of the Palestinian struggle?
>
> H: Whatever I want to do, it won't change anything.
>
> J: Do you think most people here feel the same way that you do in terms of whether their actions can change anything?
>
> H: Well, maybe the one who carried out the suicide operation inside Tel Aviv thought he could change something. . . . But Hamas did all these things, and they couldn't even get their own leader released from prison. Now if *all* the people wanted to do something, then things could change.

In light of such statements, attempts to "move the goalposts" come across as efforts to work out, through the mechanisms of popular memory, the frustrating question of what to "do" when it feels like there is "nothing to do."

# 7

# Postscript
## *A Permanent State of Emergency (continued)*

A thirty-three-year-old man is speaking to a reporter from the *Toronto Star* in Balata camp, which the reporter refers to as a "destitute rabbit's warren of back alleys." The young man, who calls himself "Abu Walid" in the *nom de guerre* tradition of an earlier generation, is one of the leaders of the al-Aqsa Martyrs Brigades, formed by Fateh activists in the midst of the "second intifada." Israel, in his view, is a "spoiled child that will give us nothing," and he vows that he and his comrades will continue to launch attacks as long as Israel continues its oppression of the Palestinian people. When speaking of the Palestinian leadership, he is both defiant and occasionally deferential, but his claim of independence is unmistakable:

> They offered us large sums of money to annex us into the Palestinian Authority infrastructure. They wanted to buy our obedience. It was an insult. We don't want their money. We are people who have lost all our friends, our leaders, our relatives. Some are dead, others are in jail. . . . We are not in a position to embarrass Arafat. If he approached us, we would give him the utmost respect. But even Arafat has no control in the field. We do not work on remote control for anybody.

"Abu Walid" is a member of the "intifada generation," born in the early years of the Israeli occupation. He has seen Israeli and Palestinian leaders alike try to bring some "order" to Balata while speaking of "peace," yet his words suggest a confidence that it is he, not they, who will determine the future of Palestine.

Meanwhile, Balata residents come by the hundreds to view a special exhibition devoted to the "martyrs" of the latest intifada. They do so, no doubt, after making sure that it is safe to go outside, for the *mukhayyam* remains subject to regular invasion by the IDF. The soldiers, in turn, are increasingly subject to the critical gaze of international solidarity activists, many of whom—like Rachel Corrie, who was crushed to death by an Israeli bulldozer while her own leaders in Washington kept silent—are in their late teens and early twenties. One such activist, John Heaney, sends a dispatch from Balata:

> It's 1:30 a.m. and I'm sitting in a plastic chair on the roof of the house that I sleep [in]. I'm terrified, chain smoking, even though I don't smoke, listening and waiting and preparing myself for what might happen at any moment. The army are in the camp where my house is, forty foot soldiers making their way through the narrow alleys. . . . The only time I break the silence is when I go into the small room with a sink in it beside my bedroom to get sick. . . . Out of the seven weeks I was in Balata Refugee Camp there were two nights that the Israeli army actually did carry out a "genuine" operation. On one of these nights they entered the camp to arrest a wanted man, a twenty-two-year-old vegetable lorry driver. When they finally got to the house of the wanted man at 3 a.m. they discovered he wasn't there, but they remained in the house for two hours questioning and terrorising the family and beating [another] son until he had a fit. All this was done after they seemingly mistakenly entered three other houses but admitted each time that they were wrong. Despite being at the wrong house the terror was no less. At the second house rather than banging on the door with their M16s they set explosives at it and blew it off, destroying the door and damaging the walls inside and the walls of the house opposite. The explosive also smashed a window of the house, covering the mother who was sleeping inside under it with broken glass. At the third house, discovering again they had made a mistake they took the father of the house at gunpoint and used him as a human shield to the house where the wanted man lived.

This is the situation in Balata as this book goes to press. As David Byrne might ask, how did we get here? Indeed, after all that has passed since December 1987—the battles large and small, the countless deaths, the false euphoria of "autonomy," the endless handshakes and "peace plans," the U.S. wars—have we gotten anywhere? If we know anything, we know that the answer is closely tied to the fate of the *jīl al-intifāda,* for it is they who understand as well as anyone that "peace" can be a weapon, and that the "state of emergency" in Palestine can be permanent.

## Oslo, the PA, and the "Intifada Generation"

The seeds of "Abu Walid" lie, of course, in the very events that are the subject of the memories explored in this book. More fundamentally, the seeds lie in the history of a movement (Zionism) whose historical trajectory leads from nineteenth-century European racism and colonialism to a full-scale attempt at what Baruch Kimmerling (2003) calls the "politicide" of the Palestinian people. In a more immediate sense, however, the seeds also lie in the Oslo agreements and in the creation of the PA. In hindsight it is clear that the promise of Oslo—that it would end the Israeli occupation and pave the way for real Palestinian independence—was as much of a myth as its initial critics said it was. In the agreements, the Palestinian leadership put their signatures to measures that actually formalized many basic elements of the colonial regime. In this sense, the comparison commonly made between Israel/Palestine and South Africa, which was going through its own transition in the 1990s, was temporally misplaced: on the ground, post-Oslo Palestine looked more like the South Africa of the 1950s, after the apartheid system was consolidated, than the "new" South Africa of 1994.[1]

As Graham Usher (1999) has noted, for example, the creation of Palestinian security forces represented not an Israeli concession to the PA, but rather the operational face of the PA's major obligation to Israel under the asymmetrical terms of Oslo II: to carry out "internal security" functions within the territories under Palestinian "autonomy." At the time, many Palestinians saw the creation of the security forces—of which there were twelve branches by late 1996—as a source of pride and a symbol of impending national sovereignty.[2] Structurally speaking, however, the forces functioned as something akin to a "native police force" essentially subcontracted to take over counterinsurgency tasks which the occupying army was only too glad to relinquish after the intifada. The late Israeli Prime Minister Yitzhak Rabin admitted as much in September 1993, arguing that the PA "will be better at it than we were because they will allow no appeals to the Supreme Court. . . . They will rule by their own methods" (quoted in Usher 1999, 154). It did not take long for residents of the West Bank and Gaza to understand what Rabin was talking about. When I began my conversations with Palestinians in the aftermath of the September 1996 clashes, many scholars were busy analyzing the dynamics of Palestinian "state building," but the young people I interviewed saw little reason for optimism. Instead I found members of the *jīl al-intifāda* reacting to the emerging statelike structure of the Authority—the formal institutional embodiment of their national liberation struggle—with what might be described as a collective shrugging of the shoulders.

In some cases, using its Oslo-enshrined authority, the PA was initially able to neutralize or even incorporate much of the political power residing in the erstwhile "children of the stones." At the same time, some of the PA's early attempts to demonstrate the extent of its limited territorial sovereignty backfired, often because many young people were unwilling to countenance the arbitrary exercise of power by any authority, Israeli or Palestinian, in the absence of a more equitable political solution. Conflicts between the PA and the "intifada generation" contributed to the generational fragmentation discussed in chapter 6 and arose, provocatively, in some of the same locations that figure so prominently in memories of the intifada: schools, prisons, and the streets. Young people who had once joined together to confront soldiers, negotiate with teachers and headmasters, and mobilize against prison authorities suddenly found themselves facing each other as demonstrator and policeman, employed and unemployed, prisoner and interrogator.

The security forces, then, are important not only for what they do, but also for who they are. While there is no available data on the makeup of the various branches, it is clear that in addition to longtime PLO fighters brought in from outside, these forces included large numbers of former intifada activists who were looking for work. The starting monthly salary of 800 shekels (roughly $250) for a soldier in the regular Palestinian police, while not enough to support a family, nonetheless represented a significant upgrade for those who were previously jobless. For its part, the PA also got something out of the arrangement: an opportunity to limit and channel the energies of thousands of potentially active young people.

The primary example of this, according to Usher, was the Preventive Security Forces (PSF), which were formed largely through the wholesale incorporation of the groups of militant intifada activists known as the Fateh Hawks and Black Panthers, thereby giving these men "a political and social status commensurate with their former role as fighters."[3] It is this "former role" that constituted the value of these men as intelligence operatives—after all, they "knew the street"—but also their potential threat to the PA. Complicating this picture even further was the fact that young people in the security forces obviously still had close connections with their age-mates outside the Authority; consequently, many internal "security operations" carried out by PA forces involved bringing these two very different trajectories of the "intifada generation" into contact with each other, with unpredictable and potentially explosive results.

There are indications that this tension spilled into the open during the September 1996 clashes, when the leadership was unable to prevent PSF members from weighing in on the side of Palestinian demonstrators.[4] This outbreak of violence, however, was preceded earlier in the year by a series of events involving Palestinian students and PA and Israeli security forces, events which affirmed the continuing importance of schools (or in this case, universities) as sites of post-intifada struggle. PA-Israeli security collaboration had increased dramatically following a series of suicide bombings in late February and early March 1996 which killed more than fifty Israelis. On 28 March, a month of mass arrests culminated in Israeli troops staging a predawn raid on three villages near Birzeit University and detaining 370 Palestinians, including 280 students (roughly 10 percent of the entire student body) who were "tied up, blindfolded and led to a football field for questioning."[5] Given the large number of Fateh supporters who were detained, it appears that the action was designed in part to impress upon those students the cost of failing to cooperate with efforts to combat the "terrorism" of the Islamist movements.

By this time it was clear that the PA itself was taking steps to demonstrate its own cooperation, having arrested some fifteen Birzeit students during March.[6] On 29 March, a day after the Israeli raid on Birzeit, Palestinian police forcibly dispersed a crowd of five hundred people who rallied outside Nablus prison to demand the release of jailed Hamas supporters. The following day, in an unprecedented show of force, hundreds of uniformed and plainclothed members of the PA security forces entered the campus of An-Najah University in Nablus. The circumstances of the raid are the subject of some dispute: one source, quoting American news reports, claims the police were attempting to put down a "pro-Hamas demonstration,"[7] while a local human rights group counters that the "demonstration" was a press conference called by students "from all major political parties" to air their grievances concerning the continuing detention of dozens of students in Israeli and PA facilities.[8] Several of the young people I interviewed were on the campus that day, and their recollections add to the uncertainty. Samira describes the occasion as a joint "celebration" (*ihtifāl*) by Hamas and the PFLP; Ashraf says that Hamas and Fateh were holding a public "dialogue" (*hiwār*), with some journalists present, about issues of democracy and interfactional cooperation; and Intissar remembers only the violence and panic that ensued once the police entered the grounds of the university. On the latter point, there is much more consistency among available sources, including the initial LAWE press release:

> [A]rmed plain-clothed security forces raided the university and began shooting in the air. Regular security forces entered the university directly afterwards, also began shooting in the air and beating panicking students with clubs. The police also beat at least one journalist, and confiscated the cameras of several others. Security forces shot tear gas into the crowd, injuring 10 people. Two students were injured from the gunfire.

In such accounts, the unstated parallel with intifada events is plain: with descriptions of tear gas, beatings, injuries, and the harassment of journalists, one could easily be reading a description of Israeli troops attacking demonstrators in the streets of any Palestinian town, village, or refugee camp.

It is significant that even though PA actions have been roundly criticized in the growing literature on the post-Oslo period, the police raid on An-Najah has largely disappeared from the record. In direct contrast to this absence, the events of 30 March play a pivotal role in oral testimony precisely because of the ways in which police actions provoked a renewed generational solidarity among students of all political persuasions:

> Eventually the police were evacuated, because of phone calls from the President [Arafat], and we stayed in the university [i.e., as a sit-in], and we found that while they were justifying themselves by saying that they stormed the university in order to beat Hamas people, most of the people injured were from Fateh, not from Hamas. (Ashraf)

> At first we couldn't believe [what was happening]. . . . I was in a lecture, and it was at the end of the lecture, so we went out, and all the students—even those who were supporters of the Authority—had turned against the Authority, because they are not supposed to enter the Univer-

sity. We've known for a long time that it's forbidden for the Israelis or any strangers to enter the campus . . . so it really astonished us. (Intissar)

If we take these personal narratives seriously, then we must at least consider the possibility that the primary significance of the An-Najah raid lies not in its relationship to the "peace process," but rather in the PA's decision to storm what was, for students, a protected space where political differences are often superseded by the perceived need for student unity. Ashraf, Intissar, and Samira all imply that this unity is justified by the fact that the security forces, in point of fact, acted not to intimidate students from a particular faction or factions, but instead attacked indiscriminately. Looking at it from the PA's point of view, one can see that the raid may have served a dual purpose: to Israeli and American authorities, the action could be sold as an attempt to crack down on Hamas, while to the Authority's Palestinian supporters, it could be sold as an effort to demonstrate that internal dissent would not go unpunished—with the implication that all students, by the simple fact of generational (as opposed to factional) identity, were potential objects of suspicion and repression.

In the eyes of many students, this kind of interpretation was bolstered when twenty-two-year-old Fateh activist Taysir al-Lawzi was shot dead on 1 April at a checkpoint in al-Bireh. Fateh accused the PA's General Intelligence of carrying out the killing, but the PA initially offered no explanation.[9] Armed with a growing list of grievances, the students took action, and they appear to have done so in a largely nonpartisan fashion. On 2 April, Fateh and Hamas supporters at An-Najah launched a boycott of classes, calling for the identification and punishment of individuals responsible for the attack on their campus. The next day, a reported one thousand students from several institutions (Birzeit, Bethlehem University, and Abu Dis Law College) converged on Ramallah and demanded to speak with President Arafat to air their concerns.[10] Those who came from Birzeit were rebuffed in their efforts to hire transportation to take them to Ramallah, alleging that the local bus company, having been threatened by PA security forces, had refused to provide buses for the trip. The students then walked to Ramallah, surging past police officers who briefly fired in the air but "utilised enormous restraint," according to one university employee. Upon arriving at the PA General Headquarters (a former Israeli prison) in Ramallah, the demonstrators presented their demands: an end to restrictions on students' freedom of movement, the release of all political prisoners, and public disclosure of the results of the investigation into the raid on An-Najah. In a remarkable concession to the "intifada generation" and an admission of the potential for political disruption it still represented, Arafat—the closest thing Palestinians have to a head-of-state—arrived on the scene within an hour:

> [T]he soldiers returned in a convoy of cars . . . and Palestinian President Yasser Arafat alighted to speak to the students. A woman shouted, "All we wanted to do was to come and speak with you but the Authority interfered with our buses." Arafat responded, "The second I heard that you were all here, I left the Council meeting to come and speak with you."

After Arafat addressed the crowd briefly, he agreed to meet with a delegation of representatives from each school. "The meeting was frank and friendly," reported a Birzeit public relations officer who was present for the students' conversation with Arafat:

> He [Arafat] spoke about the critical times in which we were living. "There are so many restrictions," Arafat told us. "I am not talking to you as a president, but as a comrade and we all have to work hard to build the Palestinian state. Please understand the situation." . . . Arafat promised to call for another meeting with the students or to send a reply to the demands in three days.

In this account, one is reminded of Hatem's memories of "negotiating" with school headmasters, shopkeepers, and other adults during the intifada, when the demands of the *shabāb* routinely carried the day. In this case the results appear to have been somewhat different. Arafat's reported words ("I am not talking to you as a president, but as a comrade") can be read as an attempt to defuse student anger vis-à-vis the PA—feelings rooted in a hierarchical relationship of ruler and ruled—by appealing to the horizontal solidarity of "comradeship." By all accounts, the strategy was successful, at least in the short term: "The overall feeling of students," the press release continues, "was that the whole day's events were very positive and a step in the right direction for Palestinian democracy."

When I arrived in September, however, students were talking bitterly about how Arafat had failed to keep his promises. Karim, a longtime Fateh activist at Birzeit, still had a photo of himself shaking hands with

Arafat mounted on the wall of his apartment, a sight which elicited sarcastic comments from the other young men who often congregated there to watch the television news, drink tea, and talk politics. By early November, many of the student detainees—as well as others who had been arrested for their involvement in the march to Ramallah—were still behind bars.[11] In Balata, young people talked about the long-term effects of the PA's decision to send its security forces into their university. Isam, for example, argues that the raid "damaged the Authority a lot," not only with students but also throughout the entire Nablus area, where Fateh is traditionally dominant. When the president came to Nablus shortly after the raid, Isam says, "no one came to see him"—this in sharp contrast to Arafat's triumphant first visit to the city, when residents turned out by the tens of thousands to welcome their returning leader.

One aspect of the An-Najah raid not mentioned in any documentary accounts of the event demonstrates the extent to which students are aware of their generation's growing fragmentation and are prepared to react strongly when confronted with its potential consequences. According to Isam, the security forces who stormed the campus that day were anything but an alien force unknown to the students. "Most of those who entered the university are people I know personally, and it really surprised me," he says, adding that in attempting to explain this situation to himself, he concluded that these police officers were clearly trying to "imitate" their Israeli counterparts: "They looked at the organization, the way of walking, the behavior of the occupation army, and it made an impression on them." During the raid, one individual in particular seems to have attracted the attention of students. This young man embodied both sides of the divide I have been describing: he was both a student at An-Najah and an employee of the security forces. On that day, Ashraf recalls, the student-soldier was off-duty—but armed—and was attending classes with the rest of the student body. When the police entered the campus, he apparently made his choice, taking out his pistol and shooting in support of his fellow PA employees. Other students such as Ashraf made a clear distinction when assigning blame, singling out the one person who had, in their minds, betrayed his fellow students. "He participated out of his own personal choice, not because he was under military command," Ashraf emphasizes. "And he was beaten, he was badly beaten [by the students]."

We find similar tensions in the prison, which during the intifada was a place to organize, to learn, and to continue the battle against the occupier on another terrain. After Oslo, this organic relationship between activism and imprisonment broke down, and prisoners—their location no longer a primary site of struggle within the context of a changing national project—were left waiting, hoping that their name would be called when the next round of releases was announced. The marginalization of these prisoners, of course, is partly a function of the fact that under the "peace process," the entire prison system was effectively divided into Israeli and Palestinian sections, with the PA often taking over many of the very facilities once used by the occupier. Not surprisingly, the early years of the PA saw prisoners using many of the same resistance tactics they had used in Israeli prisons, including hunger strikes.

A more disturbing continuity, even more sensitive for the PA, is the issue of Palestinians torturing other Palestinians. Whether we view these as cases of victims identifying with their oppressors or as manifestations of a deliberate PA policy (as some of the Authority's most vocal critics have charged), or both, there is little disagreement that the Palestinian security forces have joined their Israeli counterparts in using torture as part of their interrogations.[12] Even Samer, a loyal employee of the PSF, admits that torture has been a problem inside the security forces:

> J: There are a lot of psychologists who are trying to understand the effect of the intifada and the effect of being in prison on people here, and I think a lot of them have this idea that if someone is a victim of violence, whether it's in prison or somewhere else, that they may become that way toward someone else. They may—one way that they deal with the experience is by taking it out on someone else. I just want to get your opinion about that, whether you think that that's a danger for people here.
> S: Just like the Israelis did to us.
> J: Do you worry about that?
> S: Of course. . . . Take a small child—when he sees his father or his mother do something, he will try to imitate them. And the same goes for us, especially a people who has lived its whole life under occupation and injustice.

He then acknowledged explicitly the torture and killing of Yusuf al-Baba,[13] a case which had been in the news shortly before our interview, but insisted that the PA was taking steps to prevent the recurrence of such incidents. This view was in line with the most forthcoming of the various positions taken at the time by his superiors in the PA, namely, that cases of torture were aberrant reflections of individual behavior, not regular features of the new security regime. In an interview following the death of al-Baba, Attorney General Khaled al-Qidreh took the curious position that torture is wrong primarily because it can lead detainees to lie in order to stop the violence being visited on them. Some interrogators, he said, "do not understand the true nature of interrogation or that violence, which can result in extracting the truth, can also extract false information."[14]

At the time, the standard PA line on this question was that people suspected of Islamist sympathies were being detained without charge for their own "protection," that is, to keep them from being arrested by Israeli forces.[15] The notion of "protection" falls neatly into line with the idea of the state (or in this case, the Authority) as a paternal figure, recalling the case of one Palestinian detainee quoted in Amnesty International's (1996) report on PA human rights abuses. After undergoing sixteen hours of interrogation and torture in a PA detention facility, the man recalls, "They took me to an office and my interrogator said: 'I hope you did not mind this, please forgive us and take it as though you were hit by your father or brother.' He warned me not to tell anyone about this and then I was released" (19). If, as Samer suggests, Israelis taught their Palestinian captives to practice torture as a parent teaches his or her child, then it seems, to follow this educational-generational metaphor, that while some Palestinians were "growing up" and become "teachers" themselves, others were being forced to repeat their lessons.

Clearly, however, not all members of the *jīl al-intifāda* are comfortable with this endless hierarchical reproduction. Even among those young people who do not identify themselves with the opposition, the mass arrests and reports of torture were troubling developments. In interviews, some explicitly referred to the Authority's treatment of the opposition as a source of concern to them; others, perhaps making a concession to the climate of fear the PA was fostering through its security forces, spoke more vaguely of "wrong practices" and "mistakes." Ironically, Hamas supporters such as Qassem and Majid may have had the least to fear by speaking out, if only because their political affiliation alone made them suspect regardless of their opinions. For his part, Majid pointedly argued that while being in prison was an "honor" during the intifada, "nobody cares" about those prisoners who are held by the Authority because of their political views. While many Palestinians would undoubtedly view this as an exaggeration, Majid's distinction between two very different political contexts—yet another example of a "moral chronology"—suggests a concern that is common to many members of the "intifada generation" from across the political spectrum: the fear that the very establishment of the PA, regardless of the benefits it may bring to some, represents the eclipse of mass politics and the creation of a new apparatus that is disturbingly similar to the Israeli occupation in terms of the methods it uses to maintain "security" and crack down on dissent.

## (Re)emerging Discourses on Generation

1995: Researcher Sara Roy reports that the "institutionalization of violence" under the PA is creating a growing level of "militarization" throughout Gazan society, including in schools. She quotes a report by the Palestinian Center against Violence indicating that some 87 percent of schoolchildren claim to have been beaten in the classroom by teachers who, Roy suggests, are trying to "take back power" they lost during the intifada (1995, 77–78).

January 1996: The PA releases *Agenda for Social Renewal,* laying out "a five year programme to promote the welfare of Palestinian children." Despite its stated focus on "children," the report contains a section on youth. "For youth, the inheritance of the *Intifada* is, on the one hand, that of a group which has been *mobilized, empowered and toughened* by years of struggle and resistance," the authors acknowledge. "On the other hand, however, the same group has lost something in terms of educational and social development opportunities available in a more stable childhood. The channelling of the energies and commitment of this group into *socially constructive activities* is the challenge for this generation of young people" (1996, 35, emphasis in the original).

August 1996: The PA announces its intention to create a special police unit known as the "University Guards."[16] Students and administrators are swift and unanimous in their condemnation of the plan. "The formation of this apparatus constitutes a direct interference in the affairs of the students and their freedom," comments the head of Bethlehem University's student council, while another student leader asserts that "the practice of political freedom on campus should remain absolute," not subject to the "protection" of the PA.[17] By all indications, the plan is shelved.

September 1996: In conjunction with the "Day of Palestinian Youth"

*Figure 6.* PA Ministry of Youth and Sport poster commemorating Palestinian Youth Day, September 1996. (Tara LaFredo)

(*yōm al-shabāb al-falastīnī*), the PA Ministry of Youth and Sport produces a remarkable piece of political iconography (see Figure 6): a poster featuring a young man and woman depicted as national superheroes, resolutely facing forward, hands gripping the Palestinian flag as they lead the nation into the future. Their particular features—the man is strong and visibly muscular, the woman beautiful and wearing a traditional embroidered dress, both working together—suggest an uneasy mixture of conservative and progressive nationalist elements. The message, in other words, is inherently ambiguous: the young heroes are liberated, in the sense that they are sharing the load of political action; yet their resemblance is close enough that they may be brother and sister, and there is nothing to indicate that they are threatening to anyone but the nation's external enemies.

November 1996: Usama Bolos, the nine-year-old son of a prominent Ramallah restaurateur, is reportedly abducted on his way to school and held briefly before escaping or being released (it is unclear which) and subsequently becoming "a bit of a local celebrity" for his "poise and cocky resilience."[18] The impact of the kidnapping is perhaps magnified by the deaths, only two days before, of two thirteen-year-old boys who apparently discovered an Israeli land mine near the village of Anza, near Jenin.[19] In the public reaction to these two events, one senses a profound adult fear that society is losing its ability to protect its youngest members.

April 1997: Hussein, an eighteen-year-old Balata resident, says that many teachers are using "new rules" as an excuse to punish students, thereby exacting "revenge" for past humiliation at the hands of the students. The teachers' interpretations of these "new rules," he says, are often backed up by the threat of police intimidation; some students, he said, have actually received "notices" from the PSF warning them not to misbehave.

May 1997: In a group interview, three secondary school teachers in the Nablus area argue that extra "disciplining" of students is necessary as an antidote to negative changes that took place during the intifada. Nidal, a religion teacher who lives in Balata camp and is sympathetic to Hamas, pointedly notes that while many of his students still see themselves as "leaders" and have a "feeling of superiority" vis-à-vis their elders, they actually lack "discipline." His colleague Riyad, an Arabic teacher, agrees, asserting that these student attitudes have created a kind of "chaos" (*fawda*) in the schools.

January 1998: "The Younger Generation: Uncouth and Irresponsible," reads the headline of a 1998 *Jerusalem Times* op-ed piece whose author refers to changes in the behavior of young Palestinians as a "developing nightmare" with national implications: "This issue is of great importance, as the young generation of today will affect the futures of our brothers, sons, and the future of coming generations, who, ultimately constitute the future of our country."[20]

July 1998: A *Christian Science Monitor* feature article tells the story of Wael Hashash, a young Hamas supporter and Balata resident, who was married in a Hamas-sponsored mass wedding held in a Nablus stadium.[21] The event, which is described as an awkward mixture of secular celebration (fireworks and disco lights) and religious symbolism (security guards with T-shirts reading "Islam is the solution"), allowed thirty-five couples to get married for a fraction of the cost that is typically required for such an undertaking. Said Hashash, "If I wanted to make a wedding by myself, it would cost me $3,000. Instead, it's $70."

March 1999: Birzeit University holds its Student Council elections, traditionally seen as a bellwether of Palestinian public opinion.[22] Despite varying positions on the "peace process" (the primarily national issue at stake), all the parties take great pains to emphasize students' rights and the continuing political role of students after the intifada. "The unhealthy psychological atmosphere at the university does not help students in achieving their desired level of knowledge," argues the Change Bloc. "We see this as one of the main issues students are now facing, since youth and university students are supposed to be able to generate solutions for problems facing society and political movements and be able to pull society out of the situation it is in now." Candidates with the Jerusalem Bloc (affiliated with Fateh) stake out a cautious position, expressing support for the PA but admitting "reservations" related to "certain issues in the Oslo agreements." The An-Nahda Bloc (representing the Islamists) strongly critiques the PA's heavy-handed treatment of the political opposition, while the leftist Democratic Pole issues a cartoon using the image of Naji al-ʿAli's Hanzalla to highlight the danger which the PA's security apparatus poses to students. Sitting under a sign that reads "Intelligence Branch in the service of the people," a security official instructs his men in the treatment of a Palestinian prisoner: "Be careful not to insult him, hurt his feelings or torture him . . . bury him alive!" An-Nahda wins just under 45 percent of the vote, followed by the Jerusalem Bloc with 36 percent, the Democratic Pole with 18 percent, and the Change Bloc a distant fourth.

11 September 2001: Like everyone at my university, I am reeling from the shock of the attacks in New York and Washington. An angry colleague confronts me—I am well known on campus as a supporter of Palestinian rights—and says, "Did you see? The Palestinian children are dancing in the streets!" By the end of the week, the editor-in-chief of the *New Republic* has proclaimed that "We are all Israelis now." By the end of the year, as the frightening outlines of the "war on terrorism" come into view, it has become clear that we are all Palestinians now, for we are all potential targets of those who fight "terrorism."

April 2003: Eighteen-year-old Ahmed Khaled Khatib, a Balata resident whose family fled the town of Kfar Saba in 1948, blows himself up in the Kfar Saba train station. "You could sense a great sorrow in him," his aunt tells a British reporter. "He had no future, he could not love, he could not work, and he could not get married."[23]

July 2003: House Majority Leader Tom DeLay (R-Texas), a member of the Christian Zionist movement who has never set foot in Balata, critiques the Bush Administration's policy on Palestinian statehood. "I can't imagine this president supporting a state of terrorists, a sovereign state of terrorists," he argued. "You'd have to change almost an entire generation's culture."[24]

### *"Peace" as a Weapon*

In the process of completing this book, I have often thought of Khaled, the disgruntled former Fateh activist in Balata, who told me that soon there would be no more members of the "intifada generation" in the camp for me to interview. He was being facetious, but there is more than a grain of truth to his point. Since that time, the pattern of deaths, injuries, arrests, and other marks of political repression has only accelerated, and men and women of Khaled's age remain at the center of Palestinian attempts to resist their continuing dispossession at the hands of an Israeli state that is reckless, militarized, and ultimately suicidal. Events such as the September 1996 clashes and the early conflicts between students and the PA now undoubtedly pale in light of the killings in Jenin, the siege of Yasser Arafat's headquarters, the massive destruction in the Old City of Nablus, and the rest of Israel's Operation Defensive Shield.

That all this has taken place during a period when there is constant talk of "peace" on the lips of reporters, commentators, and politicians is an irony almost too disturbing to contemplate. Yet Palestinians are not unique in confronting this Orwellian reality; on the contrary, a look at cases from Latin America to Southeast Asia indicates that "peace" can, indeed, be a weapon, with devastating consequences for local communities, when it is actualized in the form of rampant privatization, systematic injustice, and the "war on terrorism." In the Palestinian context, Ariel Sharon has demonstrated in recent years that he is extremely adept at wielding the weapons of "peace," making regular trips to Washington even as he escalates his policies of colonial brutality. Sharon's political comeback in 2001, combined with the ascendance of a neoconservative agenda in Washington, has left Palestinians more impoverished, more desperate, and more demoralized than they have been in recent memory. Indeed, the emerging alliance between right-wing forces in the United States and right-wing Zionists in Israel suggests the troubling possibility that the so-called "Bush doctrine" is nothing more than a U.S. adaptation of long-standing Israeli policy—what we might call the "Sharon doctrine"—and that the Palestinians have been, in essence, the test subjects for the project that is now unfolding in Afghanistan, Iraq, and elsewhere.

We come back, then, to "Abu Walid" and to the "permanent state of emergency" I described, following Walter Benjamin, in the Prologue of this book. Many members of the "intifada generation" are now in their early thirties. Some, like Balata resident Nasser Awais, have responded to their "state of emergency" by taking up arms. Awais spoke defiantly to reporters ("Israeli troops will not enter the camp except over dead bodies") as the IDF assaulted Balata in March 2002 and subsequently declared himself the leader of the al-Aqsa Martyrs Brigades, saying it was a "medal of honor" to be designated a "terrorist organization" by the Bush Administration. The IDF demolished his home and Awais was soon arrested, allegedly wearing an explosives belt, and eventually sentenced to fourteen consecutive life sentences, plus fifty years, by an Israeli court after being convicted of planning a series of attacks inside Israel.

The Brigades are the product of continuing divisions within Fateh, and thus a product of Oslo and all that has come after it. The U.S. media typically shows little interest in understanding why such groups exist, investigating only the question of whether the PA is doing its post-9/11 duty and "cracking down" on its "militants." Yet these "militants" are, in a fundamental sense, no different from the rest of their generation. All are the product of the same set of historical and ideological forces: Zionism, the Israeli occupation, Palestinian nationalism, and, as I have tried to demonstrate in this book, the intifada experience that constitutes the "drama of their youth." All have witnessed things that no one should have to witness. "I have just seen them shoot a little girl in the street," said one thirty-five-year-old Balata resident as Israeli troops invaded the camp in June 2003. "They are trying to provoke us so that they can say that we are the terrorists."[25]

In the end, we must recognize that the "intifada generation" is both one and many. It is Nasser Awais, who sits defiantly in an Israeli prison; it is Ahmed Khaled Khatib, full of "great sorrow," who became a suicide bomber; it is Jamila, who chose to make a career out of dealing with the mental and physical scars of the intifada; it is Hatem, who feels betrayed by his own leadership; it is Isam, who lost his first chance at love and marriage after being arrested; it is Samer, who admits that his fellow security officers have tortured other Palestinians; it is Khaled, who insists that "the harvest is always for the rich." Most of all, it is a generation whose very existence is a contradiction between memories of the past, the injustices of the present, and the promises of a future that never arrives. "This world has to see your blood in order to believe you," said Ghassan as we discussed the willingness of so many young Palestinians to put their bodies on the line. As he continued, however, he made it clear that he held out little faith in his own statement. "The whole world will not give us our rights, and we know that—I'm sure of that," he said. "All the Palestinian people know that the world can't give us our rights, doesn't want to give us our rights. So we will continue to struggle." In such statements, one hears echoes of Benjamin, who argued that when faced with a "permanent state of emergency," one has a responsibility to "bring about a real state of emergency" in order to "improve our position in the struggle against Fascism." One also hears the words of Antonio Gramsci: "Pessimism of the intellect, optimism of the will." It could well be the motto of the *jīl al-intifāda*.

# Appendix
*The Intifada: A Brief Overview*

The misleading language of the "peace process" notwithstanding, the Palestinian struggle continues to be an anticolonial one rooted in the historical and material realities of Israeli domination. In this context, Israel's capture of the remaining territories of historic Palestine during the 1967 War appears not as an accident of war, but rather as an extension of a process of settler-colonialism whose scope was envisioned by Israel's founding fathers even before the establishment of the state in 1948. Zionist/Israeli policy in Palestine is perhaps best symbolized by inaugural Prime Minister David Ben-Gurion's deliberate decision not to declare any borders for the new state and by his stated attraction to the idea of "transferring" the Arab population out of Palestine through war, intimidation, or economic incentive. Ben-Gurion's successors have been strikingly consistent in holding to the basic aim of the Israeli state with respect to the Palestinians: the relentless pursuit of military and demographic superiority through an interlocking process of settlement, immigration, territorial expansion, and ideological work. Through numerous wars, seemingly endless rearrangements of governing coalitions, internal conflicts over issues of secularism and national-religious identity, and the rise of a determined Palestinian nationalist movement, the logic of "another goat and another acre" has continued to drive the colonization of Palestine.[1] Given this reality, Palestinian resistance appears not as rejectionism or obstructionism, but rather as a determined reminder to Israeli policy makers that conquered land is also populated land.

This history of Zionist/Israeli settler-colonialism also provides what is arguably the most relevant context in which to view the "peace process" of recent years. While Palestinians have refused to be "transferred" out of their homeland, Israel's policy of building settlements throughout the West Bank and Gaza (as well as new "bypass" roads which serve the settlements and further divide Palestinian communities from one another) has essentially negated the possibility of a true partition—that is, a division of the land into two fully sovereign states—by returning Palestine to the status it held under the British Mandate (1920–48) as a single territorial unit. Israel's leadership, realizing the implications of this—that it would eventually require either giving all Palestinians full political rights as Israelis (thereby negating Israel's identity as a Jewish state), or else removing them through expulsion or mass murder—has dealt with this dilemma by accelerating the process of granting "autonomy," and perhaps nominal "statehood" at some point, to selected Palestinian areas, hoping that the Palestinian leadership will accept such an arrangement as the "final status" of the West Bank and Gaza. It is not surprising, therefore, that many Palestinians have begun to speak of their situation in South African or Native American terms, viewing their disconnected population centers as "Bantustans" or "reservations" and talking once again about some version of a binational state—an idea firmly opposed by both national leaderships—as the only viable long-term solution to the conflict.

The fact that Israel and the Palestinians have waged this colonial-anticolonial struggle in a region that has long drawn an inordinate amount of attention from historians, journalists, religious sympathizers, and superpower strategists, perhaps helps explain why the intifada (now known as the "first intifada") is also one of the most heavily documented social movements of the twentieth century. The combined coverage of a few major newspapers, for example, provides a remarkably detailed history of the intifada, including everything from small skirmishes to major battles, from the initial demands of Palestinian activists to the secret negotiations that produced the Oslo accords. The picture is enriched and expanded by the wealth of available human rights information, which documents the vast array of less visible practices—mass arrests, torture, deportations, undercover assassinations, house demolitions, land confiscations—that constituted the bulk of Israel's counterinsurgency strategy during the uprising. Numerous scholarly monographs and edited collections, which continue to proliferate, offer yet another level of analysis.

Given the extent to which the intifada has been covered in these ways, I will give only a skeletal overview of the uprising here. Most observers credit an 8 December 1987 traffic accident, in which an Israeli truck driver struck and killed four Palestinians and injured several others in Gaza, with having sparked the intifada. The Israeli Defense Forces (IDF) attempted unsuccessfully to quell the subsequent protests with overwhelming force: the first six months saw nearly three hundred Palestinians killed, thousands injured, and over eight thousand arrested.[2] By early January 1988, the United National Leadership of the Uprising (UNLU), an underground group of leaders representing the four largest factions within the PLO, emerged to coordinate decisions and strategies concerning the uprising, which had come to be known as the *intifāda* (from the Arabic verb meaning "to shake off"). The UNLU functioned as a national counterpart to the many popular committees (*lijān shaᶜbiyya*) that had been formed in the preceding weeks in local communities throughout the West Bank and Gaza to deal with health, security, food distribution, and other pressing matters arising in the new situation. In order to publicize its specific directives, the UNLU issued regular, numbered leaflets (*bayanāt*) beginning on 8 January. Two political movements offering Islamist alternatives to the primarily secular UNLU, Hamas (the Islamic Resistance Movement) and Islamic Jihad, also made their appearance in the first year of the intifada via their own *bayanāt* and, later, a series of kidnappings, armed attacks, and suicide bombings.

From its inception, the intifada involved resistance strategies that can be grouped into three broad categories. *Local organization* took concrete form in the popular committees and built upon grassroots efforts that had been growing throughout the 1970s and 1980s; the uprising provided an opportunity, and an obvious need, to expand significantly the numbers of Palestinians involved in fashioning local control over their daily lives. This growing emphasis on self-reliance, manifested in everything from backyard gardens to clandestine education (in response to Israel's mass closure of schools), is directly related to resistance tactics focused on *disengagement* from the Israeli economy and Israeli control more broadly. By March 1988, Palestinians working for the Israeli Civil Administration (set up in 1981 to replace Israel's direct military rule of the Occupied Territories) had begun to resign in large numbers. Individuals who had worked within Israel's elaborate system of collaborators were publicly identified, and in some cases violently attacked; many took the opportunity to cut their ties with the occupation.

On an economic level, a variety of measures, including strikes, tax revolts, and product boycotts, drew even more Palestinians into the uprising and saddled the Israeli state with significant losses. *Direct actions* against the occupation forces, such as the famous street battles in which Israeli troops faced crowds of stonethrowing Palestinian demonstrators, received the greatest amount of media attention. In some cases, these confrontations arose spontaneously when soldiers entered a community, or when residents reacted to the news of specific Israeli actions elsewhere; in other cases, activists planned clashes in advance, with roles carefully assigned to particular individuals based on age and level of experience. Overall, the frequency of such events suggested a conscious attempt by Palestinians to meet the occupier directly (one word commonly used to describe confrontations with soldiers, *muwājahāt*, connotes a literal "facing" of the other), whether through nonviolent political marches, coordinated demonstrations involving the use of stones and Molotov cocktails, or simply the actions of individual Palestinians who were increasingly emboldened to challenge Israeli soldiers in the streets.

The response of the Israeli government to the intifada was, in the end, predictable and recognizable as an amalgam of the types of policies used to combat anticolonial movements and civil insurrections in contexts as diverse as French-ruled Algeria, apartheid South Africa, and the United States during the antiwar and civil rights protests of the 1960s and 1970s. Demonstrations were met with bullets, beatings, tear gas, helicopters, and even special truck-mounted rock launchers designed to emulate (with greater efficiency) the Palestinians' ability to hurl pieces of the natural landscape at the occupying army. In keeping with the government's general policy of overwhelming response, honed during Israel's 1982 invasion of Lebanon, the IDF systematically used tools of collective punishment—mass arrests, twenty-four-hour curfews, house demolitions, school closures—in order to penalize entire communities for resistance activities. Thousands of Palestinians passed through the Israeli penal system as political detainees, charged and uncharged, subject to abuses ranging from personal humiliation to torture. Intifada organizers in particular were targeted for arrest, deportation, and assassination by clandestine Israeli hit squads often disguised as Arabs. There is significant evidence that the weight of repression with respect to the most dedicated cadres, particularly the sheer volume of arrests, along with Israel's success in rebuilding its network of collaborators, played an important role in sapping the uprising's strength.

On a broader, regional level, it did not take long for the intifada to have a lasting political impact. In July 1988, Jordan's King Hussein, whose country had ruled the West Bank from 1948 until the start of the Israeli occupation in 1967, announced that Jordan was renouncing its claims on the territory; his decision eased the long-standing rivalry between Jordan and the PLO over representation of the Palestinians, and paved the way for a PLO diplomatic offensive. The Palestine National Council, the PLO's parliament-in-exile, met in Algiers in November 1988 and produced two important documents, a Declaration of Independence and a Political Communiqué, that represented an attempt to capitalize on the momentum of the intifada and a political vision for the future of the West Bank and Gaza. While these statements did lead to the opening of an unprecedented public dialogue between the United States and the PLO, a positive Israeli response to the official Palestinian peace initiative was not forthcoming.

Direct negotiations between Israeli officials and Palestinian representatives did not begin until the post–Gulf War 1991 Madrid Conference, a largely symbolic forum that was arguably doomed by the fact that the right-wing Israeli government still refused to talk with PLO representatives. In the end, it was the Norwegian-brokered "back channel" negotiations between the PLO and Israelis affiliated with the Labor-led government of Yitzhak Rabin, in power in Israeli after mid-1992, that led to mutual Israel-PLO recognition, the subsequent Oslo accords of 1994–95, and the creation of the Palestinian Authority (PA). As for the intifada, most analysts agree that it had begun to implode as early as 1990, though it continued in some form for at least two more years. The factors that contributed to this breakdown—Israeli repression, simple fatigue, growing factional divisions that sometimes turned violent, the devastating economic impact of Iraq's invasion of Kuwait, and the subsequent U.S.-led war against Iraq—are undoubtedly as manifold and complicated as the causes of the uprising itself.

# Notes

NOTES TO THE PROLOGUE

1. For a brief overview of the intifada, see the Appendix. Readers who would like a more detailed account of this period may consult any number of existing books on the uprising, its roots, and its effects on Israel/Palestine and the wider region (Aburish 1991; Al-Haq 1990; Aronson 1990; Bennis 1990; Brynen 1991; Cohen and Wolfsfeld 1993; Emerson 1991; Finkelstein 1997; Frisch 1998; Gordon 1995; Gunn 1995; Hunter 1993; Lockman and Beinin 1989; McDowall 1989; Mishal and Aharoni 1994; Nassar and Heacock 1991; Peretz 1990; Robinson 1997; Sharoni 1995). The uniformly outstanding coverage found in *Middle East Report* is also an excellent place to start.

2. As I have argued elsewhere (Collins 2002), the discourse of "terrorism" that seemed to arise out of nowhere in the post-9/11 period has a much longer genealogy. While the concept itself dates to the late eighteenth century, the current notion of "terrorism" was an invention of the late 1960s and early 1970s, when it was constituted as an object of study and policy through the work of individuals working in and between major institutions in the United States. Since that time "terrorism" has been the ultimate floating signifier, applied selectively and with devastating effect to a host of movements across the globe, even as the concept remains perpetually undefined.

NOTES TO CHAPTER I

1. In one recent text on nationalism, for example, Spencer and Wollman (2002) draw on feminist scholarship in discussing how nationalism typically relies on patriarchal constructions of women as childbearers. The obvious corollary to this argument—that the same ideological structure also assigns a national significance to the children—is never made. A notable exception to this rule, and a welcome addition to the literature on Israel/Palestine, is Rhoda Ann Kanaaneh's *Birthing the Nation* (2002). Kanaaneh's chapter on "Babies and Boundaries" is the most comprehensive discussion available of the role pronatalism plays in both Zionism and Palestinian nationalism. See also Kahn (2000).

2. A notable exception that implicitly underpins my own work is the kind of

critical ethnographic work on generation done in the British cultural studies tradition. Cultural studies researchers (Austin and Willard 1998; Hall and Jefferson
1976; Hebdige 1979; Pilkington 1994; Willis 1977) have been unusually sensitive to the ways in which the generational identities of youth are creative constructions fashioned within politicoeconomic structures and in particular historical moments (e.g., Thatcherist Britain), always in a complicated relationship
with the changing dynamics of popular culture (e.g., styles of music and fashion)
and various public discourses concerning everything from national identity and
gender roles to pedagogy and social welfare policy to crime and "deviance."
Jenks (1995) and Wulff (1995) provide other useful theoretical perspectives on
generation.

3. A novelist, teacher, and journalist, Kanafani also served as spokesman for
the leftist Popular Front for the Liberation of Palestine (PFLP) until he was assas-
sinated in Beirut in 1972. It is generally believed that Israeli agents were responsible for the car bomb that killed Kanafani and his niece.

4. That this generational dichotomy was of political import at the time is
suggested by the report of British intelligence officer J. N. Camp on the First
Palestinian Arab Congress, held in Jerusalem in early 1919 as the Paris Peace
Conference was debating the political future of the region. Despite the official
supremacy of the older, pro-British delegates, Camp reported that others attending the Congress were professing their intention to "forcibly resist" the Zionist
project. "The pan-Arab young bloods, very bold in speech, say so openly, the elderly declare that they will sell out and leave the country," he observed. "I do
not think the threat of the young Arabs is to be taken lightly" (Kayyali n.d., 61).
The position of the "young bloods" initially carried the day, but the notion of a
Greater Syria including Palestine was short-lived: the subsequent actions of European powers left the Arabs of Palestine to fend for themselves under British
mandatory rule and its sponsorship of the emerging Zionist project.

5. British documents from the period suggest a structured inability to conceive of young Palestinians as anything resembling self-motivated political actors. Edward Keith-Roach (1994), who served as Deputy District Commissioner
of Jerusalem, describes Palestine's Arab children as "fighting and clawing each
other like wild beasts" whenever he visited a village and "scattered a few
sweets" (148). Humphrey Bowman (1942), the government's first Director of
Education in Palestine and also the head of the Scouting movement, saw colonial education as the key to inoculating youth against what he called the "virus"
of nationalist politics. "Agitators are only to be found among the discontented,"
he wrote. "Do away with the cause for discontent, make your peasant happy
and prosperous, and agitation will cease. . . . In a single generation much can
be achieved." The young generation in Palestine was, in his words, a *"tabula
rasa."*

While Bowman lacks the undisguised imperial arrogance found in Keith-Roach's memoirs, he shares the latter's view of Palestine's young people as political pawns.

> [T]he Arab leaders in Palestine did their utmost to make the schools the nucleus of nationalist inspiration. . . . Their aim was to embarrass the Government by giving the schools a nuisance value; and, at the same time, to inculcate in the Arab youth a passionate nationalism which would show itself in overt acts whenever an opportunity served. To achieve this end, they tried by every means in their power to persuade the children to strike; to influence the teachers to suborn their pupils, and to force the parents by threats to support them. In view of these subversive measures, it is scarcely a matter of surprise that strikes did occasionally take place.

6. See Amos (1980) and Sayigh (1979). The use of the term *ashbāl* to designate youthful apprentices of larger paramilitary groups dates at least to the mid-1940s, when rival Palestinian factions set up militias in what was apparently a halfhearted attempt to counter the Jewish community's growing military power. Salah Khalaf reports that he joined, and became a leader of, the "lion cubs" associated with one of these militias, the *Najjādah,* of which the principal of his school was a founding member (Abu Iyad 1981).

7. "Countless examples could be given," Khalaf argues, "to illustrate the popular dictum that 'all revolutions conceived in Palestine abort in the Arab capitals'" (32). I heard echoes of this metaphor when I interviewed Ashraf, who insisted that the PLO had "aborted" the intifada (see chapter 6).

8. Swedenburg (1995a) provides an indispensable overview of this narrative field in Chapter 1 of his book.

9. The study of popular memory remains a relatively small academic subfield, located in a floating space between history, ethnography, and cultural studies. Key texts in this field include Passerini (1987), Portelli (1997), Popular Memory Group (1982), and Swedenburg (1995a). More broadly, however, the interdisciplinary study of memory has exploded in recent years, fueled by a growing interest in the way wars, genocides, national liberation struggles, and other violent periods are remembered (Amadiume and An-Na'im 2000; Cairns and Roe 2003; Cohen 2001; Feldman 1991; Fentress and Wickham 1992; Lorey and Beezley 2002; Lykes 1996; Minow 1998; Nuttall and Coetzee 1998; Pohlandt-McCormick 1999; Sanford 2003; Slyomovics 1998; Zerubavel 1995).

10. According to Taysir Daoud, Camp Service Officer for Balata, the camp's population as of late May 1997 included 16,629 registered refugees, plus approximately 350 persons classified either as nonrefugees or as nonregistered refugees. The more recent figure of 22,000 is taken from Toufic Haddad, "Balata: Belly of the Beast," *News from Within* 26, 3 (2000).

11. Linda Ammons, who did field research in Balata village during the

1970s, notes that the villagers whose land was taken in this process were only marginally compensated for their losses (Moors 1995).

12. The most detailed published account of the events of 11 December is to be found in the independent Israeli weekly *News from Within,* 6 January 1988. American press reports, while somewhat more skeletal, nonetheless confirm this version. See Glenn Frankel, "Israeli Troops Kill 3 in Refugee Camp Protest," *Washington Post,* 12 December 1987. In my interviews in Balata, numerous residents offered narratives of this initial intifada clash that generally parallel these published accounts, though several provided higher estimates of the number of fatalities.

13. My decision to focus primarily on young men was partly a practical one—based on the recognition that as a man, I would have difficulty setting up open-ended interviews with young women—but also an intellectual one. While public discourse on Palestine undoubtedly privileges men's actions, feminist researchers have made great strides in redressing this imbalance. As a result, the presence of women's voices is now one of the primary strengths of the *scholarly* literature on the intifada, whereas the stories of men have not received sustained, critical attention from scholars to match their ubiquity in popular accounts. I have included analysis of the few interviews I did with young women in part to demonstrate the ways in which certain generational experiences and narrative patterns do cross gender lines. At the same time, I have tried to point out some of the ways in which structures of gender may also lead to important differences between men's and women's testimony.

NOTES TO CHAPTER 2

1. In similar vein, Chris Jenks (1995) identifies two "codes" that, in his view, have tended to frame dominant representations of children. The "Dionysian" code "rests on the assumption of an initial evil or corruption within the child," while the "Apollonian" code views children as "angelic, innocent, and untainted by the world that they have recently entered." Given the archetypal (or mythological, in Jenks's view) nature of these "codes," it is not surprising that we find echoes of both in portrayals of young Palestinians.

2. As noted in chapter 1, the PLO used the term *ashbāl* (lion cubs) when referring to young fighters-in-training during the early phase of the armed struggle in the 1970s. On the use of *ashbāl* during the intifada, see Rouhana (1989). In an interesting parallel, Jeremy Seekings (1993) notes that young supporters of the African National Congress (ANC) in South Africa were often praised as "young lions" during the politically turbulent 1980s.

3. In Los Angeles, the April 1992 street demonstrations following the verdict in the Rodney King beating case, and the counterinsurgency tactics used by the

police in response to these demonstrations, led one activist to refer to the unrest as "an American urban Intifada" (Katz and Smith 1992). For a further discussion of L.A.–West Bank parallels, particularly as elaborated in Davis's work, see Swedenburg (1995a). In South Africa, the local ANC branch in Orange Farm, a squatter community of 250,000 residents, announced its intention to rename the area "Palestine" in 1994 in solidarity with the "homeless and marginal" status of Palestinians (see "The Highway of Zinc," *Weekly Mail and Guardian,* 30 September 1994). Ian Lustick (1993, 561) notes that the intifada was "the first of many mass-based, illegal, nonviolent or semiviolent challenges to nondemocratic governing structures to burst upon the world scene at the end of the 1980s," preceding (and, he suggests, perhaps inspiring) subsequent movements in Burma, Eastern Europe, China, and elsewhere. Finally, in a considerably more chilling example, there is the case of the Israeli man who reacted to the murder of three Palestinian workers in the city of Or Yehuda by saying, "This is our intifadah." According to an Israeli newspaper report, the three men were burned alive as they slept (Burning Hate 1988).

4. Psychologist Eyad Sarraj, who has long been at the forefront of efforts to provide post-traumatic therapy and counseling to Palestinians in Gaza, recalls how he once found himself squeezed between these two poles. "During the violent days of the intifada, I was told by a PLO official . . . that he was concerned about the damage being done to the national spirit of the struggle by the portrayal of our heroic Palestinian children as victims," writes Sarraj (1996). "At the same time . . . I still had to deal with the Israeli occupation authorities who were accusing me of using children and their alleged trauma for political propaganda." Sarraj's dilemma points to the multiple ways in which children can serve as powerful symbols in the context of violent political conflict, particularly when the children themselves are involved in the conflict as direct participants or affected bystanders. In such cases, it is common to find more than one protagonist—in this case, Sarraj as well as the Israeli state—claiming to speak in defense of "victimized" children, albeit for very different reasons.

5. The same logic is at work in the advertising campaigns of humanitarian organizations, which regularly use Palestinian children to attract readers' attention. A case in point is the special double issue of *Middle East Report* (Nos. 164–165) devoted to the intifada: of the three advertisements in the magazine placed by Palestine-related charities (Jerusalem Fund, United Palestinian Appeal, and American Near East Refugee Aid), each features a picture of a Palestinian child. The photos—a young girl holding a small bowl of food, a sixteen-year-old boy from Gaza who was seriously wounded in the intifada, and a young refugee boy in a classroom—contrast sharply with the pictures of young intifada activists scattered throughout the magazine's articles, which provide excellent social and political analysis of the uprising as it stood in mid-1990.

6. To put it another way, the fundamental nature of the occupation is the same, whether those bearing the brunt of Israeli repression are young or old, male or female, rich or poor. Yet the sheer number of organizations devoted to the defense of children's rights suggests the troubling possibility that Israel might have faced less international criticism for its occupation policies had young people not played such a central role in the intifada.

7. The Gaza Community Mental Health Programme, headed by Eyad Sarraj, continues to sponsor and publish extensive psychological research on the intifada. Much of this work is available, either in full or abstracted form, on the Programme's website at http://www.gcmhp.net/main.htm. For other published psychological research see, inter alia, Baker (1990); El-Helou and Johnson (1994); and Odeh and Arafat (1989).

8. Two significant amendments were later made to the original order. First, the definition of "security offenses" was broadened to include "any action . . . which may disturb public order or the security of the state" (Military Order 1275, 28 April 1989). Second, the period of bail—that is, the period during which the parents are legally required to prevent further "offenses"—was raised from one year to two years (Military Order 1336, 28 April 1991). For more information, see Rishmawi (1996); and Jerusalem Media and Communication Centre (1989).

9. For a useful discussion of the complexities of Israeli responses to the morally troubling aspects of the occupation, as well as the hypocrisy lying at the root of many of these responses, see Cohen (2001).

10. "Shooting and Crying," *News from Within*, 31 May 1988, 11.

11. "What Israel Is Losing," *New York Times*, 31 January 1988, 24.

12. Reprinted in *News from Within*, 14 October 1988, 5.

13. "For generations we have been taught in school that history is a narrative of kings and wars; the child's question—"Daddy, what did you do in the war?"—is an embryonic way of phrasing the larger question: What is our place in history, and what is the place of history in our lives?" (1997, ix).

14. Yesh Gvul (There Is a Limit), a movement of conscientious objectors founded in response to Israel's 1982 invasion of Lebanon, received a boost in membership during the first six months of the intifada, with some five hundred reservists signing a petition pledging their refusal to serve in the Occupied Territories. As a consequence, many of these "refuseniks" received brief prison sentences, often equivalent to the one-month tour of duty they were opposing; a few were singled out for longer prison terms, while others managed to work out an "arrangement" allowing them to serve in another capacity (Kaminer 1996). Yesh Gvul has also been active during the second intifada, and its motto ("We don't shoot, we don't cry, and we don't serve in the occupied territories!") suggests a critical engagement with the discourses of guilt and shame I have been discussing. For a critical assessment of how some segments of the Left have has-

tened their own decline by failing to support the conscientious objection movement, see Kimmerling (2003).

15. U. Yasmin, "Words to the Weeping Soldier," *News from Within,* 9 February 1988, 14.

16. In another birth story, two women are giving birth in a hospital. One of the women, an Egyptian, accuses the other, a Palestinian, of making too much noise. The latter's riposte: "Well, giving birth to a *mulathem* [a "masked" youth, referring to activists who covered their faces to avoid being identified during the intifada] is not as easy as giving birth to a belly dancer" (Kanaana 1993, 50).

17. "Clearly, if we do not bring about the departure of the Arabs," wrote Eilan Tor in 1982, "the day will come when they will be able, democratically, to destroy the state of Israel" (Lustick 1988, 132–133). Tor's use of the word "destroy" rather than "dominate" is significant, and speaks to the anomalous status of Palestinians living in a state whose identity is defined in ethnoreligious terms rather than politico-territorial ones; Palestinians may be "citizens" of the state, but because they are non-Jews, they can never be "nationals" of it.

18. Naji al-ᶜAli, who grew up in the Palestinian refugee camps in Lebanon before going into exile, died on 29 August 1987 in London, six weeks after being shot by an unknown assailant. Given that he had staked out a fiercely independent, critical position vis-à-vis both Israel and the Arab states, his death provoked a great deal of finger-pointing and discussion about the often violent intersections of culture and politics (Harlow 1994).

19. When I asked one of my interviewees, Ashraf, to describe what he remembered of the first days of the intifada, he began by listing a series of Israeli actions (beatings, school closings) which sparked popular anger in Balata before the uprising began, then broke off his narrative to make a pointed comment about the veracity of his own testimony. "All these incidents were happening before our eyes," he said. "We didn't just hear about it."

20. Wark (1994) provides a provocative discussion of this issue, noting, for example, the dilemma the British government faced when it tried to organize an airlift of orphans during the height of the war in Bosnia: "Very few of the refugees waiting forlornly for a ticket out of hell had that wide-eyed look that comes across so well in medium close-up, shot against a background of dirt or dinge. Being certified refugees, they were for the most part adults who had done something to make themselves refugees. . . . The refugees were more than a little annoyed that British baby-hunters passed them over in favor of pinching a few infants" (39–40).

21. Titles of paintings featured in the book range from generic categories representing agricultural and social activities ("The olive harvest," "Bride and groom") and political events ("Funeral procession," "Confronting the army") to detailed descriptions of intifada scenes ("Checking the identity of the man returning from the market, blindfolding another, beating a third").

NOTES TO CHAPTER 3

1. Approximately two dozen Balata residents fell as *shuhadā* during the uprising. While the majority of these were boys and young men, the number also includes at least two older men, two older women, and one teenage girl.

2. Mothers in Palestinian society are typically known by the name of their eldest son—hence Imm Ashraf ("mother of Ashraf").

3. The photographic juxtaposition of body and political cartoon also posits an organic link between Nizam's death and the ongoing national struggle. Orayb Aref Najjar (1996), analyzing a series of "Martyrs' Lists" that appeared in the Palestinian magazine *al-Kateb* during the uprising, notes that popular representations of martyrdom fostered exactly these kinds of connections between the individual and the national community in a number of related ways: by placing the deaths within the context of the repressive political measures meted out to all Palestinians living under Israeli occupation; by referring to martyrs' bodies as "bridges," as metaphorical trestles over which the road to national liberation would pass; and by highlighting the continuity of the national struggle as a series of personal and collective sacrifices, effectively linking each death with those that had gone before. As Najjar notes, *al-Kateb* accomplished this latter task formally, by presenting each death in exactly the same way (e.g., "Sunday 1/8/1989. Naim Ahmad Abu Neim (11 years) Maghir Village/Ramallah. Was martyred in al-Makased Hospital after settlers fractured his skull on 12/31/1988"), packaging each list graphically in a box with a mourning band across the corner, and concluding each list with the same message: "The editorial family of *al-Kateb* bows in respect to the reverent martyrs and extends its sincere condolences to our Palestinian people and the families of the martyrs" (510).

4. One father reported being visited by the *mukhābarāt* shortly before his son's death: "The *mukhābarāt* agent told me that if Abd al-Qader didn't immediately surrender to the Civil Administration, he would be killed. Then they searched the house. They overturned all my possessions. They threw everything down onto the floor. . . . This *mukhābarāt* agent did not say who would kill Abd al-Qader if he didn't surrender. He simply told me, Abd al-Qader will come home dead if he doesn't turn himself in" (Human Rights Watch 1993, 132).

5. Quoted in *News from Within*, 14 October 1988, 3.

6. As evidence of this shift in Israel's counterinsurgency strategy, Human Rights Watch (1993) reports that the number of undercover killings in the West Bank and Gaza jumped from eight in 1988 (the year Nizam died) to forty-three in 1992.

7. "Dum-dum" is the name Palestinians use to describe what is generally known as an "exploding bullet," a special type of ammunition designed to explode and fragment on impact, thereby causing a maximum amount of damage to the victim's body.

8. Janet Varner Gunn (1995) uses this phrase to describe Mohammad Abu Aker, a young resident of Dheisheh Refugee Camp whose case drew international media attention. Abu Aker, like Nizam, was shot and seriously wounded in 1988 after spending months on the run from Israeli security forces; against all predictions, he lived for two more years, receiving extensive medical treatment in the United States before dying in 1990 at age nineteen.

9. For a cinematic portrayal of a similar event, see *Children of Fire* (1990), an intifada documentary directed by Mai Masri and Jean Khalil Chamoun. The film opens with the Israeli army returning a slain son's body to a family in the middle of the night.

10. This notion of identity-as-performance derives from Judith Butler's work on the construction of gender as a sort of self-fulfilling prophecy. "There is no gender identity behind the expressions of gender," writes Butler (1990); rather, "that identity is performatively constituted by the very 'expressions' that are said to be its results" (24–25). Though I do not subscribe fully to the most thorough-going poststructuralist critiques of subjectivity, I do find Butler's work suggestive in terms of explaining the production of Palestinian identities through what might best be described as a dialectical relationship between "inside" and "outside." It is worth noting that stories of "resistance" and "suffering" may in fact be two sides of the same coin, and that attempts to elicit the former from Palestinians do not necessarily enable the observer-researcher to escape the ethical dilemma suggested by this line of analysis.

11. Julie Peteet (1993), who has done extensive oral history research among Palestinian refugees in Lebanon, makes a similar point regarding her interactions with camp women who were regularly called on to "represent" the culture of the Palestinian Resistance to outside visitors. "The setting," she notes, "defined the nature of the dialogue" (54).

12. This is not to say that Imm Ghassan's view on the subject is shared by all Palestinian women; on the contrary, the existing literature amply demonstrates a tremendous diversity of opinion among women. At the same time, much of this literature is also too quick, I believe, to conclude that the mutual constitution of gender and national identities can be explained without some reference to the issue of generational identity. A proper treatment of this issue would require much greater attention to the actions and opinions of the group that is most absent from research on the intifada to date, namely, older men.

13. On Rabin's plan to use what he called "force, power, and blows" to quell the uprising, see Hunter (1993). The beatings policy, which was designed to deter stonethrowing and to improve Israel's international image by limiting shooting deaths, backfired for a number of reasons: the widespread, indiscriminate use of beatings served to mobilize ever-wider segments of the Palestinian population; beatings caught on tape by television crews were beamed around the world, further eroding Israel's credibility; and, perhaps most interestingly,

Palestinians were able to redefine the experience of beating as a "rite of passage" (Peteet 1994).

14. Isam's account of this first clash is consistent with those of other Balata residents I interviewed, and with the narrative of events offered in the Israeli weekly *News from Within* (see chapter 1).

15. As Islah Jad (1998) points out, not all women would agree with this characterization: "The atmosphere of constant mourning in addition to frequent strikes all led to the presence of men and children inside the house for longer periods of time, which burdened women with new housework and limited their movement" (60–61).

16. According to Glenn Robinson (1997), "The list of those imprisoned in the Negev read like a Who's Who of Palestinian political life: student activists, labor leaders, university professors, doctors, journalists, and the like" (22).

17. As Gunn (1995) writes: "I could have written about the Big News: deaths, injuries, collective punishments, detentions, beatings, house demolitions, land confiscations. Some of that breaks into my narrative, but I was more interested in the Small News about ordinary life" (xxxvi).

18. "There can be no orderly sequence of time," writes Edward Said (1985, 25). "You see it in our children who seem to have skipped a phase of growth or, more alarming, achieved an out-of-season maturity in one part of their body or mind while the rest remains childlike."

19. For an overview of marriage trends and attitudes based on a 1992 Norwegian-Palestinian survey, see Hammami (1993).

20. Several commentators refer to the data from the Bethlehem and Tulkarem districts reported in the August 1989 issue of *al-Kateb* indicating that the average marriage age of women during the intifada dropped below eighteen years, and perhaps as low as fourteen in some rural areas (Jad 1998). For a limited discussion of additional survey data reported in the Palestinian press, see Ya'acov Lamdan, "Love, Marriage and the Intifada," *Jerusalem Post,* 18 May 1989, 7.

21. As reasons for optimism, Strum (1998) suggests that during the intifada, more women felt empowered to make their own decisions regarding the choice of a husband and the use of the *mahr*; more generally, she foresees the intifada leading to greater involvement of women in public political life, since "women who have been 'talking politics' are unlikely to be satisfied with a purely private persona" (74).

22. Dick Doughty's (1995) fascinating book on everyday life in the Gaza Strip contains an almost identical story, suggesting that the interruption of love by imprisonment may have been a common experience during the intifada. It may also be the case, of course, that the circulation of such stories has shaped the memories of young men like Isam and Doughty's interlocutor.

23. By signing the two Oslo agreements, the PLO consented to Israel's definition of the West Bank and Gaza as "disputed" rather than "occupied" territories. The implications of this compromise are twofold: first, the status of the territories is made subject not to international law or to relevant UN resolutions (which would insist on the full return of the land in question), but rather to a negotiation process in which the balance of power is grossly asymmetrical. Second, by implication, this shift gives official Palestinian approval to the Israeli government's long-standing claim that it is not bound by international agreements (primarily the Fourth Geneva Convention) aimed at protecting human rights in, and preventing the illegal settlement of, territories occupied by force.

24. See Benjamin (1968c, 258). The "conception of history" to which Benjamin refers is the "historicist" tendency to treat history as linear, progressive, and chronological, and historiography, by extension, as the "science of progress" (Osborne 1994).

NOTES TO CHAPTER 4

1. "He who seeks to approach his own buried past must conduct himself like a man digging," writes Benjamin (1978) in a famous passage from his Berlin memoir. "He must not be afraid to return again and again to the same matter; to scatter it as one scatters earth, to turn it over as one turns over soil. For the matter itself is only a deposit, a stratum, which yields only to the most meticulous examination what constitutes the real treasure hidden within the earth: the images, severed from all earlier associations, that stand—like precious fragments or torsos in a collector's gallery—in the prosaic rooms of our later understanding" (25–26).

2. According to the human rights group B'tselem, the number of administrative detainees had risen to fourteen thousand by October 1992. Ansar III, which is part of a large military base inside Israel, embodies a basic violation of international law: under the Fourth Geneva Convention, it is forbidden to transfer residents of occupied territories into the occupying state. The camp, set up in March 1988 specifically in response to the intifada, is not part of the regular Israeli prison system; consequently, intifada detainees were forced to live in conditions that drew sharp criticism from a wide range of observers, including human rights groups, the International Committee of the Red Cross, and, to a more limited extent, some Israeli politicians and Supreme Court justices. In an extremely harsh climate—scorching desert heat during the day, temperatures often below freezing at night—detainees were held, in groups of approximately twenty-five, in tents measuring five by ten meters. In addition to this intense overcrowding, the camp was marked by abysmal sanitary conditions and medical services, the use of forced labor and collective punishment, and a general atmosphere of fear

enforced by the presence of armed guards. From the opening of the camp until October 1991, detainees were allowed no family visits. See B'tselem (1992); and Lawyers Committee for Human Rights (1988).

3. Ofer, located near Jerusalem, was opened in mid-1988 for precisely this purpose; according to one report, "the gaolers and detainees prefer to call it 'the kindergarten of the intifada,' or 'Little Ansar.'" See "Children's 'Ansar,'" *News from Within*, 31 May 1988, 8.

4. Though Ra'id is not from Balata camp, I interviewed him because of his work at the Palestinian Prisoners' Club (*nādi al-ʾasīr al-falastīni*), which provides a variety of services to prisoners, former prisoners, and their families. A strong Fateh supporter, he grew up in a village outside Nablus and spent five and a half years in prison during and after the intifada before starting to work at the club's Nablus office. His time in prison included eighteen months of administrative detention at Ansar III, during which he was not allowed a single visit from his family.

5. One of the most infamous aspects of life in detention camps such as Ansar III, for example, involved forcing detainees (who were known primarily by identification numbers rather than by their names) to be counted three or four times a day, an exercise in disciplinary power marked by the strict attention paid to the placement and movement of the prisoners' bodies:

> Each time, even at night, the detainees must leave their tents and sit cross-legged on the floor in rows of five in assigned compounds even though their hands are behind their backs and their heads are bowed. No movement is allowed during the count. . . . When a detainee hears his number called out by the soldiers, he must shout out his name and turn to face in the opposite direction. After this process is completed, the prisoners must call out their numbers in sequence. The prisoners are not allowed to move until the soldiers leave the compound. . . . Some detainees collapse and faint during the noon count, as they cannot stand the heat and the tension.

("The Main Entrance to Hell," *News from Within*, 4 September 1988, 4–7) Given the long-standing Zionist/Israeli policy of maintaining Jewish demographic superiority in Israel (see chapter 2), the practice of "counting" prisoners appears not only as a disciplinary act, but also (however unconsciously) as a kind of obsessive act of national panic.

6. Shimon Alkabetz, *Hadashot*, 17 December 1987, quoted in *News from Within*, 6 January 1988, 9.

7. For an extended analysis of the hunger strike by Irish Republican paramilitaries, twelve of whom eventually died in the campaign, see Feldman (1991).

8. On the increasing use of solitary confinement and its role in the 1991 strike, see Graham Usher, "Killing Souls: Palestinian Prisoners' Hunger Strike," *Middle East International*, 6 November 1992.

9. See Daoud Kuttab, "Prisoners' Hunger Strike Reignites the *Intifada*," and

Peretz Kidron, "Israel's Conciliatory Tactics," *Middle East International,* 23 October 1992; Usher, "Killing Souls"; Jon Immanuel, "Protest over Palestinian Security Prisoners Escalates as Students Join Hunger Strike," *Jerusalem Post,* 8 October 1992; and Raine Marcus and Jon Immanuel, "Concessions Bring End to Jail Hunger Strike," *Jerusalem Post,* 13 October 1992.

10. For a useful discussion of "emplotment," particularly as it relates to the project of integrating a narrative concept of identity into the social sciences, see Somers and Gibson (1994).

NOTES TO CHAPTER 5

1. Note the use of a generational metaphor that follows directly from Fasheh's observation just quoted: the "seeds" planted by the young eclipse the "dead product" of the older generation.

2. "Two Birzeit [University] students accompanying an NBC crew to their closed campus in late January [1988] encountered a barricade in the road near the small village of Abu Qash 'manned' by a boy so young he had to stand on his tiptoes to look in the car window and check out the passengers. 'Go back, go back,' he commanded imperiously. 'We are all on strike'" (Johnson, O'Brien, and Hiltermann 1988, 7).

3. For an early report detailing the specific roles played by young people of different ages in street demonstrations and other activities, see Daoud Kuttab (1988). The practice of using graffiti to mark political territory and mobilize the public for particular actions is explored in Oliver and Steinberg (1990); and Peteet (1996).

4. In addition to facilitating the resistance movement itself, such qualities can also help foster a sense of generational consciousness. In their comparative study of youth subcultures in Britain, researchers from the Center for Contemporary Cultural Studies note that young people's sense of "difference" was especially strong "when this difference was inscribed in activities and interests to which 'age,' principally, provided the passport" (Hall and Jefferson 1976, 52).

5. See Kanaana (1990) for a useful discussion of the intifada's "intragroup humor," much of which took the form of biting jokes aimed at the children of the wealthy.

6. Within this literature, one can trace dominant lines of analysis from euphoria and optimism through to disappointment and critical reassessment. Compare, for example, two accounts—one written early in the intifada, the other shortly after it—written by the same authors (Giacaman and Johnson 1989; 1998). See also Abdulhadi (1998), who argues that political changes during the intifada's second year "directly altered gender dynamics, thus crushing Palestinian women's hopes for liberation" (657).

7. For the full text of this story, collected in 1989 from a twenty-year-old

woman in Nablus, see Kanaana (1993). The story, the general outlines of which are common to a number of tales circulating in the West Bank, concludes with the young man returning to the house and asking to marry the daughter.

NOTES TO CHAPTER 6

1. My use of the designation "soldier" is a function of the fact that all those working for the PA in my interview cohort did so in a security capacity. The term is also obviously gendered: while there are a limited number of women working as police officers, the vast majority of individuals employed by the security forces (including both "soldiers" in my cohort) are men.

2. More than anyone else I spoke with, Samer clearly saw himself as performing a defensive function in relation to critiques of the official nationalist movement. When I first met him, I had already conducted the bulk of my interviews in the camp, and I suspect that as a well-connected political operative (and an employee of the intelligence service), he had already learned a great deal about me and about the lines of questioning I had been pursuing with others.

3. Here I have used an idiomatic English expression to approximate Nabil's words. The adjective he uses to describe the "support" in question is *ghamziyya,* which is derived from the verb meaning "to wink." Sometimes, he says, families would simply receive "fifty [Jordanian] dinars in an envelope" from a young man acting as a sort of undercover courier.

4. Here Hassan acknowledged explicitly that he was quoting (or paraphrasing) a famous saying he attributed to Mao Zedong.

5. While it is theoretically possible that Leila's use of the term "outside forces" is a veiled reference to the PA, a more likely explanation is that she is misremembering the timing of the event (placing it before the PA's arrival) and accusing Israel or Iran (via its backing of Hamas) of fomenting tension in Gaza. It is significant in this context that in the aftermath of the clash, the notion of "outside forces" proved equally useful for supporters and critics of the PA's actions. In a statement issued the day after the battle, the Fateh movement implicitly invoked the specter of Iranian support for Hamas when it warned Palestinians against taking part in "conspiratorial plans on behalf of foreign parties," while other observers, such as one young Gazan quoted in the *New York Times,* suggested a different conspiracy: "This was all done on the orders of [then-Israeli Prime Minister] Rabin and [U.S. President] Clinton." See Clyde Haberman, "12 Die as Arafat's Police Fire on Palestinian Militants," *New York Times,* 19 November 1994.

6. On 24 February 1994, Baruch Goldstein, an American-born settler and member of the far-right Kach movement, opened fire on worshipers at Hebron's Ibrahimi mosque—located in one of the most bitterly contested religious sites in Palestine, the "Tomb of the Patriarchs"—before he was beaten to death by sur-

vivors. Most accounts list the death toll at twenty-nine individuals, a number of whom were killed by soldiers while attempting to flee the area.

7. Sartre writes:

It is the moment of the boomerang . . . it comes back on us, it strikes us, and we do not realize any more than we did the other times that it's we who have launched it. . . . The Left at home is embarrassed; they know the true situation of the natives, the merciless oppression they are submitted to; they do not condemn their revolt, knowing full well that we have done everything to provoke it. But, all the same, they think to themselves, there *are* limits; these guerillas should be bent on showing that they are chivalrous; that would be the best way of showing they are men. Sometimes the Left scolds them . . . "You're going too far; we won't support you any more." The natives don't give a damn about their support; for all the good it does them they might as well stuff it up their backsides. (Fanon 1963, 20–21)

8. Those concerned with historical accuracy will note—as Abdul-Jabbar, who was the interpreter for the interview, did when he interrupted Ayman to correct him at this point in the interview—that Ayman exaggerates the number of people killed in the Hebron massacre. Ayman's error of fact is significant in a narrative sense, for the point of revenge discourse in this case is to portray suicide attacks first and foremost as Palestinian responses to escalations of violence from the Israeli side.

9. The "letter of recognition" to which Usher refers was one of two such documents exchanged between Arafat and then-Israeli Prime Minister Yitzhak Rabin. Among the terms contained in Arafat's letter was a confirmation that references to "armed struggle" in the PLO charter would be considered null and void.

10. Jon Immanuel, "Arafat Hints at Renewal of Intifada," *Jerusalem Post*, 1 September 1996.

11. Once again we see how Ashraf speaks in terms which call to mind Fanon's discussion of the Algerian revolution, in this case the latter's description, in *A Dying Colonialism*, of the heterosexual couple as the "fertile nucleus of the nation." On this point, see Mowitt (1992).

12. On 3 April, teachers in most of the West Bank responded to the PA's offer of a 10 percent salary increase by declaring a strike; the Authority responded immediately by suspending nineteen of the strike organizers. As the protest continued, an Arafat spokesman accused the teachers of "damaging state security" through their labor action, and the PA eventually arrested at least twenty-five teachers on 21 April. After two days they were released in exchange for ending the strike, which failed to achieve its declared goals. See LAWE press release, 22 April 1997; and Shyam Bhatia, "Jailing of Teachers Fuels Discontent with Arafat," *Guardian* (London), 5 May 1997.

13. See Hammami (1995) and Sullivan (1996). For a useful critique of Sullivan's position on the relationship between NGOs and "civil society," see the letter by Julia Hawkins in the autumn 1996 edition of *Journal of Palestine Studies*. For a brief overview of attempts by the PA to exert control over NGOs—and the international funds flowing to them—see Robinson (1997).

14. In addition to works cited in the previous note, see Muslih (1993); Giacaman and Lønning (1998); and Parker (1999).

15. Here Khaled is referring to divisions that have arisen with the coming of the PA. To illustrate this point, he invoked the contradictory position of a colonel in the security forces who achieved his high rank because of political connections. On the one hand, said Khaled, this man has less military training than many of his subordinates, a situation which creates a significant amount of resentment; on the other hand, the colonel also feels powerless vis-à-vis his own superiors because the autocratic structure of the PA doesn't allow anyone to raise questions without being accused of national treason.

NOTES TO CHAPTER 7

1. Tanya Reinhart (2002) goes even further, arguing persuasively that Israel is now engaging in measures that even the apartheid regime in South Africa never used. The West Bank and Gaza are, in her view, Israel's "penal colonies." For other perspectives on the linkages between Israel and South Africa, see Collins (1996); Greenstein (1995); Marshall (1995); and Shafir (1999).

2. According to Amnesty International (1996), the total number of police rose from 12,000 at the PA's inception to more than 40,000 by September 1996. In Gaza, the report notes, "there is one law enforcement officer for every 50 people, possibly the highest ratio of police to civil population in the world" (8).

3. By mid-1995 the PSF employed more than 4,000 men operating beyond the reach of any independent legal authority, making it the largest branch in the security forces (Usher 1999).

4. According to Mouin Rabbani (1996), "The West Bank Commander of the Palestinian Police, Haj Isma'il Abu-Jabr, almost ignited civil war when he arrived to threaten punishment for those who continued firing. He was chased away unceremoniously, and other orders to desist were similarly ignored. Subsequently, the Preventative Security Force . . . joined the exchanges as an organized force. It appears that their participation was imposed upon, rather than ordered by, Arafat" (3).

5. Press release, Birzeit University Public Relations Office, 30 March 1996.

6. Press release, Birzeit University Public Relations Office, 26 March 1996. According to Human Rights Watch (1997), at least 2,000 Palestinians were arrested by the PA during the first eight months of 1996; between 900 and 1,200 of these were detained in the three months following the suicide bombings.

7. *New York Times* and *Washington Times* reports (from 3 April and 31 March, respectively), cited in "Chronology," *Journal of Palestine Studies* 25, 4 (summer 1996): 172. The *Jerusalem Post* featured a similar report ("PLO Police Raids Hamas Student Rally," 31 March 1996).

8. Press release, Land and Water Establishment (LAWE), 1 April 1996.

9. See LAWE press release, 3 April 1996; and press reports cited in "Chronology," *Journal of Palestine Studies* 25, 4 (summer 1996): 173. According to Amnesty International (1996), two members of the security forces were eventually found responsible for al-Lawzi's death at a military trial in July 1996; both men were sentenced to eighteen months in prison.

10. The following account is taken from the Birzeit University Press Release dated 3 April 1996.

11. Islah Jad reports that at least two of the students involved in the march were held for more than six months. See Jad, "A Victory for the Youth Movement," *News from Within* 13, 2 (February 1997): 12, n. 2.

12. Human Rights Watch (1997), relying on testimony gathered in mid-1996, argues that "detainees who undergo interrogation by the Palestinian security forces are commonly tortured, while detainees who are not interrogated—the vast majority—are generally not physically ill-treated" (16). Among the victims of torture, the report alleges, are at least fourteen individuals who died while in custody during the first three years of PA rule. The death of Mahmud Jumayal, a member of the Fateh Hawks who was tortured by the Coastal Police near Nablus, provoked a public outcry and led Fateh to call for a general strike.

13. According to LAWE, al-Baba died of a "massive internal hemorrhage" after being tortured while in the Palestinian prison in Nablus. The PA Justice Minister acknowledged that al-Baba had been arrested without charge, and admitted that after al-Baba's body was taken to a Nablus hospital, the file on the case mysteriously "disappeared." LAWE press release, 4 February 1997.

14. "A-G Says PA Has No Human Rights Problem," interview by Asya Abdul Hadi, *Palestine Report,* 28 February 1997, 6–9.

15. This was also the response of Prisoners' Club official Ra'id Amr when I asked him about the number of prisoners being held by the PA. Anxious to demonstrate his concern for the well-being of all prisoners, he insisted that prison was the safest place for these opposition supporters. In this light, it is interesting that a number of detainees were reportedly required, upon their release from Ramallah prison in September 1996, to sign a "loyalty pledge" indicating their willingness to support the PA's program of political negotiation. See Peter Dickie, "Loyalty Pledge for Released Prisoners," *Jerusalem Times,* 6 September 1996, 1.

16. As noted above, exact information on the composition and function of the PA security forces is difficult to obtain. When the announcement regarding the "University Guards" was made, one source speculated that the new unit

would be the eleventh "secret service" within the security apparatus. See Ata Mana', "Students Reject Security Unit," *Jerusalem Times*, 6 September 1996, 2.

17. Quoted in Mana', "Students Reject Security Unit." See also Mousa Qous, "University Guards 'Rejected,'" *Palestine Report*, 13 September 1996, 16.

18. Muhammed El-Hasan, "Palestinians Stunned by Abduction of Local Boy," *Palestine Report*, 29 November 1996, 12.

19. Hatem Lutfi, "Israeli Army Mine Claims the Lives of Two Children," *Jerusalem Times*, 29 November 1996, 1. The front page article in the *Times* features a striking photograph taken at the boys' funeral, showing a crowd of similarly young boys leading the funeral procession; according to the caption, the funeral "was attended mainly by children."

20. Salwa Al-Shahabi Al-Ghawanmah, "The Younger Generation: Uncouth and Irresponsible," *Jerusalem Times*, 16 January 1998, 5.

21. Ilene R. Prusher, "Budget Weddings by Hamas," *Christian Science Monitor*, 27 July 1998.

22. All materials related to the Birzeit elections were accessed in March 1999 at http://www2.birzeit.edu/scouncil/elections/1999.html.

23. Quoted in the *Observer* (London), 27 April 2003, 21.

24. David Firestone, "DeLay Is to Carry Dissenting Message on a Mideast Tour," *New York Times*, 25 July 2003, 1.

25. Quoted in the *Guardian* (London), 5 June 2003, 15.


NOTES TO THE APPENDIX

1. The phrase "another goat and another acre" is attributed to Chaim Weizmann, Israel's first president and a key Zionist diplomat in the decades leading up to 1948. Edward Said (1994) refers to the Zionist practice deriving from Weizmann's homespun philosophy as "a Benthamite policy of detail," sharply different from and more successful than the Palestinian tendency to "rely on unassailable general principles" (33).

2. Figures on deaths and arrests are taken from Wenger and Niva (1988). Figures on injuries—which range, in this context, from shootings to beatings to tear gas inhalation—are notoriously variable and difficult to obtain. Julie Peteet (1994), using conservative estimates from the Palestine Human Rights Information Campaign, quotes a figure of 106,600 Palestinians injured in the first three years of the uprising.

# Glossary of Arabic Terms

*ahdāf* (sing. *hadaf*): goals

*ʿamaliyyāt intihariyya*: suicide operations

*ʾamen wiqāʾi*: Preventive Security Force (PSF), one of several intelligence and law enforcement bodies set up under the Palestinian Authority (PA)

*ashbāl*: "lion cubs," a nickname given to young Palestinian men who were trained as guerrilla fighters after the formation of the PLO

*atfāl al-hijāra*: the "children of the stones," a popular nickname given to the young Palestinian stonethrowers who confronted Israeli troops during the intifada

*awlād* (sing. *walad*): boys

*bayanāt* (sing. *bayān*): leaflets issued by Palestinian political factions during the intifada

*diʿam*: support

*fidāʾīyīn*: guerrilla fighters

*hamel*: pregnancy

*idāra*: administration (e.g., in a prison)

*ihtijāj*: protest (n.)

*ihtirām*: respect

*ijhād*: abortion

*intiqām*: revenge

*istiqrār*: stability

*iʿtiqāl idāri*: administrative detention

*jāmiʿa*: university

*jīl al-intifāda*: the "intifada generation"

*jīl al-thawra*: the "generation of the revolution," referring to those who grew up during the armed struggle of the late 1960s and 1970s

*jīl al-nakba*: the generation formed by the Palestinian experience of dispossession in 1948

*khalas*: colloquial expression roughly translated as "forget it!"

*lāje³*: refugee

*lijān shaᶜbiyya*: popular committees

*madrasa*: school

*mahr*: brideprice

*majmūᶜa*: group

*marāhel* (sing. *marhala*): stages

*mas³ūl*: responsible

*masāri*: money

*masrahīya*: drama

*mudīr al-madrasa*: school headmaster

*mukhābarāt*: secret police, intelligence services

*mukhayyam* (pl. *mukhayyamāt*): refugee camp

*mukhtār*: village headman

*mutaradīn* (sing. *mutarad*): wanted, chased; name for Palestinians who were actively sought by Israeli authorities during the intifada

*nakba*: catastrophe; used by Palestinians to refer to the 1948 war and the dispossession of the Palestinian people

*nidā³* (pl. *mnādā*): call, appeal; used to refer to intifada leaflets (*bayanāt*)

*shabāb* (sing. *shab*): young men

*shahīd/shahīda* (pl. *shuhadā³*): martyr

*shāreᶜ*: street

*sirrīya*: secrecy

*taᶜlīm*: education

*taᶜlīq*: suspension (e.g., of classes)

*taᶜzīb*: torture

*tafāwada*: to negotiate

*tahqīq*: interrogation

*tawjīhī*: exam given at the conclusion of secondary school

*thimār*: fruits

*ᶜumala*: collaborators; used specifically to refer to those who collaborate with Israeli occupation authorities

*³ustāz/³ustāza*: teacher, professor

*al-wadeᶜ*: the political situation

*zahrāt*: "flowers," a nickname given to young Palestinian women who were trained as guerrilla fighters after the formation of the PLO

*zawāj badri*: early marriage

# Bibliography

INTERVIEWS

*Note*: Names in quotation marks indicate pseudonyms, which I am employing in accordance with assurances given to the individuals interviewed. Ages at the time of the interviews, when known, are indicated parenthetically.

Abu Mohammed Sharake (53), 18 October 1996, Jalazon Refugee Camp.
"Ghassan" (23), 3 November 1996, Birzeit.
"Hassan" (26), 31 January and 8 March 1997, Birzeit.
"Issa" (25), 28 February and 4 April 1997, Balata.
"Samira" (22), 2 March and 7 March 1997, Balata.
"Khaled" (26), 6 March, 11 March, and 18 March 1997, Balata.
Isam Abu-Hawila (25), 6 March, 13 March, and 10 April 1997, Balata.
"Ashraf" (24), 14 March, 21 March, and 28 March 1997, Balata.
"Ayman" (18), 18 March, 27 March, and 3 April 1997, Balata.
"Nabil" (25), 21 March and 2 April 1997, Balata.
"Hussein" (18), 25 March and 1 April 1997, Balata.
"Intissar" (23), 1 April and 8 April 1997, Balata.
"Majid" (27), 2 April, 10 April, and 15 April 1997, Balata.
"Iyad" (27), 3 April and 24 April 1997, Balata.
"Leila" (25), 4 April and 12 April 1997, Balata.
"Jamila" (25), 10 April and 21 April 1997, Balata.
Imm Ghassan Abu-Hawila (62), 15 April and 22 April 1997, Balata.
"Salim" (23), 20 April and 4 May 1997, Balata.
"Hatem" (23), 20 April and 25 April 1997, Balata.
"Samer" (25), 25 April and 2 May 1997, Balata.
"Ibtissam" (25), 30 April 1997, Balata.
"Fida" (20), 30 April 1997, Balata.
"Ramzi" (20), 1 May 1997, Balata.
"Qassem" (25), 1 May 1997, Balata.
Family of Sahar al-Jirmi, 4 May 1997, Balata.
Ibrahim Abu-Lughod (Vice-President, Birzeit University), 5 May and 26 May 1997, Birzeit University.

"Abu Nimr" (56), 6 May 1997, Balata.
Ra'id Amr (30), 8 May 1997, Nablus.
Talal Sidr (PA Minister of Youth and Sport), 26 May 1997, Ramallah.
Eyad Sarraj (Director, Gaza Community Mental Health Programme), 28 May 1997, Ramallah.
Taysir Daoud (Camp Service Officer, Balata Refugee Camp), 29 May 1997, Balata.
"Yousef" (21), 2 June 1997, Birzeit.
Mutawakil Taha (PA Deputy Minister of Information), 4 June 1997, Ramallah.
"Nidal" (secondary school teacher), 5 June 1997, Balata.
"Riyad" (secondary school teacher), 5 June 1997, Balata.
"Mousa" (secondary school teacher), 5 June 1997, Balata.

NEWSPAPERS AND MAGAZINES

*Al-Fajr* (English, Jerusalem), 1986–1993.
*Jerusalem Post,* 1989–1992.
*Jerusalem Times,* 1996–1998.
*Middle East International* (UK), 1987–1999.
*News from Within* (Jerusalem), 1988–2000.
*New York Times,* 1988–2003.
*Palestine Report* (Jerusalem), 1996–1999.

BOOKS AND ARTICLES

Abdo, Nahla. 1991. Women of the *Intifada*: Gender, Class and National Liberation. *Race & Class* 32 (4):19–34.
———. 1999. Gender and Politics under the Palestinian Authority. *Journal of Palestine Studies* 28 (2):38–51.
Abdulhadi, Rabab. 1998. The Palestinian Women's Autonomous Movement: Emergence, Dynamics, and Challenges. *Gender & Society* 12 (6):649–673.
Abrams, Philip. 1982. *Historical Sociology.* Ithaca: Cornell University Press.
Abu Iyad, with Eric Rouleau. 1981. *My Home, My Land: A Narrative of the Palestinian Struggle.* Translated by Linda Butler Koseoglu. New York: Times Books.
Aburish, Said. 1991. *Cry Palestine: Inside the West Bank.* Boulder: Westview Press.
Al-Haq. 1990. *Punishing a Nation: Israeli Human Rights Violations during the Palestinian Uprising, December 1987–December 1988.* Boston: South End Press.
Amadiume, Ifi, and Abdullahi An-Na'im, eds. 2000. *The Politics of Memory: Truth, Healing & Social Justice.* London and New York: Zed Books.

Amnesty International. 1996. *Palestinian Authority: Prolonged Political Detention, Torture, and Unfair Trials*. London: Amnesty International.

Amos, John. 1980. *The Palestinian Resistance: Organisation of a Nationalist Movement*. New York: Pergamon Press.

Anderson, Benedict. 1991. *Imagined Communities: Reflections on the Origin and Spread of Nationalism*. Rev. ed. London: Verso.

Aronson, Geoffrey. 1990. *Israel, Palestinians, and the Intifada: Creating Facts on the West Bank*. London: Kegan Paul International/Institute for Palestine Studies.

Austin, Joe, and Michael Nevin Willard, eds. 1998. *Generations of Youth: Youth Cultures and History in Twentieth-Century America*. New York: New York University Press.

Awwad, Nariman. 1992. *The Effect of Israeli Violence on the Children of Dheisheh Refugee Camp during the Intifada*. Jerusalem: Women's International League for Peace and Freedom.

Baker, Ahmad M. 1990. The Psychological Impact of the Intifada on Palestinian Children in the Occupied West Bank and Gaza: An Exploratory Study. *American Journal of Orthopsychiatry* 60 (4):496–505.

Balibar, Etienne. 1996. The Nation Form: History and Ideology. In *Becoming National: A Reader*, ed. Geoff Eley and Ronald Grigor Suny, 132–149. New York: Oxford University Press.

Barghouti, Hussein. 1989. A Song for Childhood. In *Intifada: The Palestinian Uprising against Israeli Occupation*, ed. Zachary Lockman and Joel Beinin, 42. Boston: South End Press.

Bargouti, Husain Jameel. 1991. Jeeps versus Bare Feet: The Villages in the *Intifada*. In *Intifada: Palestine at the Crossroads*, ed. Jamal R. Nassar and Roger Heacock, 107–123. New York: Praeger.

Ben-Ari, Eyal. 1989. Masks and Soldiering: The Israeli Army and the Palestinian Uprising. *Cultural Anthropology* 4 (4):372–389.

Benjamin, Walter. 1968a. On Some Motifs in Baudelaire. In *Illuminations*, ed. Hannah Arendt, 155–200. New York: Schocken Books.

———. 1968b. The Storyteller: Reflections on the Works of Nikolai Leskov. In *Illuminations*, ed. Hannah Arendt, 83–109. New York: Schocken Books.

———. 1968c. Theses on the Philosophy of History. In *Illuminations*, ed. Hannah Arendt, 253–264. New York: Schocken Books.

———. 1978. A Berlin Chronicle. In *Reflections: Essays, Aphorisms, Autobiographical Writings*, ed. Peter Demetz, 3–60. New York: Schocken Books.

Bennis, Phyllis. 1990. *From Stones to Statehood: The Palestinian Uprising*. Brooklyn: Olive Branch Press.

Birzeit University. 1989. The Criminalization of Education: Academic Freedom and Human Rights at Birzeit University during the Palestinian Uprising. Birzeit: Birzeit University Public Relations Office.

Boullata, Kamal. 1990. *Faithful Witnesses: Palestinian Children Recreate Their World*. New York: Olive Branch Press.

Bowman, Humphrey. 1942. *Middle East Window*. London and New York: Longmans, Green and Co.

Brown, Ken. 1989. "Transfer" and the Discourse of Racism. *Middle East Report* (157):21–22, 47.

Brynen, Rex, ed. 1991. *Echoes of the Intifada: Regional Repercussions of the Palestinian-Israeli Conflict*. Boulder: Westview Press.

B'tselem. 1992. Detained without Trial: Administrative Detention in the Occupied Territories since the Beginning of the Intifada. Jerusalem: B'tselem.

Bundy, Colin. 1987. Street Sociology and Pavement Politics: Aspects of Youth and Student Resistance in Cape Town, 1985. *Journal of Southern African Studies* 13 (3):303–330.

Burning Hate. 1988. *Washington Report on Middle East Affairs*, October 1988.

Butler, Judith. 1990. *Gender Trouble: Feminism and the Subversion of Identity*. London and New York: Routledge.

Cairns, Ed, and Micheal D. Roe, eds. 2003. *The Role of Memory in Ethnic Conflict*. New York: Palgrave Macmillan.

Cohen, Akiba, and Gadi Wolfsfeld, eds. 1993. *Framing the Intifada: People and Media*. Norwood, N.J.: Ablex.

Cohen, Stanley. 2001. *States of Denial: Knowing about Atrocities and Suffering*. Cambridge: Polity.

Collins, John. 1996. Exploring Children's Territory: Ghassan Kanafani, Njabulo Ndebele and the "Generation" of Politics in Palestine and South Africa. *Arab Studies Quarterly* 18 (4):65–85.

———. 1998. Fixing the Past: Stockpiling, Storytelling, and Palestinian Political Strategy in the Wake of the "Peace Process." Paper presented to the conference "Legacies of Authoritarianism: Cultural Production, Collective Trauma, and Global Justice," University of Wisconsin–Madison, April 1998.

———. 2002. Terrorism. In *Collateral Language: A User's Guide to America's New War*, ed. John Collins and Ross Glover, 155–173. New York: New York University Press.

Darwish, Mahmoud. 1973. *Selected Poems*. Translated by Ian Wedde and Fawwaz Tuqan. Cheadle, Cheshire: Carcanet Press Limited.

Doughty, Dick, with Mohammed El Aydi. 1995. *Gaza: Legacy of Occupation— A Photographer's Journey*. West Hartford, Conn.: Kumarian Press.

El-Helou, Mohamed W., and Peter R. Johnson. 1994. The Effects of the Palestinian *Intifada* on the Behaviour of Teenagers in the Gaza Strip. *Journal of Child and Youth Care* 9 (4):63–70.

Elmessiri, Abdel-Wahab. 1996. Checking Out of Hotel Zion. *al-Ahram Weekly*, 26 December 1996–1 January 1997, 12.

Emerson, Gloria. 1991. *Gaza—A Year in the Intifada: A Personal Account from an Occupied Land.* New York: Atlantic Monthly Press.

Fanon, Frantz. 1963. *The Wretched of the Earth.* Translated by Constance Farrington. New York: Grove Press.

Faris, James. 1989. Reading an El Al Ad. *Middle East Report* (158):32–33.

Fasheh, Munir. 1989. Al-Intifada and a New Education. In *Occupation: Israel over Palestine,* ed. Naseer Aruri, 537–560. Belmont, Mass.: Association of Arab-American University Graduates.

Feldman, Allen. 1991. *Formations of Violence: The Narrative of the Body and Political Terror in Northern Ireland.* Chicago: University of Chicago Press.

Fentress, James, and Chris Wickham. 1992. *Social Memory.* Oxford: Blackwell.

Finkelstein, Norman. 1997. *The Rise and Fall of Palestine.* Minneapolis: University of Minnesota Press.

Foucault, Michel. 1979. *Discipline and Punish: The Birth of the Prison.* Translated by Alan Sheridan. New York: Vintage Books.

Frisch, Hillel. 1998. *Countdown to Statehood: Palestinian State Formation in the West Bank and Gaza.* Albany: State University of New York Press.

Giacaman, George, and Dag Jorund Lønning, eds. 1998. *After Oslo: New Realities, Old Problems.* London: Pluto Press.

Giacaman, Rita, and Penny Johnson. 1989. Palestinian Women: Building Barricades and Breaking Barriers. In *Intifada: The Palestinian Uprising against Israeli Occupation,* ed. Zachary Lockman and Joel Beinin, 155–170. Boston: South End Press.

———. 1998. Intifada Year Four: Notes on the Women's Movement. In *Palestinian Women of Gaza and the West Bank,* ed. Suha Sabbagh, 216–230. Bloomington: Indiana University Press.

Goffman, Erving. 1974. *Frame Analysis: An Essay on the Organization of Experience.* Cambridge, Mass.: Harvard University Press.

Gordon, Haim. 1995. *Quicksand: Israel, the Intifada, and the Rise of Political Evil in Democracies.* East Lansing: Michigan State University Press.

Graff, James, assisted by Mohamed Abdolell. 1991. *Palestinian Children and Israeli State Violence.* Toronto: Near East Cultural and Educational Foundation of Canada.

Greenstein, Ran. 1995. *Genealogies of Conflict: Class, Identity, and State in Palestine/Israel and South Africa.* Hanover and London: Wesleyan University Press and University Press of New England.

Gunn, Janet Varner. 1995. *Second Life: A West Bank Memoir.* Minneapolis: University of Minnesota Press.

Hall, Stuart, and Tony Jefferson, eds. 1976. *Resistance through Rituals.* London: Hutchinson.

Hammami, Rema. 1993. Women in Palestinian Society. In *Palestinian Society in*

*Gaza, West Bank, and Arab Jerusalem: A Survey of Living Conditions,* ed. Marianne Heiberg and Geir Ovensen, 283–311. Oslo: FAFO.

Hammami, Rema. 1995. NGOs: The Professionalization of Politics. *Race & Class* 37 (2):51–63.

Harkabi, Yehoshofat. 1988. *Israel's Fateful Hour.* Translated by Lenn Schramm. New York: Harper & Row.

Harlow, Barbara. 1989. Narrative in Prison: Stories from the Palestinian Intifada. *Modern Fiction Studies* 35 (1):29–46.

———. 1994. Writers and Assassination. In *Imagining Home: Class, Culture and Nationalism in the African Diaspora,* ed. Sidney Lemelle and Robin D. G. Kelley, 167–184. London: Verso.

Hebdige, Dick. 1979. *Subculture: The Meaning of Style.* London: Methuen.

Hudson, Leila. 1994. Coming of Age in Occupied Palestine: Engendering the Intifada. In *Reconstructing Gender in the Middle East: Tradition, Identity, and Power,* ed. Fatma Müge Göcek and Shiva Balaghi, 123–136. New York: Columbia University Press.

Human Rights Watch. 1993. A License to Kill: Israeli Operations against "Wanted" and Masked Palestinians. New York: Human Rights Watch.

Human Rights Watch/Middle East. 1997. Palestinian Self-Rule Areas: Human Rights under the Palestinian Authority. New York: Human Rights Watch.

Hunter, F. Robert. 1993. *The Palestinian Uprising: A War by Other Means.* 2nd ed. Berkeley: University of California Press.

Jad, Islah. 1998. Patterns of Relations within the Palestinian Family during the Intifada. In *Palestinian Women of Gaza and the West Bank,* ed. Suha Sabbagh, 53–62. Bloomington: Indiana University Press.

Jenks, Chris. 1995. Decoding Childhood. In *Discourse and Reproduction: Essays in Honor of Basil Bernstein,* ed. Paul Atkinson, Brian Davies, and Sara Delmont. Cresskill, N.J.: Hampton Press.

Jerusalem Media and Communications Centre. 1989. *The Intifada: An Overview—The First Two Years.* Jerusalem: Jerusalem Media and Communications Centre.

———. 1995. *Israeli Military Orders in the Occupied Palestinian West Bank, 1967–1992.* 2nd ed. Jerusalem: Jerusalem Media and Communications Centre.

Johnson, Penny, Lee O'Brien, and Joost Hiltermann. 1988. The West Bank Rises Up. *Middle East Report* 18 (4):4–12.

Kahn, Susan Martha. 2000. *Reproducing Jews: A Cultural Account of Assisted Conception in Israel.* Durham, N.C.: Duke University Press.

Kaminer, Reuven. 1996. *The Politics of Protest: The Israeli Peace Movement and the Palestinian Intifada.* Brighton: Sussex Academic Press.

Kanaana, Sharif. 1990. Humor of the Palestinian *Intifada. Journal of Folklore Research* 27 (3):231–240.

———. 1993. The Role of Women in Intifadah Legends. *Contemporary Legend* 3:37–61.

———. 1995. The Role of Women in Intifada Legends. In *Discourse and Palestine: Power, Text, and Context*, ed. Annelies Moors, Toine van Teeffelen, Ilham Abu Ghazaleh and Sharif Kanaana, 153–161. Amsterdam: Het Spinhuis.

Kanaaneh, Rhoda Ann. 2002. *Birthing the Nation: Strategies of Palestinian Women in Israel.* Berkeley: University of California Press.

Kanafani, Ghassan. 1984. *Palestine's Children.* Translated by Barbara Harlow. London: Heinemann.

———. 1990. Thoughts on Change and the "Blind Language." *Alif: Journal of Contemporary Poetics* (10):132–157.

Katz, Cindi, and Neil Smith. 1992. L.A. Intifada: Interview with Mike Davis. *Social Text* (33):19–33.

Kayyali, A. W. n.d. *Palestine: A Modern History.* London: Croom Helm.

Keith-Roach, Edward. 1994. *Pasha of Jerusalem: Memoirs of a District Commissioner under the British Mandate.* London: Radcliffe Press.

Kestenbaum, Jonathan. 1988. Diary of a Soldier. *Jerusalem Post International Edition,* 24 September 1988.

Khadduri, Walid, ed. 1972. *International Documents on Palestine, 1969.* Beirut: Institute for Palestine Studies.

Kimmerling, Baruch. 2003. *Politicide: Ariel Sharon's War against the Palestinians.* London: Verso.

Kuttab, Daoud. 1988. A Profile of the Stonethrowers. *Journal of Palestine Studies* 17 (3):14–23.

Kuttab, Jonathan. 1988. The Children's Revolt. *Journal of Palestine Studies* 17 (4):26–35.

Lawyers Committee for Human Rights. 1988. Conditions of Detention at Ketziot. New York: Lawyers Committee for Human Rights.

Lesch, Ann. 1979. *Arab Politics in Palestine, 1917–1939.* Ithaca: Cornell University Press.

Liebes, Tamar, and Shoshana Blum-Kulka. 1994. Managing a Moral Dilemma: Israeli Soldiers in the Intifada. *Armed Forces & Society* 21 (1):45–69.

Linn, Ruth. 1994. Morally Puzzled Individuals in a Morally Puzzled Community: Resisting Israeli Soldiers during the War in Lebanon and the Intifada. *Psychological Reports* 75 (1):423–434.

———. 1996. When the Individual Soldier Says "No" to War: A Look at Selective Refusal during the Intifada. *Journal of Peace Research* 33 (4):421–431.

Lockman, Zachary, and Joel Beinin, eds. 1989. *Intifada: The Palestinian Uprising against Israeli Occupation.* Boston: South End Press.

Lorey, David E., and William H. Beezley, eds. 2002. *Genocide, Collective Violence, and Popular Memory: The Politics of Remembrance in the Twentieth Century.* Wilmington, Del.: SR Books.

Lustick, Ian. 1980. *Arabs in the Jewish State*. Austin: University of Texas Press.
————. 1988. *For the Land and the Lord: Jewish Fundamentalism in Israel*. New York: Council on Foreign Relations.
————. 1993. Writing the Intifada: Collective Action in the Occupied Territories. *World Politics* (45):560–594.
Lykes, M. Brinton. 1996. Meaning Making in a Context of Genocide and Silencing. In *Myths about the Powerless: Contesting Social Inequities,* ed. M. Brinton Lykes, Ali Banuazizi, Ramsay Liem, and Michael Morris, 159–178. Philadelphia: Temple University Press.
Mannheim, Karl. 1952. The Problem of Generations. In *Essays on the Sociology of Knowledge,* 276–320. London: Routledge & Kegan Paul.
Mansour, Sylvie. 1996. The Intifada Generation in the Classroom. *Prospects* 26 (2):293–310.
Marshall, Mark. 1995. Rethinking the Palestine Question: The Apartheid Paradigm. *Journal of Palestine Studies* 25 (1):12–22.
Massad, Joseph. 1995. Conceiving the National: Gender and Palestinian Nationalism. *Middle East Journal* 49 (3):467–483.
Mazrui, Ali. 1990. *Cultural Forces in World Politics*. Portsmouth, N.H.: Heinemann Educational Books.
McCole, John. 1993. *Walter Benjamin and the Antinomies of Tradition*. Ithaca: Cornell University Press.
McDowall, David. 1989. *Palestine and Israel: The Uprising and Beyond*. Berkeley: University of California Press.
Minow, Martha. 1998. *Between Vengeance and Forgiveness: Facing History after Genocide and Mass Violence*. Boston: Beacon Press.
Mishal, Shaul, and Reuben Aharoni. 1994. *Speaking Stones: Communiques from the Intifada Underground*. Syracuse: Syracuse University Press.
Moors, Annelies. 1995. *Women, Property and Islam: Palestinian Experiences, 1920–1990*. Cambridge: Cambridge University Press.
Morgan, Robin. 1989. *The Demon Lover: On the Sexuality of Terrorism*. New York: W. W. Norton & Company.
Mowitt, John. 1992. Algerian Nation: Fanon's Fetish. *Cultural Critique* (22): 165–186.
Muslih, Muhammad Y. 1993. Palestinian Civil Society. *Middle East Journal* 47 (2):258–274.
Najjar, Orayb Aref. 1996. "The Editorial Family of al-Kateb Bows in Respect": The Construction of Martyrdom Text Genre in One Palestinian Political and Literary Magazine. *Discourse & Society* 7 (4):499–530.
Nassar, Jamal R., and Roger Heacock, eds. 1991. *Intifada: Palestine at the Crossroads*. New York: Birzeit University and Praeger Publishers.
Nixon, Anne Elizabeth. 1990. *The Status of Palestinian Children during the*

*Uprising in the Occupied Territories.* 2 vols. East Jerusalem: Rädda Barnen/ Swedish Save the Children.

Nuttall, Sarah, and Carli Coetzee, eds. 1998. *Negotiating the Past: The Making of Memory in South Africa.* Oxford: Oxford University Press.

Odeh, Jumana, and Cairo Arafat. 1989. Health Conditions of Palestinian Children during the Uprising: Reflections on Physical and Psychological Well-Being. Jerusalem: Union of Palestinian Medical Relief Committees.

Oliver, Anne Marie, and Paul Steinberg. 1990. *The Graffiti of the Intifada: A Brief Survey.* Jerusalem: PASSIA.

Osborne, Peter. 1994. Small-Scale Victories, Large-Scale Defeats: Walter Benjamin's Politics of Time. In *Walter Benjamin's Philosophy: Destruction and Experience,* ed. Andrew Benjamin and Peter Osborne, 59–109. London and New York: Routledge.

Palestinian National Authority. 1996. Agenda for Social Renewal: The National Programme for Palestinian Children, Vol. 1. Ramallah: Ministry of Planning and International Cooperation.

Parker, Christopher. 1999. *Resignation or Revolt? Socio-Political Development and the Challenges of Peace in Palestine.* London: I. B. Tauris & Co.

Passerini, Luisa. 1987. *Fascism in Popular Memory: The Cultural Experience of the Turin Working Class.* Cambridge: Cambridge University Press.

———. 1989. Women's Personal Narratives. In *Interpreting Women's Lives: Feminist Theory and Personal Narratives,* ed. Personal Narratives Group, 189–197. Bloomington: Indiana University Press.

———. 1996. *Autobiography of a Generation: Italy, 1968.* Hanover: University Press of New England.

Peretz, Don. 1990. *Intifada: The Palestinian Uprising.* Boulder: Westview Press.

Peteet, Julie. 1993. Authenticity and Gender: The Presentation of Culture. In *Arab Women: Old Boundaries, New Frontiers,* ed. Judith Tucker, 49–62. Bloomington: Indiana University Press.

———. 1994. Male Gender and Rituals of Resistance in the Palestinian *Intifada*: A Cultural Politics of Violence. *American Ethnologist* 21 (1):31–49.

———. 1996. The Writing on the Walls: The Graffiti of the *Intifada. Cultural Anthropology* 11 (2):139–159.

Pilkington, Hilary. 1994. *Russia's Youth and Its Culture: A Nation's Constructors and Constructed.* London and New York: Routledge.

Pohlandt-McCormick, Helena. 1999. "I Saw a Nightmare . . .": Doing Violence to Memory: The Soweto Uprising, June 16, 1976. Ph.D. dissertation, University of Minnesota.

Popular Memory Group. 1982. Popular Memory: Theory, Politics, Method. In *Making Histories,* ed. Richard Johnson, Gregor McLennon, Bill Swartz, and David Sutton, 205–252. Minneapolis: University of Minnesota Press.

Portelli, Alessandro. 1991. *The Death of Luigi Trastulli and Other Stories.* Albany: State University of New York Press.

———. 1997. *The Battle of Valle Giulia: Oral History and the Art of Dialogue.* Madison: University of Wisconsin Press.

Rabbani, Mouin. 1996. Palestinian Authority, Israeli Rule: From Transitional to Permanent Arrangement. *Middle East Report* (201):2–6.

Reinhart, Tanya. 2002. *Israel/Palestine: How to End the War of 1948.* New York: Seven Stories Press.

Rishmawi, Mervat. 1996. Legislation relating to Palestinian Children. Birzeit: Birzeit University Law Center.

Robinson, Glenn. 1997. *Building a Palestinian State: The Incomplete Revolution.* Bloomington: Indiana University Press.

Rouhana, Kate. 1989. Children and the *Intifadah. Journal of Palestine Studies* 18 (4):110–121.

Roy, Sara. 1995. Report from Gaza: Alienation or Accommodation? *Journal of Palestine Studies* 24 (4):73–82.

Sabbagh, Suha, ed. 1998. *Palestinian Women of Gaza and the West Bank.* Bloomington: Indiana University Press.

Said, Edward. 1984. Permission to Narrate. *Journal of Palestine Studies* 13 (3): 27–48.

———. 1985. *After the Last Sky: Palestinian Lives.* New York: Pantheon.

———. 1989. *Intifada* and Independence. In *Intifada: The Palestinian Uprising against Israeli Occupation,* ed. Zachary Lockman and Joel Beinin, 5–22. Boston: South End Press.

———. 1994. *The Politics of Dispossession: The Struggle for Palestinian Self-Determination, 1969–1994.* New York: Vintage Books.

Sanford, Victoria. 2003. *Buried Secrets: Truth and Human Rights in Guatemala.* New York: Palgrave Macmillan.

Sarraj, Eyad. 1993. Peace and the Children of the Stone. Gaza Community Mental Health Programme. Accessed in March 2004 at www.gcmhp.net/eyad/stone.htm.

———. 1996. Palestinian Children and Violence. Belfast: Impact of Armed Conflict on Children conference.

Sayigh, Rosemary. 1979. *Palestinians: From Peasants to Revolutionaries.* London: Zed Press.

Schiff, Ze'ev, and Ehud Ya'ari. 1989. *Intifada: The Palestinian Uprising—Israel's Third Front.* Translated by Ina Friedman. New York: Simon & Schuster.

Seekings, Jeremy. 1993. *Heroes or Villains? Youth Politics in the 1980s.* Johannesburg: Ravan Press.

Shafir, Gershon. 1999. Business in Politics: Globalization and the Search for Peace in South Africa and Israel/Palestine. *Israel Affairs* 48 (6):103–120.

Shalev, Aryeh. 1991. *The Intifada: Causes and Effects.* Boulder: Westview Press.

Shammas, Anton. 1988. A Stone's Throw. *New York Review of Books,* 31 March 1988.

Sharoni, Simona. 1995. *Gender and the Israeli-Palestinian Conflict: The Politics of Women's Resistance.* Syracuse: Syracuse University Press.

Slyomovics, Susan. 1998. *The Object of Memory: Arab and Jew Narrate the Palestinian Village.* Philadelphia: University of Pennsylvania Press.

Somers, Margaret R., and Gloria D. Gibson. 1994. Reclaiming the Epistemological "Other": Narrative and the Social Construction of Identity. In *Social Theory and the Politics of Identity,* ed. Craig Calhoun, 37–99. Cambridge, Mass. and Oxford: Blackwell.

Spencer, Philip, and Howard Wollman. 2002. *Nationalism: A Critical Introduction.* London: Sage.

Spurr, David. 1993. *The Rhetoric of Empire: Colonial Discourse in Journalism, Travel Writing, and Imperial Administration.* Durham, N.C.: Duke University Press.

Stein, Rebecca Luna. 1995. Political Tourism in Palestine. *Stanford Humanities Review* 5 (1):176–181.

Strum, Philippa. 1998. West Bank Women and the *Intifada*: Revolution within the Revolution. In *Palestinian Women of Gaza and the West Bank,* ed. Suha Sabbagh, 63–77. Bloomington: Indiana University Press.

Sullivan, Denis J. 1996. NGOs in Palestine: Agents of Development and Foundations of Civil Society. *Journal of Palestine Studies* 25 (3):93–100.

Swedenburg, Ted. 1990. The Palestinian Peasant as National Signifier. *Anthropological Quarterly* 63 (1):18–30.

———. 1995a. *Memories of Revolt: The 1936–39 Rebellion and the Palestinian National Past.* Minneapolis: University of Minnesota Press.

———. 1995b. With Genet in the Palestinian Field. *In Fieldwork Under Fire: Contemporary Studies of Violence and Survival,* ed. Carolyn Nordstrom and Antonius C. G. M. Robben, 25–40. Berkeley: University of California Press.

Tamari, Salim. 1990. The Uprising's Dilemma: Limited Rebellion and Civil Society. *Middle East Report* (164/5):4–8.

———. 1991a. The Palestinian Movement in Transition: Historical Reversals and the Uprising. *Journal of Palestine Studies* 20 (2):57–70.

———. 1991b. The Revolt of the Petit Bourgeoisie. In *Intifada: Palestine at the Crossroads,* ed. Jamal R. Nassar and Roger Heacock, 159–173. New York: Birzeit University and Praeger Publishers.

———. 1995. Fading Flags: The Crises of Palestinian Legitimacy. *Middle East Report* (194/5):10–12.

Taraki, Lisa. 1991. The Development of Political Consciousness among Palestinians in the Occupied Territories, 1967–1987. In *Intifada: Palestine at the Crossroads,* ed. Jamal R. Nassar and Roger Heacock, 53–71. New York: Birzeit University and Praeger Publishers.

Taussig, Michael. 1992. *The Nervous System.* New York and London: Routledge.

Tekiner, Roselle. 1991. Race and the Issue of National Identity in Israel. *International Journal of Middle East Studies* (23):39–55.

Thompson, John B. 1984. *Studies in the Theory of Ideology.* Berkeley: University of California Press.

Usher, Graham. 1995. *Palestine in Crisis: The Struggle for Peace and Political Independence after Oslo.* London: Pluto Press.

———. 1999. The Politics of Internal Security: The Palestinian Authority's New Security Services. In *After Oslo: New Realities, Old Problems,* ed. George Giacaman and Dag Jorund Lønning, 146–161. London: Pluto Press.

———. 2002. Letter from Balata. *Middle East International* (671):32.

Wark, McKenzie. 1994. Fresh Maimed Babies: The Uses of Innocence. *Transition* (65):36–47.

Wenger, Martha, and Steve Niva. 1988. Intifadah Index. *Middle East Report* (154):12.

Willis, Paul. 1977. *Learning to Labour.* Farnborough: Saxon House.

Wulff, Helena. 1995. Introducing Youth Culture in Its Own Right. *In Youth Cultures: A Cross-Cultural Perspective,* ed. Vered Amit-Talai and Helena Wulff, 1–18. London: Routledge.

Ya'ari, Ehud. 1989. Israel's Prison Academies. *The Atlantic Monthly,* October 1989, 22–30.

Yahav, David, ed. 1993. *Israel, the "Intifada" and the Rule of Law.* Israel: Israel Ministry of Defense Publications.

Yair, Gad, and Nabil Khatab. 1995. Changing of the Guards: Teacher-Student Interaction in the Intifada. *Sociology of Education* 68 (2):99–115.

Yuval-Davis, Nira. 1989. National Reproduction and "the Demographic Race" in Israel. In *Woman-Nation-State,* ed. Nira Yuval-Davis and Floya Anthias, 91–109. London: Zed Press.

Zerubavel, Yael. 1995. *Recovered Roots: Collective Memory and the Making of Israeli National Tradition.* Chicago: University of Chicago Press.

# Index

1936–39 rebellion, 33, 158
1948, 25, 89, 151, 232, 252n. 1; dispossession of Palestinians in, 13, 21, 51, 111, 225; establishment of the state of Israel in, 229; war, 61, 80, 91.
1967 war, 16, 19, 26, 27, 42, 72, 80, 91, 146, 229, 232

Abdulhadi, Rabab, 247n. 6
Abortion: as political metaphor, 21, 165, 171, 172, 186, 191, 192, 195, 197, 204, 237n. 7; services for Palestinians in Israel, 60
Abrams, Philip, 100
Abu Dis Law College, 217
Abu Jihad (Khalil al-Wazir), 70; assassination of, 175
Abu-Lughod, Ibrahim, 18
Aburish, Said, 68, 69
Acre, 19
Admistrative detention, 113, 126, 131, 246n. 4
Afghanistan, 226
African National Congress (ANC), 238n. 2, 239n. 3
Age: authority of, 120, 161, 162; changing meaning attached to, 8, 140; decoupling from generation, 161; difference between *shabāb* and soldiers, 93; fusion with generation, 161; and generational identity/consciousness, 13, 14, 24, 106, 166, 202; groups and how to de-

fine/label them, 38–39, 44, 45–46, 73–74, 172; of interviewees, 31, 76; of marriage, 96–98; and memory, 24, 92, 161, 189, 202; political importance of, 18; and roles in intifada demonstrations, 232
Al-Ali, Naji, 63–65, 79, 225, 241n. 18
Al-Aqsa Martyrs Brigades, 30, 211, 227
Al-Aqsa mosque, 184, 203
Al-Baba, Yusuf, 220–221
*Al-Fajr* (newspaper), 42
Algeria, 6; anticolonial resistance in, 4, 43, 232, 249n. 11; setbacks suffered by women after independence in, 97
*Al-Kateb* (magazine), 242n. 3, 244n. 20
Al-Lawzi, Taysir, 217, 251n. 9
Al-Qidreh, Khaled, 221
Ammons, Linda, 237n. 11
Amnesty International, 221, 250n. 2, 251n. 9
Anderson, Benedict, 10
Andoni, Lamis, 75
An-Najah University, 75, 129, 150; boycott by students at, 217; raided by Palestinian security forces (1996), 104, 215–219
Ansar II detention center, 131
Ansar III (Ketziot) detention center, 94, 95, 126, 127, 128, 133, 245n. 2, 246n. 4

141; intifada memories of, 53; marriages arranged by, 97, 98–99; as portrayed in popular memory, 119; praised in intifada leaflets, 42; role in war, 54; spending more time with children during intifada, 93. *See also* Parents

Feldman, Allen, 115, 121, 131, 133, 135

First Palestinian Arab Congress (1919), 236n. 4

Fisk, Robert, 1

Foucault, Michel, 112

Frames, 37, 38

Freire, Paolo, 144

Future: children as embodiment of, 59, 146, 223, 224; imagined/promised, 8, 19, 86, 103, 104, 105, 109, 205, 227; and popular memory, 22; possibilities of the, 79

Gaza Community Mental Health Programme, 240n. 7

Gaza Strip, 41, 59, 120, 179, 239n. 4; arrival of Yasser Arafat in, 186; children in, 141; everyday life in, 244n. 22; Fateh-Hamas clash in, 178–179, 248n. 5; militarization of society in, 222, 250n. 2; refugee camps in, 24, 28; "is ruled by a child," 35, 70; and start of the intifada, 28, 29, 91, 116, 203, 205, 230

Gender, 14; analysis of the intifada, 97, 154, 247n. 6; and changes in marriage patterns, 97, 99; and differences between men's and women's testimony, 238n. 13; distinction between parents in children's memories, 120; divisions, 166; and education, 150, 155; and generational categories, 39; identities, 109, 152, 156, 243n. 12; and

nationalism, 57, 243n. 12; and patriarchy, 20; as performance, 243n. 10; roles, 167, 236n. 2; "traditional" relations of, 154; and women's activism, 89–90

Generation, 9, 13, 21; "actual," 14, 15, 106, 167, 200; and class, 195–203; discourses of, 7, 15, 20, 36, 37, 112; emerging/new, 17, 19; and marriage, 99–100; and memory, 14, 24, 79, 106, 160, 162, 166; and narrative, 15, 17, 34, 165, 238n. 13; and nationalism/national identity, 13, 14, 15, 17, 34, 58, 192; -as-possibility, 14, 15, 16, 18; scholarship on, 14, 236n. 2; units, 167, 168, 202; and women's activism, 89–90. *See also* Age

Generational: authority, 8, 68, 71, 119, 149, 150, 160; categories (e.g., children, youth), 38–40, 44, 45, 106, 141; consciousness, 14, 20, 153, 158, 161, 247n. 4; continuity, 20–21; dynamics, 33, 158; failure, 101, 192; hierarchies, 8, 93, 112, 113, 114, 125, 158; identity/identities, 8, 15, 24, 100, 106, 109, 121, 139, 145, 162, 172, 176, 196, 202, 217, 236n. 2, 243n. 12; inversion/upheaval, 8, 68, 69, 112, 123, 139, 146, 147, 160; metaphors, 16, 21, 38, 221, 247n. 1; phors, 16, 21, 38, 221, 247n. 1; solidarity/unity, 152, 165, 166, 202, 203, 216. *See also* Age

Genet, Jean, 10

Geneva Convention, 245n. 2

Giacaman, Rita, 89

Girls: conflicts with parents, 72; involvement in intifada, 52, 115, 116, 150

Goffman, Erving, 37

Goldstein, Baruch, 248n. 6

78, 103, 186, 189, 227, 235n. 1;
and patriarchal constructions of
women, 235n. 1; as political project, 15, 23, 66, 67, 102, 149, 165;
and procreation/reproduction, 58,
60; promises of, 6, 8, 13, 104, 201;
and reproduction, 58; roles assigned by, 104; scholarship on/
theories of, 14, 104, 235n. 1
National liberation, 102, 103, 144,
184, 196, 208, 237n. 9, 242n. 3;
narratives of, 3, 6, 22; struggle in
Palestine, 13, 19, 146, 214
Native American reservations, 230
Negev Desert, 94, 126, 244n. 16
Negotiation: between prisoners and
the *mukhābarāt*, 136–137, 159;
between prisoners and prison administration, 135; between students
and headmasters, 146, 149–150,
159, 214, 218; between students
and teachers, 124, 149–150, 214;
between young people and shopkeepers, 124, 218; over burial of
intifada martyrs, 85; of family relationships, 69, 118; of generational
authority, 101, 113; political/peace,
8, 101, 102, 106, 165, 172, 180,
186, 187, 188, 190, 194, 200, 206,
230, 233; as theme in intifada
memories, 124, 136, 137, 149,
159, 161, 218
Netanyahu, Benjamin, 188
*New Republic* (magazine), 225
*News from Within* (magazine), 238n.
12, 244n. 14
*New York Times*, 54, 61
*Nightline* (ABC News program), 67
Non-governmental organizations
(NGOs), Palestinian, 209, 210,
250n. 13
Northern Ireland, hunger strikes in,
133

Occupation of the West Bank and
Gaza, Israeli, 1, 9, 27, 49, 80, 89,
102, 142, 151, 176, 187, 211, 213,
222, 227, 231, 239n. 4, 242n. 3;
advent of, 26, 232; criticism of, 2,
53; and erosion of parental authority, 120; growing up under, 66,
112; Israeli responses to, 240n. 9;
Palestinians living under, 41, 124,
181, 195, 207, 220; Palestinian
struggle against/resistance to, 24,
28, 29, 38, 40, 52, 64, 71, 91,
101, 104, 125, 155, 157, 174, 178,
180, 203, 204, 205, 231; structure
and maintenance of, 45, 73, 112,
240n. 6
Ofer Detention Centre ("kindergarten of the intifada"), 126,
246n. 3
Oral history, 22, 243n. 11
Osborne, Peter, 105, 106
Oslo: negotiations and agreements, 9,
30, 165, 180, 185, 186, 188, 189,
190, 191, 198, 213, 214, 225, 227,
230, 233, 245n. 23; post-Oslo period, 104, 166, 187, 190, 196, 209,
213, 216, 220

Palestine Human Rights Information
Center (PHRIC), 45
Palestine Liberation Organization
(PLO), 28, 171, 173, 181, 187,
192, 193, 204, 214, 231, 233,
239n. 4; accused by Israel of exploiting young people, 49; Arab
support of, 94; charter, 249n. 9; as
custodian of official nationalist
narrative, 22, 103; declares "generation of liberation," 36, 66; dialogue with United States, 232; leadership of, 19, 21, 70, 71, 170, 186,
195; local leaders approved by,
194; money sent into West Bank

PLO *(continued)*
and Gaza during the intifada, 93,
173, 173–178; negotiations with
Israel, 186, 190, 191, 233, 245n.
23; popular dissatisfaction with,
72; rise of the, 58; rivalry with
Jordan, 232
Palestine National Council, proclamation of independent Palestinian
state, 20, 43, 61, 233
Palestinian Authority (PA), 32, 164,
187, 191, 193, 196, 211, 215, 221,
227, 232; *Agenda for Social Renewal*, 222; arrest of Palestinian
students, 215; attempt to create
University Guards, 222; campaign
of weapons confiscation, 30; conflicts with the "intifada generation," 214–215, 226; creation of
jobs and distribution of benefits
under, 27, 195, 196, 197, 199; as
custodian of official nationalist
narrative, 103; establishment/
arrival of, 8, 149, 165, 169, 171,
186, 189, 193, 195, 204, 209, 213,
222, 233, 250n. 13; and Fateh,
170, 176, 198; and Hamas, 179,
188, 206; and the "intifada generation," 9; institutionalization of violence under, 222; limited powers of,
105, 214; local critiques and evaluations of, 104, 149, 166, 176, 184,
198, 199, 200, 205, 248n. 5; Ministry of Youth and Sport, 223;
negotiations with Israel, 183, 200,
213; and Palestinians NGOs, 250n.
13; as paternal figure, 221; Preventive Security Forces (PSF), 168,
214, 215, 220, 224; prisoners held
under the, 220, 221, 250n. 6,
251n. 12, 251n. 15; raid on An-
Najah University, 215–219; security cooperation with Israel, 215;

security forces in general, 27, 104,
128, 149, 158, 167, 168, 179, 184,
189, 197, 199, 201, 213, 215, 220,
225, 250n. 15; supporters, 173,
189, 217, 225; suspension of striking teachers, 249n. 12; taking over
former Israeli prison facilities, 220;
taxation policies, 199; torture of
Palestinians under, 220–221; young
people working for the, 8, 128,
165, 167, 183, 197, 248n. 1
Palestinian Center against Violence,
222
Palestinian Legislative Council, 30,
176
Palestinian Prisoners' Club, 128, 137,
138, 246n. 4, 251n. 15
Parents, 18, 19, 35, 37, 67, 71, 111,
114; accused of neglecting children,
49–50, 53, 73; accused of using
children as cannon fodder, 35; and
arranged marriages, 96, 97; authority of, 8, 49, 50, 69, 73, 101, 113,
119, 120, 122, 124, 161; children's
circumvention of authority of, 120;
defied/disobeyed by their children,
72, 73, 121, 122, 123; engaging in
political action with their children,
53; erosion of influence, 101;
everyday power struggles and negotiations with children, 69, 81, 115,
118, 121; giving "orders" to children, 123; held responsible for children's actions, 49, 88, 121, 240n.
9; interaction with Israeli soldiers,
119, 121; as interviewees, 31, 32,
78; kept in the dark about their
children's activities, 122, 123; of
martyrs, 31; in popular memory,
119, 120, 124; preventing children
from going outside, 8, 116, 118;
and rhetorical mode of guilt/
shame, 38; role in arranging

# About the Author

John Collins is Assistant Professor of Global Studies at St. Lawrence University in Canton, New York, where he teaches courses on Palestine, nationalism and violence, globalization, news media analysis, and cultural studies. He is the coeditor (with Ross Glover) of *Collateral Language: A User's Guide to America's New War* (NYU Press, 2002), a collection of essays critically interrogating the rhetoric used to justify U.S. military action following the September 11 attacks.